Perfect Days in ...

BERLIN

Travel with Insider Tips

www.marco-polo.com

Contents

 TOP 10   4

That Berlin Feeling   6

For chapters: See inside front cover

TOP 10

Not to be missed!
Our TOP 10 hits – from the absolute No. 1 to No. 10 –
help you plan your tour of the most important sights.

1 PARISER PLATZ ➤ 56

This square comes top of our list with its captivating mix of the Brandenburg Gate (photo left), a classy hotel, embassies and the Academy of Arts.

2 MUSEUMSINSEL ➤ 82

Five different museums boasting one of the most valuable collections of art and historical artefacts in the world! The Pergamon altar in the Pergamonmuseum and the Neues Museum's bust of Nefertiti are particularly worth a visit.

3 ALEXANDERPLATZ ➤ 88

Visit the Fernsehturm (TV Tower) for great views of the square, the World Clock, the Neptune Fountain, the Rotes Rathaus, the Alexa Shopping Centre and many department stores.

4 REICHSTAG ➤ 58

The view from the glass dome of the Reichstag lets you keep an eye on the city's government district while admiring the plenary chamber, the Brandenburg Gate and the old centre of Berlin.

5 SONY CENTER ➤ 106

Fantastic light effects make Potsdamer Platz particularly entrancing at night. The Film and TV Museum is a must.

6 GENDARMENMARKT ➤ 62

Found near Friedrichstraße, Berlin's most beautiful square is home to the historic glory of the Konzerthaus and the German and French cathedrals.

7 SCHLOSS CHARLOTTENBURG ➤ 124

Berlin's largest palace with private royal apartments, a valuable art collection and a French baroque garden. Queen Luise is entombed in the Mausoleum.

8 JÜDISCHES MUSEUM ➤ 142

Two thousand years of Jewish history are documented within Daniel Libeskind's breathtaking architectural design.

9 KAISER-WILHELM-GEDÄCHTNISKIRCHE ➤ 127

The ruined old tower rises up high into the sky like an admonitory finger while the New Church's 30,000 blocks of glass gleam next door.

10 HACKESCHE HÖFE ➤ 90

An ensemble of courtyards off the Hackescher Markt with shops, theatres and a cinema.

THAT
BERLIN

Experience the city's unique flair and find out what makes it tick – just like the Berliners themselves.

A TRUE BERLIN PASTIME

Watching the colourful hustle and bustle go by on the streets while enjoying a latte macchiato is a true Berlin pastime. **Café Manolo** is a perfect vantage point: It boasts the best window seats around. You can also sit out on the street itself (daily from 7am, Schönhauser Allee 45, U2 Eberswalder Straße, ✚ 201, north of E5). You can't leave without trying a *Currywurst* (sausage in curry sauce) from **Konnopke** opposite (Mon–Fri 9am–8pm, Sat 11.30am–8pm).

PEDAL POWER

Berlin's a great place to go cycling! Why not try having a relaxing pedal along the river Spree from the Reichstag to **Charlottenburg Palace** (▶ 124). Grab some tasty treats at **FrischeParadies** on your way there (Mon-Fri 8am-8pm, Sat 8am–6pm, Morsestr. 2) and enjoy a picnic in the palace's romantic park when you arrive. You can rent bicycles from nearly every street corner in the city (▶ 40).

SEE YOU AT THE WORLD CLOCK

Friends, acquaintances and lovers traditionally meet up at the **Weltzeituhr** (World Clock, ▶ 89) for a stroll around or a night on the tiles. Early arrivers can enjoy the lively scene on **Alexanderplatz** (▶ 88) and soak up a bit of Berlin's big city atmosphere. Crowds stream towards the station and head to the cinemas and the Alexa shopping centre. Trams push their way through at a walking pace. Many Berliners have fond memories of first dates that started here.

A SPREE ON THE SPREE

Relax on a deckchair in the sun, take the occasional dip in the turquoise water and enjoy the view with a cocktail at the beach bar. With its swimming pool in the middle of the Spree, the **Badeschiff** ("Bathing Ship", image right; ▶ 146) is the perfect place to go on hot summer days. Fancy a touch more luxury? Then treat yourself to a massage (Easter–Sept, daily 8am–midnight, weather permitting. Eichenstr. 4, S-Bahn Treptow).

FEELING

Summer in the city – Berlin is particularly beautiful by the Spree

That Berlin Feeling

A MULTICULTURAL MARKETPLACE

The scents, aromas and tasty treats here will make you feel you've been transported to the East. Dealers tout their wares at the top of their voices at Berlin's second-largest weekly market, the **Turkish market on the Maybachufer** (Tue, Fri 11am–6.30pm; ➤ 148). They sell almost everything, from fruit and veg to colourful fabrics. Enjoy the atmosphere and try a speciality or two from the snack stands. You'll find the best *Gözleme* (crispy pastries filled with spinach or cheese) at **Aycicek** (almost at the riverbank's easternmost end).

A BEER BY THE LAKE

As soon as they feel the first rays of sun, Berliners flock to the **beer garden at the Café am Neuen See** (➤ 75) in the middle of the Tiergarten. Friends welcome in the summer with sausages from the grill or simply come for a break from the noise of the city. You can go rowing (€5 for 30 min) amongst the ducks and see the magnificent natural surroundings from the water. (Restaurant daily from 9am, Beer garden Mon–Fri from 11am, Sat–Sun from 10am, Lichtensteinallee 2, U 1 or 2 Wittenbergplatz, ✚ 203 D3).

TO THE CANTEEN!

Berlin is a creative, open city. After the curtain goes down at the **Berliner Ensemble** (➤ 74), everyone heads to the theatre canteen, where you can sit right next to the actors. There's a loud, jovial atmosphere, particularly when the performance has been a success. People fortify themselves with beer, wine and tasty *Buletten* (meatballs) and relive the show once more. (Mon–Sat 9am–midnight, Sun 4pm–midnight).

FABULOUS SUNSETS

It's particularly romantic up on the **pedestrian bridge in Friedrichshain** (Modersohnstraße, U-/S-Bahn Warschauer Straße, ✚ 206 east of C3) when the sun sinks behind the Fernsehturm and into the sea of houses below. On warm evenings, musicians play guitars, Berliners and tourists blink in the sun's dying rays, and everyone enjoys the clear view while taking in the beauty of the moment.

Taking a breather at the Café am Neuen See

The Magazine

Berlin's **DIVERSITY**

Berlin is big – 891.67km² (554mi²) to be exact. At its largest, it's 45km (30mi) from east to west and 38km (23.6mi) from north to south. Each district has its own unique charm.

No one's really interested in finding out whether people come from the East or West of the city today – what's much more important is the district people call home ((are you from Tempelhof or Pankow?) If you're coming to live in Berlin or moving house within the city, your choice of area is vital – it plays a large part in determining your quality of life.

In Berlin, your "quality of life" is dictated by a district's variety of places to shop and go out, its cinemas and theatres, and how close you'll be to parks, pools and stations. If you love hustle and bustle and enjoy going out, avoid the suburbs and head to Friedrichshain or Kreuzberg instead.

Berliners live in their *Kiez* ("neighbourhood"). This word of Slavic origin actually refers to a modest servants' settlement. In Berlin, *Kiez* just means "home". You'll find everything you'll ever need in your *Kiez*: Bakeries, churches, kindergartens, a warm welcome, a word of encouragement, a quick chat with an acquaintance on the street and your regular go-to bar.

Middle-class Charlottenburg

A wild party in White Trash, a club-restaurant in Prenzlauer Berg

Farewell... For Ever?

Anyone who makes the move from Kreuzberg to Charlottenburg, for example, will often have to leave their friends behind for good – they won't happen to bump into each other any more, and can't arrange to meet on the corner. People see each other less and less until they gradually lose touch.

Berliners move house with incredible frequency – usually to another part of their *Kiez*. Sometimes they'll end up somewhere they don't like, however. Many people from Kreuzberg moved to Prenzlauer Berg in the early 90s after the Wall came down, for instance, because it reminded them of their early days in Kreuzberg – a once wild place with an uncertain future. Many are now moving back: Prenzlauer Berg has become too tidy, too chic and too bourgeois for their tastes.

Home is Where Your *Kiez* is

The flux of inhabitants helps shape the character of each *Kiez*. People change their neighbourhood, gradually making it their very own. The formerly run-down workers' district of Friedrichshain, for example, was abandoned by many disgruntled residents. Young people – for whom Mitte was too pricey and Prenzlauer Berg too posh and intellectual – moved into the cheap flats there instead. They opened colourful shops and bars and created their very own redefined, remodelled *Kiez*. A similar change is currently taking place in the Neukölln district. Hip bars and clubs are springing up in place of workers' watering holes. Young folk are moving in, and the rent is rising. All of a sudden, *Kreuzkölln* – the north of the area near Kreuzberg – has become a chic place to live.

Experience
THE CAPITAL

Exciting museums, imposing buildings, elegant shops, fantastic events… there's so much to discover as you explore Berlin. Why not take a boat trip or climb aboard a double decker bus?

Bus Route 100

This popular city trip only costs the price of a single ticket. The yellow double decker takes around 25 minutes to show you all of the capital's most important sights. The first East-to-West route after the Berlin Wall came down, Line 100 is much more than just a bus service: Architecture, politics and contemporary history come to life as you head from Alexanderplatz, down Unter den Linden, past the Reichstag and Bellevue Palace and over to Zoologischer Garten station. Buses leave every few minutes. Beware of pickpockets. The equally popular 200 bus goes from Zoo Station to Prenzlauer Berg via Potsdamer Platz.

Boat Trips

A great way to experience the city from a whole new perspective! If you've only got an hour to spare, take the "Bridges Tour" from somewhere in Mitte. If you've got three hours to spend and want to relax and see something new, take a round trip down the Spree and the Landwehr canal. You'll pass Museumsinsel (Museum Island), new government buildings, industrial wharves and Charlottenburg Palace. You'll also see Potsdamer Platz from an unusual angle and get to peek in at the private lives of Kreuzberg's residents from the canal. Mind your head under the bridges!

Night at the Museum

Dancing in the Pergamon Museum, puppetry by ancient statues and readings with music next to Nefertiti… experience something new on the *Lange Nacht der Museen* ("Long Night of the Museums") in March and August. Shuttle buses run from one venue to the next until about 2am. For toy theatres, night-time jungle tours at the Botanic Garden, and much, much more, visit www.lange-nacht-der-museen.de.

Karneval der Kulturen

Around 503,000 foreigners from 186 countries live in Berlin. When the "Carnival of Cultures" passes through Kreuzberg at Easter, it looks as if they're all there at once! Spectators can see different groups with costumes, exotic sounding music, dances and unusual rituals from all over the world in a parade that lasts for several hours (www.karneval-berlin.de).

Summer Nights at the Waldbühne

Whether you're off to a jazz, rock or classical concert, the most important thing is to take a picnic (and perhaps a blanket if it's a little chilly outside). The Waldbühne is a mighty, circular, open-air arena in the middle of the city with seating for 20,000 people. A twin awning shelters the stage. Come early to find a good seat. Picnic until the show starts. No glass bottles. (S-Bahn: Pichelsberg; www.concert-concept.de).

The whole world comes out to play at the Carnival of Cultures

THE GOVERNMENT DISTRICT

The Chancellery, the Bundestag buildings and the Parliamentary offices are collectively known as the *Band des Bundes* ("The Federal Strip"). Green spaces stretch between the structures, and the river Spree symbolically separates the complex into two halves. Topped with its glass dome, the majestic Reichstag looks unimpressed by the young buildings around it.

Berliners and visitors in the city's top attraction – the Reichstag Dome

Everything looks new here. Well… nearly everything: Although the Chancellery was opened as late as 2001, the Reichstag – a crowd-pleasing parliamentary building designed by Paul Wallot – has been standing on this site since 1894. The *Band des Bundes*, which includes the stylistically unified Chancellery and two Federal buildings, was dreamt up by architects Axel Schulte and Charlotte Franck.

The Chancellery

When it's sunny outside, it's worth taking a walk along the banks of the Spree down past the Chancellery. You might even get to see Frau Merkel taking a phone call by a window… If you don't, you can always see her colleagues eating lunch with a river view in the cafeteria. A monumental steel sculpture by Spanish-Basque artist Eduardo Chillida stands at a height of over

The Paul-Löbe and Marie-Elisabeth-Lüders buildings form a stylistic whole

5m (16ft) by the entrance to the building. Its four arms come together, representing German unity.

Paul-Löbe-Haus

This building opposite the Chancellery was named after a former Reichstag President (1920–32). 550 offices for 275 deputies are housed here along with 450 committee bureaux. The large glass façades on the western and eastern sides unite the building architecturally with the Chancellery and the Marie-Elisabeth-Lüders-Haus on the other bank of the Spree. Public exhibitions on political themes are held in the foyer.

Marie-Elisabeth-Lüders-Haus

This building was the last to be presented to the government when it opened in 2003. It houses the world's third largest parliamentary library and boasts a public exhibition hall where temporary exhibitions of modern art are put on display. The Berlin Wall used to run where the building sits today – a memorial, open to visitors, stands in memory of this fact. Marie-Elisabeth Lüders, after whom the building was named, was the first female deputy in the German Reichstag (during the Weimar Republic).

INSIDER INFO

■ A visit to the imposing glass dome of the Reichstag is an absolute must while you're in Berlin (➤ 58).

■ The work of more than 100 renowned international artists – including the likes of Joseph Beuys, Georg Baselitz, Jenny Holzer und Gerhard Richter – are on display in the government buildings. Visitors can admire some of it on free **Art and Architecture Tours** through the Paul-Löbe-Haus and the Reichstag building. Tours are held most weekends and have to be booked ahead. English tours on request. (www.bundestag.de)

Insider Tip

An **ISLAND**
in the "Red Sea"

During World War II, the USA, the Soviet Union and Great Britain agreed to break up the German Reich and Berlin into occupied zones. When it came down to it, however, it turned out that the Eastern Power had other plans…

Berlin was placed under Allied control after the War. When the Western powers – the British, French and Americans – made the decision to rebuild West Germany at London's 6-Power Conference in March 1948, the Soviets immediately withdrew their offer of collaboration. Their military authorities blocked all land access to the city on 24 June, 1948.

Air Bridge

US military governor Lucius D. Clay organised an air bridge together with the British Royal Air Force that supplied around 2.5 million people with all the necessities of life for 11 months. From coal to toilet paper, clothes to Father Christmases, there was nothing the Americans didn't bring into Tempelhof airport. One of their planes, nicknamed *Rosinenbomber* ("Raisin Bombers") by the people of Berlin, can be seen on top of the Deutsches Technikmuseum (German Museum of Technology) near Potsdamer Platz. A memorial commemorates the operation and its victims.

A New Light in the West

The "Berlin Aid Act" of 1950 gave this "front-line city" – as West Berlin was known – billions in subsidies. The money was spent on making the city look fantastic, complete with new districts, department stores, dance

Left: Young people greet an American "Raisin Bomber"; Right: A rally in front of the war-damaged Reichstag

halls and film festivals to show West Berlin's will to survive as a self-governing entity. At the same time, firms, banks, trade associations and politicians fled to West Germany. Despite this, West Berlin – the "Showcase of the West" – celebrated its status as an economic miracle.

Cut Off

In 1952, the GDR ("German Democratic Republic", the East German State) cut all phone lines between the East and West of the city. The bus and tram links between the two halves were also shut down in 1953. Berliners had to walk over border crossings or take the U and S-Bahn trains. In a programme of "voluntary construction work", East Berliners built sports grounds, created the Freidrichsfelde Zoo and refurbished Unter den Linden boulevard, the Rotes Rathaus (Red Town Hall) and the Volksbühne theatre.

Living in Isolation

An East German workers' protest against increasing labour quotas was suppressed on 17 June, 1953, leaving at least 50 dead and 200 wounded. West Germany declared it a national holiday, the "Day of German Unity". By 1961, 2.7 million people had fled away from "the Russians" and towards the "golden West." This mass exodus put the East's reconstruction work in jeopardy, so the Soviets put up road blocks and started building the Wall around their sector on 13 August, 1961, turning West Berlin into an "Island in the Red Sea".

From left to right: Greetings over barbed wire; the Sector border after the Wall was built; a last chance to flee as the wall goes up on Bernauer Straße

CULTURE FOR ALL

A newspaper with tips on the day's events can only give you a taste of the enormous number of things to do here. In truth, Berlin's real cultural wealth comes from the whole city being like a stage – a fact for which it's envied all over the world.

Things begin to kick off as the sun sets in the sky: A colourful crowd starts to gather at the Strandbar Mitte beach bar right on the banks of the river Spree. People dance under the darkening sky as tango, salsa and swing ring out of the speakers. If you need a break, spend some time waving at the passengers on the passing tour boats or enjoy the light effects projected onto the façade of the Bode Museum. If you like your melodies a little more civilised, the Berlin Philharmonic puts on free musical lunch breaks for your delectation on Tuesdays (➤ 109).

INSIDER INFO

The Neuköllner Opera has been the talk of the town for many years thanks to its entertaining performances and soap operas. Its "Berlin Opera Prize" – a competition for young composers – is a unique institution in Germany. (Neuköllner Oper: Karl-Marx-Str. 131–133, tel: 030 68 89 07 77, www. neukoellneroper.de, U-Bahn: Karl-Marx-Straße)

Insider Tip

Give your Imagination Wings!

A ruined department store in Oranienburger Straße became the Tacheles Art House after the Wall came down. It was taken over by people from all over the world and used as a place for sculpture, painting, showing films, dreaming up inventions and partying. They sought inspiration here, letting their creativity, music, dance, video art and fashion run wild in spaces behind wooden partitions and in the abandoned cavities of buildings. Different art forms continually pop up like will-o'-the-wisps in new venues, however, and the old haunts gradually fade away. That's what happened to the Tacheles, which was abandoned in September 2012. Some of the artists have found new creative spaces at the site of a former stockyard in the eastern district of Marzahn.

High and Fringe Culture

There are three major opera houses and a number of other stages – perhaps around 50? – that even most Berliners don't know the names of. Most of them are fringe theatres with unusual monikers: Vagantenbühne ("Journeymen Stage"), Theater unterm Dach ("The Theatre in the Roof"), and Zum Westlichen Stadthirschen ("To the Little Western City Stag"), for example. There are also around nine cabarets, but these are now being upstaged by comedy events. In addition, you'll also find puppet shows, classical comedy venues and revue theatres in Berlin alongside various houses of so-called high culture and 200 museums.

Creative Diversity

Berlin is full of different cultures happily existing in the same space – some of them interact, some of them keep to themselves. Chinese, Russian, Polish, American and African communities go about their lives without mingling or being influenced by the mainstream. A small slice of this cultural landscape takes part in the annual Carnival of Cultures at Easter – everyone's welcome, from Samba dancers to Native Americans (▶ 13).

Dancing by the Spree – the Strandbar Mitte beach bar

The Magazine

Many Actors, Few Stars

Hundreds of actors put on events in bars, halls, galleries, clubs, parks and cellars every day to compete for the public's attention. They get good and bad reviews and decide whether to carry on or give up. Their efforts mean there's always something going on in Berlin to make your evenings exciting. Some of the actors will shine as Berlin's stars – at least for a short time. The rest content themselves with air guitar competitions, cockroach racing and readings from telephone directories.

Home-grown Talent: Books, Culture, Fashion

It's probably due to nostalgia for such cultural heydays as the much-vaunted 'Golden 20s' that reading fever has broken out in the city – both in posh "salons" and trashy bars alike. DIY has become the new high culture in Berlin. It's a craze that takes many forms – the city's awash with home-grown hip hop talent (check out "Fler", "Pyranja" and "K.I.Z"), local fashion labels and young poets trying to capture the essence of the city with their words. The cultural ideal in Berlin is to be part of something new – at least as an on-screen extra. Thousands find jobs in films every year, and shoots often close off whole streets. There are numerous casting agencies, although the money isn't particularly good.

The Party and Music Capital

Berlin is one of Europe's most celebrated club and party capitals. Countless legal and illegal locations invite you in to party and dance the night away – and not just at the weekend. The highlights of this scene can be found are found in the Friedrichshain district and round the Oberbaumbrücke bridge. Party till dawn at Watergate (➤ 156) with its view of the Spree, for example, and you'll get to see the city from its best side. Berghain (➤ 174) – a monstrous, chic factory filled with booming techno beats near the Ostbahnhof station – draws an international crowd. And of course there are also the secret venues that play host to illicit clubs. Only a select few know of their whereabouts.

INSIDER INFO

Berlin's gastronomic scene keeps on getting more and more creative, too. **Street Food Thursday**, held in Kreuzberg's historic Markthalle 9 (Eisenbahnstr. 42, Thursday 5pm–10pm) has quickly become the hottest food event in the city. The selection ranges from Korean Tacos and New Zealand meat pies to Taiwanese burgers and American barbecue sandwiches. Wash it all down with a glass of wine or a Heidenpeters craft beer.

Two Berlins:
BATTLE of the BUILDINGS

The history of every city is reflected in its architecture. Each structure is a product of the era in which it was built. This makes Berlin's cityscape doubly rich in meaning – the Cold War was partly fought with bricks and mortar.

Soviet architecture with a twist of Schinkel: "People's Palaces" on Karl-Marx-Allee

Until World War II there was only one Berlin – a city with a prestigious classical centre built by the Hohenzollern dynasty. In the 19th century, *nouveau-riche* citizens filled Berlin (and the area around the Kurfürstendamm in particular) with ornate structures in a mix of neo-baroque and neoclassical styles, gaining Berlin the mocking nickname "Parvenupolis". Expressionism has left few architectural traces here, although Daniel Libeskind's Jewish Museum (► 142) has brought its spirit back to life.

Fortunately, the Nazis' most ambitious architectural dreams never saw the light of day. Much was destroyed in the war, but some of their monstrosities remain. The Reich Air Ministry in Leipziger Straße, built in 1935–6 and home to the Ministry of Finance today, is a gigantic complex. Five to seven storeys high, it's built around three closed and five open courtyards. Near the airfield at Tempelhof Airport (opened in 1923, closed since 2008) is another Nazi-built structure. Measuring in at 1.2km (0.75mi) long with 500 rooms, it's the largest office building in Europe.

The Magazine

"Berlin" (1987), a sculpture on the Kurfürstendamm

An Architects' War

After Berlin was split in two, the Cold War wasn't restricted to politics: It was also fought on drawing-boards and in the cityscape itself. The East set up the architectural "Competition for Berlin" in 1950, for example. The GDR's most significant urban development project was the building of Stalinallee (now Karl-Marx-Allee), where "People's Palaces" were built in a Soviet neoclassical, Schinkel-inspired style to house workers and their families. These massive housing blocks rose out of the rubble on either side of a 90m-wide traffic artery from 1952. For a low rental fee (and countless hours of work) you could get a modern apartment complete with a roof terrace, refuse chute and an internal telephone in these 100–300m-long, 7–9 storey buildings clad with Meissen porcelain tiles.

The West Replies

In 1956–7, the West responded with "Interbau", a development by international architects meant to bare the soul of this "forward-looking city." The projects built included the Hansaviertel (Hansa District, U-Bahn: Hansaplatz) by such modern masters as Walter Gropius, Alvar Aalto, Egon Eiermann and Bruno Taut.

IN MEMORIAM

Several monuments were erected in Berlin in honour of the Soviet soldiers killed during World War II. The largest of them all – a memorial complex dominated by a two storey-high sculpture of a soldier – can be found in **Treptower Park**. Standing on an elevation, he looks out across a giant field where some 5,000 men are buried. Reliefs carved into stone sarcophagi depict events from the war (S-Bahn: Treptower Park).

Showcase

When the Europa-Center (➤ 129) – the first high-rise in West Berlin – was built from 1963–1965, no one suspected that covered shopping arcades would one day become commonplace. With an ice rink, eateries and nearly 100 shops, this 22-storey, steel and glass-clad structure was the epitome of a new kind of "experiential shopping".

Just Keep Building!

Berlin's Fernsehturm (TV Tower) is the tallest building in Germany – it's a full 44m (144ft) taller than the Eiffel tower in Paris! The 368m (1,207ft)-high structure was designed to show the West exactly what the GDR was capable of. Opened in 1969, the tower was designed by architect Hermann

Young people meet at the Fernsehturm (TV Tower) on Alexanderplatz. Tourists prefer to see the view from up top.

Henselmann. On clear days, visitors to the 207m (679ft)-high viewing platform with a café can enjoy some fantastic views of the city (www.tv-turm.de).

The Same for Everyone

The competition between the two political systems still defines the city-scape today. The Berlin Philharmonie is just as much a child of the Cold War as the TV Tower. Separating the city led to the duplication of zoos, operas, museums, concert halls, observatories and theatres, etc. Anything that existed on one side of town had to be built on the other to show that both could get along perfectly well on their own.

Designers come in Droves

After the Wall came down, Berlin's empty spaces made it a paradise for architects from all over the world. This designing frenzy presented politicians with difficult decisions as to how they should proceed. Bold architectural creations began flooding the city, so it was to the relief of many when Berlin architect Hans Kollhoff came out and said: "It's a city, not an international exhibition."

BERLIN'S
HISTORY

Berlin is a young place – it's not even 800 years old – and the Cold War wasn't the first time in its history that it's been a double city. You can best see the traces of its eventful past from a bird's eye view (up on the TV Tower in Alexanderplatz, for example).

Can you spot the 8-lane concrete strip going over the Spree with two towers behind the Rotes Rathaus (Red Town Hall) and the Nikolaikirche (Church of Saint Nicholas)? That's the Mühlendamm bridge where the city began. It started out as a mere marshland ford halfway between the forts of Spandau and Köpenick. A colony of merchants were the first people to settle here alongside fishermen on a nearby Spree island.

A Tiny Triangle

The fishing island of Cölln was first mentioned as a town in 1237. Berlin, next to the ford, wasn't written about until 1244. If you imagine the island and the town hall at two corners of a triangle, the third point would lie where you can make out the mighty ruins of a Franciscan monastery church. This gives you an idea of how small Berlin was: Medieval mendicant monks lived on the outskirts of towns.

The town of Spandau was a long way from Berlin in the 1640s; it became part of Greater Berlin in 1920

Tolerance Pays Off

When Electoral Prince Friedrich Wilhelm took over in 1640, Berlin had already suffered significant damage in the Thirty Years' War. He married a Dutch princess, Louise of Nassau, whose fortune included the province of Brabant with its supplies of livestock and vegetables. Religious refugees from Austria and France were welcomed to Berlin with open arms. By the time Friedrich Wilhelm ("The Great Elector") died following a victory against Sweden, Berlin had grown into a town of 20,000 inhabitants. New citizens continued to arrive from France, Italy, Belgium, Switzerland, Poland and Bohemia – there were 30,000 Berliners by 1700.

Expansion from 1710

The Great Elector's successors were just as tolerant. In 1701, his son, nicknamed *der schiefe Fritz* ("crooked Fritz") because of his hunchback, chose to be crowned Friedrich I of Prussia in Königsberg Castle. This stronghold, dating from 1443, was remodelled and the Arsenal and the Gendarmenmarkt's two churches were built. The districts of Cölln, Friedrichswerder, Dorotheenstadt and Friedrichstadt were incorporated into Berlin on 1 January, 1710, and Berlin became the Royal city of residence.

A Peaceful Army

King Friedrich Wilhelm I (1713–40), the miserly "Soldier King" who was hated by Berliners, only ever saw fit to spend money on the military. His army was so precious to him that he never let it fight in any wars.

Unexpected Power Politics

When Friedrich II came to the throne, Berliners looked forward to having an artistic, peace-loving king. However, the young ruler, later known as Friedrich the Great, marched into Silesia and waged wars that made Prussia

Left: Friedrich Wilhelm welcomes the Huguenots to support the nation and its economy; Right: The Stadtschloss (City Palace) in Mitte, 1788; it's been undergoing work to turn it into the Humboldtforum since 2013 (end date: 2019)

The Magazine

more powerful than ever. To make up for the loss of money and men, Friedrich welcomed refugees into Berlin, just like his predecessors had done before him. His nephew, Friedrich Wilhelm II (1786–97), ruled over one of the most important – and, with 150,000 inhabitants, one of the most populous – cities in Europe.

Twice Crowned the Capital City

The Rotes Rathaus (Red Town Hall) was finished in 1870. The city, known as the "Athens by the River Spree", was connected to the outside world by 8 main railway lines. In a surprise move, King Wilhelm was crowned German Kaiser far from home in Versailles in 1871. Berlin, which had been named capital of the North German Confederation in 1866, now suddenly became capital of a new German Empire. The Empire's boom years began after defeating the French at Sedan in 1871. The Kurfürstendamm was extended in a Parisian style, the first U-Bahn lines were laid and the sewage system and market halls were built. Berlin was now a true world city.

The Boom is Over

The sudden boom came to an equally sudden end. Banks and stock exchanges faltered and commercial bankruptcies led to mass redundancies and unemployment. The first peace rally was held in July 1917, three years into World War I. Revolution broke out on 9 November, 1918. Workers went on strike. Social Democrat Philipp Scheidemann declared a Republic from the Reichstag, and Karl Liebknecht proclaimed a Free Socialist German Republic from the balcony of the City Palace. The Kaiser abdicated soon afterwards. Street fights, political assassinations, a general strike and a revolt followed. The Social Democrats won an election. In 1920, the surrounding towns, rural communities and estates were incorporated into the city. Greater Berlin now had 4 million inhabitants.

A time-lapse montage of history (from left to right): Philipp Scheidemann declares the Republic; Hitler becomes Reichskanzler (Chancellor) and brown-shirted Nazi mobs

Terror Turns to War

1929 saw the world economic crisis. In 1930, 450,000 Berliners were out of a job. The Nazi Party won seats in the Reichstag. Hitler became Chancellor on 30 January, 1933. A month later, the Reichstag went up in flames, ushering in a reign of terror: Anyone suspected of being left wing was arrested, the Communist party was banned, Jews were persecuted, books were burned, and concentration camp deportations began. Hitler started World War II in September 1939.

POTSDAM GIANTS

The thrifty Soldier King allowed himself one vice in his Potsdam garrison – a regiment of very tall soldiers. The minimum height of 1.9m (6'2") he required was difficult to find, so many of the fighters were brought in from the Tsarist Empire. Friedrich Wilhelm I gave the Dutch his grandfather's stronghold in West Africa on one condition – that they present him with 12 tall African men.

Four Sectors

The Red Army entered Berlin in April 1945. Hitler and his partner Eva Braun committed suicide in a bunker north of Leipziger Platz. By that time, Berlin looked like a moon landscape. 2.5 million people still lived amidst the city's 75,000,000m³ (246,000,000ft³) of rubble. The victors divided Berlin into four parts.

The Capital Once Again

When the German Democratic Republic (GDR) was founded in 1949, East Berlin was declared its capital. The border crossing was reopened on Bornholmer Straße on 9 November, 1989. Berlin was made the capital city and the seat of government for a reunited Germany.

march through the Brandenburg Gate; books are burned on Opernplatz; Red Army soldiers hoist the victory flag; women sort through what remains of Berlin

BERLIN: ECO CITY

With fewer and fewer cars, more and more bikes, and increasing numbers of buildings employing renewable sources of energy, Berlin is the low-CO_2 capital of Germany!

Berlin is eco-friendly in terms of the number of cars on its roads: Only one in three inhabitants now owns their own automobile. Instead, people are increasingly turning to cycling, which is why dedicated bike streets where cyclists have priority have been set up over the past few years. Berlin's visitors also enjoy a pedal: As well as a great many rental shops, you'll also find a number of guided bike tours – try one from Berlin on Bike (www.berlinonbike.de) or the Fahrradstation (▶ 40), for example. Tours are also available that deal with various themes, including architecture and the history of the city.

Solar Cells and Organic Markets Galore

Berlin uses less energy and produces less CO_2 per capita than any other city or state in the whole of Germany! Lots of public institutions and large businesses are setting a good example. The Bundestag (German Federal Government), for instance, is kept warm by its own plant-oil thermal power station and uses solar cells to heat its water. The headquarters of the CDU (a large German political party) and the Heinrich-Böll foundation's new building are also equipped with photovoltaic systems and constructed using home-grown timber. As well as the usual sights, a round trip on a solar boat (www.solarpolis.de, tel: 01 51 54 22 80 44) will show you areas and buildings that have

More and more Berliners are taking up cycling

You'll spot organic sausages all over the city – this stall's on Kollwitzplatz

minimised their energy consumption. You can also go on your own adventure by hiring a solar vessel yourself (▶ Insider Info).

Like organic, locally sourced food? Then Berlin is the place for you! Countless organic markets and supermarkets provide Berliners with a selection of fresh produce. One of the largest organic supermarkets is found in Prenzlauer Berg (www.lpg-biomarkt.de). It's also where the original branch of Europe's first vegan supermarket chain opened in 2011 (www.veganz.de). Berlin's largest weekly eco market attracts a sustainably minded crowd. You'll find such tasty treats as *Currywurst* (sausage with curry sauce) made with organic meat (Thu noon–7pm, till 6pm in winter).

Swimming in the Spree?

Berlin Engineer Ralf Steeg wants to make the Spree – the best-known river in Berlin – suitable for swimming once again. He's developed a system of collecting pools that would prevent raw sewage from getting into the river during periods of heavy rain. This waste would then be cleaned in purification plants. The Berlin Senate likes the idea; the only problem is finding the funding. It would be great to get people swimming in the river again more than 80 years after it was originally banned.

INSIDER INFO

Located on the banks of the Dahme near Köpenick Palace, Berlin's first **solar boat rental shop** hires out boats for up to 8 people by the hour or per day. From late March till early October you can charter vessels ranging from little two-seaters to big yachts and and take them on a tour round Berlin – all without need of a licence. The boats are CO_2 neutral, don't use any oil and glide quietly over the water (Solarboot Pavillon Berlin Köpenick, tel: 01 60 6 30 99 97, www.solarwaterworld.de).

BBQS, JOGGING, Drinking COFFEE

There's only one city in the world with over 400,000 trees, parks on every corner and even an airstrip used as an open-air playground. Its name? Berlin!

Berlin is full of green spaces where you can have a barbeque. On sunny summer weekends, people head out to take part in a true Berlin ritual: In the early afternoon, couples, families and groups of friends of all ages grab their rugs, garden chairs, crockery, grills, charcoal and food and hunt for the best place to set up camp. They then spend the whole day eating, drinking, daydreaming under the trees and playing Frisbee.

> "countless cafés and watering holes set up shop"

Green spaces are a vital part of Berlin life: As soon as the sun starts shining, locals head outside. They're spoilt for choice: Nearly a third of the city is covered in parks and woodland!

A Peaceful Paradise

Hordes of joggers and walkers use the city's green spaces every day. Idlers can also have fun under the trees, however – in the idyllic rose garden in Humboldthain Park, for example, or at the edge of the Märchenbrunnen (Fairy-tale Fountain) in the Volkspark Friedrichshain. Fancy a cold drink

or a cappuccino? You won't have far to go. Countless cafés and watering holes set up shop as soon as the first ray of sun hits the foliage. You can enjoy this outdoor world late into the night – sit with a beer under the tapestry of stars at the fishing huts by Schlachtensee lake, for example, and watch lovers rowing across the water.

Parks: Something for Everyone

The city's natural side isn't just popular with Frisbee and volleyball enthusiasts: Berliners also relax by doing Yoga, Tai Chi and Qi Gong in many of the parks. Kiteboarders flit over the former landing strips at Tempelhof airfield, open-air Karaoke fans meet in the Mauerpark on Sundays, and jugglers get their balls out in the morning sun long before the young men arrive to bronze themselves in the altogether on the screened-off *Schwulenwiese* ("Gay Meadow") in Neukölln's Hasenheide Park.

A Sunday Picnic in the Tiergarten

Beach Bars ("Strandbars") draw people to Berlin's waterways in summer

BERLIN:
CAPITAL of IDEAS

Berlin, a UNESCO City of Design, is home to more creative types than most other places in the world. Innovative products are created by the hour. You can admire them – and buy them! – all over the city.

Fancy some book ends in the shape of the Berlin Wall? Or perhaps a belt made from an authentic Berlin bike tyre would be more your cup of tea? There's no end to the the range of design souvenirs you can buy in Berlin. And if you arrive into the Hauptbahnhof (Central Station) or Tegel Airport, check out the design vending machines that display a selection of what Berlin's creatives have to offer. As well as getting your hands on a bike tyre belt, you'll also find pillowcases with pictures of Berlin buildings and bags with punning local phrases.

Kitchen Table Creations
The careers of many Berlin designers get started at at the kitchen table – you don't need a lot of money to achieve a great deal in this self-appointed

INSIDER INFO

Countless celebrities and notables from the international fashion scene all flock to the city at the end of January and the start of July for **Berlin Fashion Week**. They're here to party and spot the latest trends (www.fashion-week-berlin.com). **Bread & Butter** (www.breadandbutter.com), the largest streetwear fair in the world, is a real crowd-puller. Some fashion shows are always held in such surprising locations as aircraft hangers, churches, clubs and in the U-Bahn, for example. You can also visit **The Key.to** (thekey.to), which displays the very latest in eco fashion.

Fashion: Made in Berlin

European Capital of Creatives. The metropolis on the Spree draws in young designers from all over the world as if by magic: Over 800 fashion labels toil away creating the newest outfits, for example. The possibility of renting cheap shop/studios, the diversity of marketing platforms for small fashion labels, and the city's openness to new trends all make Berlin an ideal breeding ground for inventiveness and innovative products. It's little surprise that UNESCO named Berlin a "City of Design".

Fashion from Berlin

Many well-known Berlin fashion labels sell their clothes in the Spandauer Vorstadt district between the Hackescher Markt and Rosenthaler Platz in Mitte. You'll find row after row of fashion emporia in the city – there's a particularly high density of these stylish boutiques in Alte Schönhauser Straße and the Hackesche Höfe. The latter is home to the cult shoe label **Trippen** (▶ 98). Young designers also abound in Kastanienallee and Oderberger Straße in Prenzlauer Berg and around Boxhagener Platz in Friedrichshain. Less established creators sell their wares at such events as the flea markets in the Mauerpark (▶ 167) and Boxhagener Platz (▶ 164).

I Want to be a Designer!

Around 5,500 students study at Berlin's nine fashion schools and enhance the clothing scene with their fresh ideas and debut collections. No other city in Europe trains as many fledgling designers!

WATERSIDE CITY

Berlin has 190km (120mi) of waterways and nearly 1,000 bridges – it's a perfect place for houseboats and long walks along the river.

A boat rocks on the Havel river. A man is reading a newspaper under a parasol while his wife chats to a neighbour. She's standing with her legs below the waterline – and so is her friend. An hour later, nothing much will have changed. Not all boat owners are quite as relaxed as that, but on summer days when it's boiling hot in the city, the ducks seem to be the only things moving on the water. As soon as the good weather starts to kick in, boat owners have a quick check to see that their craft are actually still mobile.

Dreamboat

German writer Kurt Tucholsky once wrote that he dreamt of a "villa in the country with a large terrace; the Baltic in front of you, Friedrichstraße

Every Berliner's Dream: A houseboat on the Spree

behind; a place of rural chic with great views – you can see the Bavarian Alps from the bathroom window…" If you take a boat trip to Charlottenburg, you'll see that some people have actually created their own dream residences on boats in the Spree. You'll also see washing drying on board ships at Plötzenseer Kolk next to Saatwinkler Damm road. The owners of these vessels must not only be skilled craft-speople but also masters of diplomacy when dealing with officials and the authorities – strictly speaking, their house-boats shouldn't exist.

BY the Water, Not ON the Water!

The concept of a "waterside city" assumes that people live *by* the water, not *on* it. Once the first companies and embassies had gobbled up all the best conventional sites, developers started to build housing right on the river bank. People have now begun to clamour for floating houses

Above: A cooling jump in the Spree;
Below: Relaxing at Kreuzberg's Urbanhafen ("Urban's harbour")

(not normal houseboats – properly designed homes bobbing in the water!) It's said that "Berlin was built from barges," and it's true that the water has always been a major transport artery for the city, but whether you'd actually want to live there is another matter altogether!

Floating Homes

The "Floating Homes" architectural competition has been held, and the designs have been seen by the authorities. The only problem – they haven't yet decided what to do. Until they make up their minds, you can enjoy the hotel boats by Oberbaum bridge, the floating restaurants in the Urbanhafen, the open-air cinema on the "Insel der Jugend" (Island of Youth) opposite Treptower Park, and Berlin's 40 or so river beaches and 31 outdoor pools.

DID YOU KNOW…

- … that you can sleep in Karl Lagerfeld's bed in the Schlosshotel if you don't mind splashing out? When designing the rooms, the fashionista took out a lifetime reservation on one of the suites!

- … that there are 70,000 allotment holders in Berlin? They are a powerful political force and protest vehemently against any proposal to use their beloved land for any other purpose. They saved a site from being developed with 700 apartments in 2014, for example.

- … about the remarkable Noack foundry? They made Rainer Fetting's statue of Willy Brandt that's found in the Kreuzberg offices of the SPD (Social Democratic Party), and cast the *Quadriga* on the Brandenburg Gate. They also have a statue of Friedrich the Great and sculptures by Henry Moore, Georg Kolbe and Joseph Beuys in their workshop.

- … that Europe's largest Chinese Garden (2.7ha/6.5 acres) is located in Berlin's Marzahn district?

- … that the geographical centre of Berlin is on Alexandrinenstraße in Kreuzberg? If you want to be extremely exact, you'll find it at 52°, 30', 10" north, 13°, 24', 15" east.

- … that a World Cup ski race was held on the Teufelsberg in Grunewald in 1987? It took place on grass!

Berliners love their dogs – there are over 105,000 in the city.

- … that Berlin has the Allies to thank for not having a closing time imposed on its bars? Heinz Zellermeyer, head of the German Hotels and Inns guild, helped have it abolished in 1949. After years of curfews, Berliners wanted to go back to the way they ran their watering holes before the War.

- … that a dog tax was introduced to Berlin on 20 April, 1830? There were more than 6,000 dogs registered in the city back then (the total stands at more than 105,000 today). Some politicians wanted to ban poorer people from having dogs at all. Their reasoning? They didn't need them because they didn't have any property worth protecting!

Finding Your Feet

First Two Hours

Tegel Airport

Berlin has two airports. Tegel "Otto Lilienthal" Airport (TXL) deals with internal German connections and international flights to Western Europe and the USA. It's located about 8km (5mi) away from west Berlin and 10km (6mi) from the eastern side of the city.

Airport Transfers

- Depending on the time of day and the traffic, a **taxi** to the city takes 15 to 30 mins and costs around €20 to the west and €25 to the east.
- The **JetExpressbus TXL** connects Alexanderplatz and Unter den Linden with the airport. The journey takes 40 minutes.
- The **Expressbus X9** goes to Zoologischer Garten station.
- **Bus 109** goes to Jakob-Kaiser-Platz, where you can change to U-Bahn train U7.
- Buses depart approx. every 10 minutes (20 mins at the weekend).

Schönefeld Airport

Around 20km (12mi) southeast of the city centre, Schönefeld Airport (SXF) receives flights from the Near East, Asia, and eastern and south-eastern Europe. It also deals with charter flights. It's right next to Berlin Brandenburg (BER), an international airport that's currently under construction.

Airport Transfers

- Depending on the time of day, a **taxi** into the city takes around 40 minutes and costs about €40.
- The **Airport-Express** departs for the city centre every half an hour (takes 20 minutes to Alexanderplatz, 30 minutes to Zoologischer Garten station). The trains are called RE 7 and RE 14 in the timetable.
- The **S9** train travels via Friedrichshain (Ostkreuz) and Prenzlauer Berg (Schönhauser Allee) to Pankow. Going to the Messe (Trade Fair)? Take the S45 and change to the S41 at Südkreuz.

Central Airport Information

☎ 030 60 91 11 50.

Railway Stations

IC and ICE trains stop at the Hauptbahnhof (Central Station), Ostbahnhof and Spandau Bahnhof stations. Fast trains also call at Gesundbrunnen (Wedding) and Südkreuz (Tempelhof). Regional and S-Bahn trains currently stop at Zoologischer Garten station. The Hauptbahnhof is Europe's largest station.

- For train times and ticket prices, call 0180 6 99 66 33 (€0.20 per call from a German landline; max. €0.60 from a German mobile) or visit www.bahn.de.

Coaches

Long-distance national and international coaches stop at the **Zentraler Omnibusbahnhof** (ZOB, Masurenallee 4–6) near the Funkturm tower and the International Congress Centre (ICC). For information, call 030 3 01 03 80, or visit www.iob-berlin.de.

Cars

All main roads and motorways join the **Berliner Ring** road (A10). Branch off to head to your destination.

Tourist Information

You can get a lot of information about Berlin on the Internet (www.visit-berlin.de), over the phone (030 25 00 23 23), at airports and from Berlin's Tourist Information offices: at the Brandenburg Gate (Apr–Oct 9.30–7, Nov–Mar until 6pm), at the Fernsehturm (TV Tower, Apr–Oct 10–6, Nov–Mar 10–4), at the Hauptbahnhof (Central Station, 8–8) and in the Neues Kranzler Eck on the Kurfürstendamm (Mon–Sat 9.30–8).

Museumspass (Museum Pass)

The Berlin Museum Pass (€24) grants culture vultures access to the permanent exhibitions of over 50 museums for three consecutive days (passes are on sale at museums and tourist information centres).

Getting Around

Berlin has an excellent U-Bahn (underground) and S-Bahn (local commuter railway) system complemented by bus and tram routes and a good cycle network. Cycle taxis ferry people around from spring to autumn (predominantly through parks). Most of Berlin's boats are pleasure cruisers, but there are also ferry lines in Köpenick and Wannsee.

Public Transport

- The Berlin **U-Bahn** celebrated its centenary in 2002. Around 906 million passengers travel on approx. 144km (90mi) of track each year. There are 173 stations, 79 of which are listed historic buildings.
- Nine U-Bahn lines run from **4 in the morning until 2am the next day**. A 24-hour service has been introduced on Saturday and Sunday nights and during public holidays. Routes that aren't serviced by the U-Bahn are covered by night buses.
- 15 **S-Bahn lines** run partial routes twenty-four hours a day. A circle line travels round the city centre.
- 15 **MetroBus** and 9 **MetroTram lines** supplement the U and S-Bahn routes.
- There are three **price zones**: A lies inside the S-Bahn circle line, B ends at the city limits, and C covers the surrounding areas. An AB ticket is valid for the whole of Berlin (with the exception of Schönefeld Airport).

Tickets

- **Single tickets** are valid for two hours, but not for return journeys. A **Kurzstreckenkarte** ("short trip ticket") allows you to travel 3 stops with the U or S-Bahn and up to 6 stops with the bus or tram.
- You can buy tickets from the machines in railway stations, on trams and from bus drivers. You can also get them from kiosks, tobacconists and anywhere you see signs advertising "**BVG-Karten**".
- **Children aged 6 and under** travel for free. There are reduced tariff tickets for those aged 7 to 14.
- A bike ticket is required to take a **bicycle (Fahrrad)** on public transport. You also need to pay for **larger dogs**.

Finding Your Feet

- You can buy **Zeitkarten** ("Timed Tickets") for 1–7 days.
- The **WelcomeCard** allows tourists to discover Berlin with free travel on the city's public transport for two, three or five days. You also get a discount at many cultural institutions and museums. The cards are available online at www.visit-berlin.de or from BVG ticket machines.
- **Rail tickets** are only valid after they've been stamped by the red ticket validating machines on the platform.
- The **penalty for traveling without a ticket** is €40.

City Bus Tours

Numerous companies offer bus tours of the city.. Lasting between 1.5 and 3 hours, they start from the **Kurfürstendamm** (on the corner of Fasanenstraße, opposite Breitscheidplatz and across from the Europa-Center, for example) and from **Unter den Linden** (at the corner of Friedrichstraße). The tours have live commentaries, sometimes in two languages. You can often also listen to information in several languages via headphones, but the recordings are sometimes out of date.

Cycling

- The German railway system has 1,700 "**Callbikes**" spread over the city centre. After a one-time registration (e.g. at www.callabike.de), you can hire and return bikes by phone (you'll find the number on the bike itself). Payment is carried out electronically.
- You can now also **hire bikes** in every central city district, including at various cycle stations in Mitte (Auguststr. 29a, tel: 030 22 50 80 70; Dorotheenstr. 30, tel: 030 28 38 48 48; Leipziger Str. 56, tel: 030 66 64 91 80) and in Kreuzberg (Bergmannstr. 9, tel: 030 2 15 15 66).

Taxis

There are taxi ranks at airports, railway stations, shopping centres, event venues and larger squares. If a taxi's yellow light is illuminated it means it's empty and available to be flagged down. The large Berlin taxi firms can be contacted using two free centralised numbers: 0800 2 22 22 55 and 0800 0 26 10 26.

Velotaxi (Cycle Taxi)

High-tech tricycles have been ferrying people along bus lanes, cycle tracks and through parks since 1997. If they're empty, just wave them down. There are ranks at Wittenbergplatz, Adenauerplatz, the Zoo, the Brandenburg Gate and Alexanderplatz. You can also book by calling 0178 8 00 00 41.

By Car

Berlin's traffic is less dense than most other big cities, but parking is just as much of a problem. Although many areas allow some free parking (evenings, Saturday afternoons, Sundays), you always have to pay in the city centre. 30 mins will cost at least €1. An *Umweltplakette*, a sticker displaying your car's environmental rating, is required if you want to drive in the city. You'll need a green (highest level) sticker to drive within the S-Bahn circle line. Info: www.environmental-badge.co.uk.

By Plane

Air Service Berlin can help you out if you fancy clambering aboard a biplane, a helicopter or a sea plane and experiencing Berlin from the air. Tel: 030 53 21 53 21 or visit www.air-service-berlin.de.

By Boat

Almost 200km (125mi) of waterways are used for tours and excursions by shipping companies of all sizes. The outings on offer include trips through historic Berlin, tours through the city, seven lake expeditions, excursions to Köpenick and Potsdam, jaunts round the canal locks in Brandenburg and voyages at night. The biggest firms are Stern and Kreis Schifffahrt (sales office in Treptow harbour, tel: 030 5 36 36 00; www.SternundKreis.de) and Reederei Riedel (030 6 91 37 82; www.reederei-riedel.de). Brochures are available from tourist information centres (➤ 39).

Berlin on Foot

A whole host of operators offer city walking tours with **various themes**. They'll take you through the historic city, to government departments and embassies, round famous cemeteries, up hills, into single districts and following the footsteps of poets. There are English language tours alongside outings in German, French and Italian. Info and times can be found in *tip* and *zitty* magazines.

Accommodation

With over 800 places to stay – including designer hotels, women-only hotels and hotels geared to kids – you'll truly be spoilt for choice. The abundant selection just keeps on growing, with luxury hotels and cheap backpacker hostels leading the way.

City Districts

Almost all the hotels found in Mitte have been opened (or at least modernised) in the last ten years. Those in Prenzlauer Berg are all new. Nearly all of the city's backpacker hostels are found in the hip districts of Kreuzberg, Friedrichshain and Prenzlauer Berg. Some of the hotels around the Kurfürstendamm continue to uphold the traditions of the past with spacious, somewhat grandiose suites that play host to celebs – and not just when there's a film festival in town. You'll still find guest houses with attentive landladies and places kitted out with plush sofas and inherited works of art. Berlin is known around the world for its big gay and lesbian scene and its associated festivals. It even has its very own special range of LGBT hotels (the Pink Pillow Berlin Collection).

Reservations

Berlin Tourismus & Kongress GmbH (Am Karlsbad 11, 10785 Berlin) has partner hotels that can be booked at any time by phoning 030 25 00 25 or visiting www.visitberlin.de, where you can also get a guide to the hotels they represent. All other accommodation can be booked independently on the Internet.

Private Accommodation

Guest rooms and apartments – with or without host families – can also be rented privately. You can find out about them from displays in Tourist

Finding Your Feet

Information Centres (▶ 39). The Berlin Inn letting agency (Feilnerstraße 1, 10969 Berlin, tel: 030 3 39 88 77 80; www.berlin-inn.de) also provides rooms and apartments by the night.

Campsites

Berlin has 8 campsites, almost all of which are located in the the suburb of Spandau. They're also popular with Berliners in the summer. Details can be found at www.visitberlin.de and from the Deutscher Camping Club Berlin (www.dccberlin.de).

Hotels

The hotel prices in Berlin are relatively cheap. Unless there's a big event in town (such as a trade fair, etc.), you'll have a good chance of negotiating special rates.

Accommodation Prices
Price for a double room per night (incl. breakfast)
€ under 70 euros
€€ 70–120 euros
€€€ 120–180 euros
€€€€ over 180 euros

---

acksel Haus Berlin €€–€€€

A very beautiful, privately run little hotel in an excellent location in Prenzlauer Berg. It's just a few minutes' walk from Kollwitzplatz and the Wasserturm with its numerous cafés and restaurants. Most of the rooms are individually themed: You can sleep surrounded by animal motifs in the "Africa" room, share the "Movie" room with framed pictures of stars of the silver screen, and enjoy the free-standing bathtub and playful décor when you spend the night in "Rome". You can relax on a divan amidst the greenery of the pretty interior courtyard in summer.

➕ 201 F4 ✉ Belforter Str. 21
☎ 030 44 33 76 33; www.ackselhaus.de
Ⓜ Senefelder Platz

Adlon €€€€

This hotel – a new version of the legendary old Adlon which hosted the likes of Einstein, Charlie Chaplin and Thomas Mann – was where Michael Jackson caused quite a stir in 2002. The opulence of a golden age survives here un-changed: Liveried butlers lead you to rooms and suites glistening with gilded finery and the latest in luxury. The presidential suite has views of Unter den Linden and the Brandenburg Gate.

➕ 200 B2 ✉ Unter den Linden 77
☎ 030 2 26 10; www.hotel-adlon.de
Ⓜ Brandenburger Tor

Alexander Plaza €€–€€€

It's only a few steps away from this inviting hotel in the centre of Mitte to Alexanderplatz, Unter den Linden, the Synagogue in Oranienburger Straße and the Hackescher Markt. The recently renovated rooms are soundproofed and decorated in pleasant red and neutral tones. You can relax after a hard day's sightseeing in the hotel's own sauna or head to the fitness centre to pump yourself up for your evening ahead. The info boards in the foyer are worth a look to find out about the moving history of the hotel's location.

➕ 201 D3 ✉ Rosenstr. 1
☎ 030 24 00 10; classik-hotel-collection.com
Ⓜ Hackescher Markt

Arte Luise Kunsthotel €–€€€

Whether it's an attic room with a shared shower or a suite with its very own bath – there's a different world behind every door in this hotel. Each room is an individual work of art. You can check them all out online; the selection includes a cabaret room, a spy room, a colourful room in homage to Edward Hopper, and a black and white room by Elvira Bach. A small amount of money from the price of each residence goes to the artist involved.

🏠 200 B3 ✉ Luisenstr. 19
☎ 030 28 44 80; www.luise-berlin.com
🚇 Friedrichstr.

Baxpax Mitte hostel €

A nice backpacker hostel with individually styled rooms and shared bathrooms down the corridor. The themed accommodation includes the Honeymoon Suite for two people and the Four Elements room for groups. Located in an inexpensive part of Mitte, it's a great place for travellers on a budget and makes an ideal starting point for sightseeing and nightlife. The amenities include free WiFi, bike hire and reduced-price tickets to clubs.

🏠 200 B4 ✉ Chausseestr. 102
☎ 030 28 39 09 65; www.baxpax.de
🚇 Naturkundemuseum

Bleibtreu €€–€€€

This pleasant, central hotel has a beautiful, flower-scented lobby and a romantic courtyard. Situated in a side street off the Kurfürstendamm, it's been furnished with the goal of promoting the health of its guests. You can sleep, eat, relax and shop all under one roof. The Turkish bath (included in the price) *Insider Tip* and the health therapist can help you forget a stressful day's sightseeing. It also boasts the new Dudu 31, a branch of a hip restaurant in Mitte which serves healthy, tasty Asian fusion food in a chic urban atmosphere.

🏠 202 A3 ✉ Bleibtreustr. 31
☎ 030 88 47 40; www.bleibtreu.com
🚇 Uhlandstr.

Casa Camper €€€

This designer hotel is just as unconventional as the Camper brand's range of shoes itself. Located a few steps away from Hackescher Markt, the rooms are creative and decorated with a real eye for detail. The lounge on the top floor – where you can serve yourself free drinks and snacks 24/7 – is a little bit special.

🏠 200 D3 ✉ Weinmeisterstr. 1
☎ 030 20 00 34 10; www.casacamper.com
🚇 Weinmeisterstr.

Die Fabrik €

This former factory dating from the late 19th century has been turned into a simple yet charming five-storey hotel. Depending on their budget, guests can spend the night in inexpensive dormitories or in nicely furnished double rooms. Breakfast and all other meals are served in the connected Fabrik Café with its Kreuzberg atmosphere. The best thing about the hotel is the studio on the top floor with its sloping glass roof and its own wash hand basin. The hot water is produced by solar panels on the roof.

🏠 206 C2 ✉ Schlesische Str. 18
☎ 030 6 11 71 16; www.diefabrik.com
🚇 Schlesisches Tor

Ellington €€

A hotel steeped in history near the Ku'damm (Kurfürstendamm). Louis Armstrong, Ella Fitzgerald and Duke Ellington once played here at the legendary "Badewanne" jazz club, and Bowie & Co partied in the equally famous "Dschungel" club on the same site in the 70s. The modern hotel boasts extremely relaxing, cosily furnished rooms

Finding Your Feet

today. The Duke restaurant serves fresh international cuisine.

🔲 202 C3 ✉ Nürnberger Str. 50–55
☎ 030 68 31 50; www.ellington-hotel.com
🅢 Wittenbergplatz

Flower's Boardinghouse Mitte €€–€€€

Generously appointed apartments in a excellent location right next to the Hackescher Markt. It's a great alternative to a hotel if you want to feel right at home while you're in Berlin. Free tea, coffee, croissants and fresh bread rolls are available to take away from reception in the morning. If you stay in the maisonette apartment on the top floor, you'll get to enjoy a wonderful view over Mitte. The reception desk is staffed from 9am till 6pm.

🔲 201 E4 ✉ Mulackstr. 1
☎ 030 28 04 53 06; www.flowersberlin.com
🅢 Weinmeisterstr.

Grand Hyatt Berlin €€€€

Spanish architect José Rafael Moneo and Swiss designer Hannes Wettstein designed and furnished this luxury hotel on Potsdamer Platz. Modern art, contemporary design and top-class materials all form part of their stylistic concept. The Olympus Spa & Fitness Club on the 7th floor is superb and boasts a pool with city views. You can enjoy sophisticated delicacies in one of the two restaurants before rounding off the evening with a nightcap in the chic Vox Bar, which boasts live jazz from Thursday to Saturday and 240 types of whisky.

🔲 204 A4 ✉ Marlene-Dietrich-Platz 2
☎ 030 25 53 12 34; www.berlin.hyatt.com
🅢 Potsdamer Platz

Hecker's Hotel €€–€€€

Renowned for its friendliness, this little hotel earns its reputation anew every single day. The double rooms are equipped with walk-in wardrobes, kitchenettes and

marble baths. The themed suites are decorated in German Colonial, Bauhaus and Tuscan styles. Enjoy a glass of wine on the roof terrace in the evening and watch the bustling Kurfürstendamm down below.

🔲 202 A3 ✉ Grolmannstr. 35
☎ 030 8 89 00; www.heckers-hotel.com
🅢 Savignyplatz

Honigmond Garden Hotel €€€ *Inside Tip*

Lovingly restored rooms located round a green courtyard garden. Instead of traffic noise, you'll hear trickling water at breakfast and croaking frogs in the evening. Nevertheless, it's only a short walk to Friedrichstraße, Hackesher Markt and Museum Island.

🔲 200 B4 ✉ Invalidenstr. 122
☎ 030 28 44 55 77; www.honigmond.de
🅢 Naturkundemuseum

Hotel de Rome €€€

Luxury holidaymakers are greeted by a packing and unpacking service, the Bebel Bar and a good Italian restaurant when they check in at the former home of the Dresdner Bank. The erstwhile vaults now boast a stylish swimming pool with a luxurious spa right next door. You can enjoy cocktails with a view of Berlin from the roof terrace in summer.

🔲 200 C2 ✉ Behrenstr. 37
☎ 030 4 60 60 90; www.hotelderome.de
🅢 Französische Str.

Hotel Gendarm Nouveau €€–€€€

This friendly, elegantly furnished hotel with 39 rooms and 3 suites has the Konzerthaus concert hall and the German and French cathedrals right on its doorstep. With a bit of luck, you'll see them from your room. With chilled beer and cool cocktails, the cosy Gendarmenbar is a great place to relax 24/7.

🔲 200 C1 ✉ Charlottenstr. 61
☎ 030 2 06 06 60; www.hotel-gendarm-berlin.de
🅢 Stadtmitte

Lette'm Sleep €

A typical backpacker hostel in the middle of Prenzlauer Berg with bars, pubs and clubs very close by. The friendly rooms, furnished with light wood, accommodate up to ten people. Bathrooms and toilets are found down the corridor. The twin rooms even come with a small kitchenette. Guests hang out in the colourful, cosy common room which boasts cooking facilities and Internet access.

🔲 201, north of F5 ✉ Lettestr. 7
☎ 030 44 73 36 23; www.backpackers.de
🚇 Eberswalder Str.

Novum Hotel Gates €–€€

This 3-star business hotel is located in a 19th-century building, parts of which are protected by a historical preservation order. Such stars as Claudia Cardinale and Marlon Brando once climbed its beautiful staircase. It was dubbed "Europe's first Internet hotel" when it opened in 2001 thanks to its progressive IT equipment. They still offer free Internet via DSL and WiFi to this day.

🔲 202 A4 ✉ Knesebeckstr. 8–9
☎ 030 31 10 60; www.novum-hotels.de
🚇 Ernst-Reuter-Platz

Radisson Blu Hotel €€

Fancy a room with a sea view? This modern hotel has the next best thing – a 25m (82ft)-high aquarium filled with tropical fish in the atrium. You can't beat its central location by Museum Island.

🔲 201 D2 ✉ Karl-Liebknecht-Str. 3
☎ 030 23 82 80; www.radissonblu.de
🚇 Alexanderplatz

Riverside Royal Hotel & Spa €–€€€

This hotel right next to the Spree (all of the rooms have balconies!) calls itself a "Wellness Hotel for Lovers". It offers large, plush rooms with such features as four-poster water beds, free-standing bathtubs and Jacuzzis on the balcony. Guests can indulge in various treatments in the hotel's own Royal Spa. Why not try a sensual Bali Royal Massage?

🔲 200 C3 ✉ Friedrichstr. 105–106
☎ 030 28 49 00; www.tolles-hotel.de
🚇 Friedrichstr.

Schweizerhof Hotel Pullman €€€–€€€€

This modern business hotel near Zoo Station looks out over the zoo and a green inner courtyard. All of the rooms are stylish and practically furnished. The dedicated business rooms offer an abundance of space to work in. A generous hotel pool helps you forget the bustle of the metropolis. The wine bar and the Mediterranean restaurant serve up some tasty treats, and you can enjoy a nightcap in the open plan lobby bar. 👪 Kids up to the age of 12 stay for free in their parents' rooms.

🔲 202 D3 ✉ Budapester Str. 25
☎ 030 2 69 60; www.pullmanhotels.com/berlin
🚇 Zoologischer Garten

Food and Drink

Meatballs, Eisbein (pork knuckle) with puréed peas, liver with apple rings and onions... Berlin's traditional cuisine hardly ever appears on the menu any more. It's all about modern fusion food today – a phenomenon that's even taking over traditional snack stands.

Berlin's snack culture is legendary. "Invented" in 1949 in homage to American spare ribs with ketchup, the **Currywurst** (sausage with curry sauce) quickly replaced cold meatballs and warm hot dogs in Berliners'

Finding Your Feet

affections. If you order a *Currywurst* you'll be asked *"mit oder ohne?"* – with or without an outer skin – and *"knackig oder labbrig?"* – with crispy skin or soft? One *Currywurst* stand, **Konnopke** in Prenzlauer Berg (➤ 171), has become famous, although Kreuzbergers prefer to get their fix from Curry 36 on the Mehringdamm. If you want organic fare, head to Witty's Bioland Imbiss on Wittenbergplatz.

Most Popular Snack: Döner Kebabs
The Döner Kebab has recently outstripped the *Currywurst* in the popularity stakes. Take a piece of pita bread, add some sliced meat, lettuce, onions, cabbage and perhaps a shot of garlic sauce and you're ready to go. Bagels, exotic soups and Asian snacks are also hot on their heels.

High-class Cuisine
Berlin is the undisputed gourmet capital of Germany. No fewer than 14 of the city's restaurants were honoured in the 2014 Michelin guide – 9 of them were awarded one star and 5 even picked up two. Such top chefs as Tim Raue, Daniel Achilles and Michael Kempf work with precision, purity and imagination to create their culinary masterpieces. Their food is served up in stylish surroundings and accompanied by a range of fine wines.

Traditional Fare, Modern Interpretations
Old Berlin recipes have been à la mode in hip restaurants for some time now. Young chefs have given them a new lease of life, preferring to work with organic vegetables and locally sourced meat and fish.

International Cuisine
Nowadays you can eat Italian, Turkish, Greek, Spanish, French, Mexican, Brazilian, African, Australian, American, Chinese, Vietnamese and Japanese food in Berlin without ever leaving the city. There's also a wide selection for vegetarians and vegans, even at a top gourmet level. Berlin is also home to Germany's first Paleo restaurant where the focus is on healthy eating following the same diet as Stone Age man.

Al Fresco Dining
As soon as the sun comes out, Berlin's landlords set up tables in the garden or outside their front door. The city's a great place to sit outside! Quick, inexpensive set menus are often up for grabs at lunchtime (usually from noon till 3pm). Many city centre restaurants are open all day, while others only open their doors at 6pm.

Fancy a day trip? There are eateries with great views by the Havel (Moorlake; Blockhaus Nikolskoe) and the Spree (Klipper in Treptow).

The Most Important Meal
If you're a breakfast fan, you're in for a treat: Most Berlin cafés serve the first meal of the day until 4pm – sometimes even later. Many offer Sunday buffets where you can eat for as long as you like for a fixed price.

Berliner Weiße (White Berlin Beer)
Beer is most Berliners' tipple of choice when the sun goes down. Although the only major brewery left in Berlin is the Berliner-Kindl-Schultheiss-Brauerei, lots of small private outfits have recently popped up. The Huguenots were the first to brew *Berliner Weiße*, a firm local favourite.

It's a top-fermented light beer that's drunk with a straw from bowl-like glasses with an added "green *(grün)* shot" (woodruff syrup) or "red *(rot)* shot" (raspberry syrup). It's low alcohol, making it a refreshing summer drink.

Restaurant Prices
Prices for a main course, not including drinks:
€ under 12 euros
€€ 12–25 euros
€€€ over 25 euros

Shopping

Most visitors to Berlin enjoy shopping. As well as the classic shopping streets of Friedrichstraße and the Kurfürstendamm, you'll also find a wealth of small stores selling out-of-the-ordinary items.

Souvenirs

■ Almost everyone buys a **souvenir** when they visit Berlin. Such keep-sakes as Berlin bears, Brandenburg Gate ashtrays, tankards with coats of arms, t-shirts and *Ampelmännchen* (traffic light men) are sold in vast quantities. Producers of "genuine" pieces of the Berlin Wall do a brisk trade, thousands of snow globes cover gaudy *Trabis* (iconic GDR cars) in exhaust-blackened flakes, and so many GDR National People's Army caps have been bought over the years it's a wonder there are any left. Nevertheless, you'll still find them for sale alongside Soviet watches emblazoned with a red star.

■ If you want a souvenir that will hold its value, check out the **porcelain** from the erstwhile Royal Factory (KPM) on Wegelistraße 1 (Tiergarten).

Fashion and Design

Fashion by designers from all over the world is sold on the "Ku'damm" (Kurfürstendamm) and on Friedrichstraße. You'll find lots of small fashion shops and witty Berlin labels on Kastanienallee in Prenzlauer Berg, Schlüterstraße in Charlottenburg and on Alte and Neue Schönhauser Straße in Mitte. Designers creating various innovative accessories for the kitchen and bathroom have opened shops on Winterfeldtplatz and Goltzstraße in Schöneberg, on Bergmannstraße in Kreuzberg and on Kastanienallee in Prenzlauer Berg.

Art

Art lovers are spoilt for choice in Berlin. International painters, sculptors, photographers and conceptual artists exhibit their work in over 400 galleries. Most are located in Auguststraße, Oranienstraße, Linienstraße and Torstraße. Artistic quarters have also sprung up along Potsdamer Straße and between Checkpoint Charlie and the Jewish Museum in Kreuzberg. In addition, you'll find a great deal of galleries north of the Kurfürstendamm between Giesebrechtstraße and Uhlandstraße.

Finding Your Feet

Markets

More than 100 markets are held in Berlin every week. They're mostly **weekly markets** of various sizes selling fruit and vegetables. Nearly every district in the city also has a **junk or flea market**, most of which take place on Sundays.

- Berlin's largest and oldest flea market is held every weekend along **Straße des 17. Juni** (see below). There's also an arts and crafts market that takes place at the same time.
- Museum Island acts as the backdrop for the **Antiques and Book Market** held near the Bode Museum (on Am Kupfergraben street) every Saturday and Sunday (see below).

Insider Tip

- The city's most beautiful **market hall** is found on Marheinekeplatz in Kreuzberg. It sells fruit and veg, meat and fish, newspapers, deli products and tasty organic treats. There's also a wide selection of snacks!
- The largest and most popular **weekly markets** take place on Maybachufer (▶ 48), on Winterfeldtplatz in Schöneberg (Wednesday and Saturday mornings) and on Kollwitzplatz in Prenzlauer Berg (Thursday afternoon and Sunday till 4pm).

Junk and Flea markets

- **Art and Flea market** (antiques, design, fashion), Straße des 17. Juni, Saturday and Sunday, 10am– 5pm.
- **Large Antique Market at Ostbahnhof station** (Sunday 9am–5pm).
- **Flea market on Boxhagener Platz** (Sunday 10am–6pm).
- **Flea market in the Mauerpark** (Sunday 9am–5pm).
- **Antiques and Book Market** by the Bode Museum, Museum Island, the Zeughaus and on Am Kupfergraben street (Sat–Sun 11am–4pm).
- **Flea market on Arkonaplatz** (Sunday 10am–4pm).
- **Flea market at Schöneberg Town Hall (Rathaus)**, John-F.-Kennedy-Platz (Sat, Sun 9am–4pm).

Opening Times

- **Normal shop opening times** are from Monday to Saturday, 9am/10am until 8pm. When you get away from the main shopping streets, some stores close as early as 7pm. Some supermarkets open until 10pm or midnight, while others are even open 24 hours a day.
- **Boutiques and smaller shops** in the city's districts don't open until 11am or noon.
- **Spätkäufe** (*"Späti"* for short) are small shops that often only open in the evening and sell beer, wine and basic items into the early hours of the morning. They're a Berlin speciality.
- Berlin has ten **shopping Sundays** when stores can open from 1pm until 8pm (German shops generally close on Sundays). They're mainly held during important trade fairs, festivals and other major events.

Entertainment

With around 3,000 events taking place here every single day, it's hard to choose what to do. Even Berliners need some help making up their minds. If you're formulating last-minute plans, you'll sometimes get lucky by flicking through the day's papers.

Berlin has three large opera houses, around 50 theatres, a great deal of cabarets, more than a dozen children's theatres, a growing number of literature festivals and reading events, hundreds of bars and clubs, and countless open-air events and movie screenings in the summer…you have to be decisive if you want to go out in this city! Comedy clubs are springing up, too – Kookaburra in Prenzlauer Berg (Schönhauser Allee 184) is one of the pioneers.

If you're studying the **listings** when half the evening's already behind you – don't panic! Midnight is still a great time to go dancing, hear some music and even see some movie previews.

Theatre

Berlin's most popular theatre is the **Volksbühne** on Rosa-Luxemburg-Platz where a younger audience enjoys spectacular productions, social satire and work by young guest directors.

The **Berliner Ensemble** (Bertolt-Brecht-Platz 1) sees Claus Peymann continuing the satirical tradition of the theatre's founder, Bertolt Brecht. For high quality *Regietheatre* (director's theatre), check out the **Deutsches Theater** (Schumannstr. 13) and the **Schaubühne am Lehniner Platz** (Kurfürstendamm 153), known for its provocative, often socially and politically engaged performances.

And don't forget the city's countless fringe theatres, puppet theatres and 🎭 children's theatres. The most famous of the latter is **Grips** (ages 6 and up) in the Tiergarten (Altonaer Str. 22).

The Music Scene

Music lovers make a beeline for Berlin's clubs and bars. Some of the more established venues include **Arena** in Treptow's Eichenstraße, **C-Halle** on the Columbiadamm in Tempelhof, **Tempodrom** at Möckernbrücke 10 and **Lido** at Cuvrystraße 7 in Kreuzberg.

Jazz fans love the long-standing scene in the west of the city. Two favourites in Charlottenburg are **A-Trane** (Bleibtreustraße 1), where you can hear modern jazz, swing or blues almost every night, and **Quasimodo**, a classic venue for live concerts and impromptu jam sessions under the Delphi Cinema (Kantstr. 12a).

You can hear live music every day of the week at the **Junction Bar** (Gneisenaustraße 18) and from Wed to Sun in **Yorckschlösschen** (Yorckstraße 15) in Kreuzberg.

Drink, Dance, See and Be Seen

If you haven't got very much time and want to get an overall impression of what Berlin's hip nightlife has to offer, head to the areas with the most bars: Torstraße in Mitte, Simon-Dach-Straße in Friedrichshain, Oranienstraße in Kreuzberg or Weserstraße in Neukölln. And then where? Those in the know just go with the flow…

Gays and Lesbians

Berlin prides itself on its big, open gay and lesbian scene. It's made its mark in **Schöneberg**, where you'll find lots of bars, cafés and even rainbow-coloured snack stands along Fuggerstraße, Eisenacherstraße and Motzstraße. Schöneberg was the best-known meeting place for gays and lesbians in the 1920s. You'll also find cool hangouts in **Prenzlauer Berg** (on Gleimstraße and Greifenhagener Straße) and in **Kreuzberg** (on Oranienstraße and Mehringdamm).

Finding Your Feet

Parks

- You don't have to wait till nightfall to go out in Berlin. Public green spaces make up 14.2% of city's total area, and they get a lot of use – particularly in summer. Workers on their lunch break, mums with kids and exhausted tourists lie on the grass in the tiny, central **Monbijou Park** (Hackescher Markt), for example. There's a small sports ground, an 🏊 outdoor pool for kids and a beach bar on the banks of the Spree.
- **Volkspark Friedrichshain** (U-Bahn: Strausberger Platz) is the go-to park for students and young inhabitants of Prenzlauer Berg and Friedrichshain. Café Schönbrunn and the beer garden are great places to party into the night. There's an open-air cinema, tennis and basketball courts, and the beautiful *Märchenbrunnen* ("Fairy-tale Fountain"). It's popular with kids by day and a hotspot for gay men at night.
- Kids throng Kreuzberg's **Viktoriapark** during the day. Long after they're tucked up in bed, you'll hear bongo drums competing with the nightingales. And the night hasn't even begun in Golgatha (➤ 50) – not by a long chalk.

Information

- Info magazines *zitty* and *tip* alternate every fortnight to give daily listings for cinema *(Kino)*, theatre *(Theater)*, music *(Musik)*, readings *(Lesungen)*, lectures *(Vorträge)* and parties *(Partys)*. They also contain daily tips, addresses and info on tours, markets, kids' events, art exhibitions and much, much more.
- You'll also find a selection of events in the **daily newspapers**.
- **Posters around the city** give notice of big events weeks and weeks in advance.
- **Theatre box offices and ticket agencies** will tell you all about upcoming events.

Advance Booking

- Concert and theatre box offices charge high advance booking fees. You'll find **theatre box offices** in the Potsdamer Platz Arcades, at KaDeWe, Karstadt and Wertheim, on the Internet (www.showtimetickets.de) and sometimes also in newsagents.
- You can also ring up and reserve tickets from most **venues**. You'll have to come and pick them up half an hour before the start of the performance.
- Berlin Tourismus & Kongress GmbH (➤ 39) sell tickets **without an advance booking fee**.

Last Minute Tickets

After two o'clock in the afternoon, **Hekticket** sells off reduced price tickets for concerts, cabarets and theatre performances the very same day. You'll find them in the foyer of the Deutsche Bank at Hardenbergstraße 29d opposite Zoo Station (tel: 030 2 30 99 30) and near Alexanderplatz at Karl-Liebknecht-Straße 13 (www.hekticket.de).

Free

Many events in Berlin are free of charge. You'll find tips on the Internet at www.gratis-in-berlin.de. There are also free lunchtime concerts held most Tuesdays at 1pm in the foyer of the Philharmonie (➤ 109; September to June).

Unter den Linden

 **Little Treats**

Time Out from the City
The **Raum der Stille** (Room of Silence) at the Brandenburg Gate (➤ 56) is an almost spiritual place of peace.

Honey, I Shrunk Berlin
The **Humboldt-Box** (➤ 66) opposite Berlin Cathedral boasts a mini model of the city centre at the turn of the 20th century.

Party in the Park
Locals flock to hear jazz and rock at the free summer concerts held in the **Englischer Garten** every Sunday (➤ 72).

Getting Your Bearings

The avenue known as Unter den Linden (literally "Under the Lime Trees") has achieved mythical status. That's because it's a visible record of all the joy and pain of centuries of German history. No one really lives here, and locals don't use it much, but they love showing it off to visitors.

Nothing happens here at night, so it's best to visit during the day. Unter den Linden shows you the Berlin of the *Kurfürsten* (electoral princes), of Prussian Kings, of the GDR, and of modern town planners. The latter have recently turned the chic avenue into a vast, dusty building site. Construction of the *Kanzlerlinie* ("Chancellor Line") – a Helmut Kohl-era U-Bahn link from Alexanderplatz to the Central Station – should be finished by 2019. Rebuilding the Berliner Stadtschloss (City Palace) opposite Museum Island has also caused substantial disruption.

The Federal Chancellery by the Spree, designed by Axel Schultes

The interesting collection of buildings on Pariser Platz – the Brandenburg Gate, the French and US Embassies and the Hotel Adlon – draw in crowds of tourists. The square also boasts Frank Gehry's design for the DZ Bank and Günter Behnisch's Akademie der Künste (Academy of Arts). If you face away from from the Brandenburg Gate and follow the road down to Schlossplatz a good kilometre (half a mile) away, you may well find yourself tempted to turn left or right into Friedrichstraße, where you'll discover architecturally interesting rows of shops hidden in the so-called *Quartieren* ("Quarters"). Head over the beautiful Gendarmenmarkt and the history-laden Bebelplatz and you'll arrive back on Unter den Linden near the equestrian statue of Friedrich the Great.

The Perfect Day

Our one-day itinerary is great for getting to know Berlin's magnificent boulevard and the surrounding area without missing any of the highlights. More info about the individual sights can be found in the following pages (➤ 56–73).

🕘 09:00

Get online and book an appointment to visit the dome of the ☆**Reichstag building** (➤ 58) – one of the best attractions to be found in Berlin. Climb to the top to enjoy some splendid views of the Tiergarten and the city.

🕙 10:00

It's still early, and Berlin is slowly waking up. In summer, stroll through the 🔢**Regierungsviertel** (Government District, ➤ 71) and over to the 🔢**Haus der Kulturen der Welt** (House of World Cultures, ➤ 72) by the Spree.

🕚 11:00

Walk back and head through the **Brandenburger Tor** (Brandenburg Gate, ➤ 56) and onwards into the famous ☆**Pariser Platz** (➤ 56). It's well worth checking out the conference hall at the DZ Bank (image below).

🕦 11:30

Wander down **Unter den Linden** and then explore ⑪**Friedrichstraße** (➤ 65) – visit the north side first before heading to the street's southern end. Go via the basement of the Galeries Lafayette to the fine shops and Venetian marble at **Quartier 206** (➤ 67).

🕜 13:30

If the appetising aromas haven't already tempted you to grab a midday snack in the basement of the Galeries Lafayette, walk to the ☆**Gendarmenmarkt** (image above right; ➤ 62), a square surrounded by eateries with relaxing terraces. Enjoy taking the time to admire what is perhaps Berlin's most beautiful plaza while eating lunch at the Brasserie am Gendarmenmarkt (➤ 74) or at Refugium (➤ 75).

🕑 14:00

Walk a short way down Friedrichstraße to **Checkpoint**

Charlie (➤ 65). Visit the Mauermuseum (Wall Museum) and you'll be amazed by the courage and ingenuity of those who risked death to escape the GDR. Next, walk or take the U-Bahn back to Französische Straße. Follow Behrenstraße down to Bebelplatz, site of the Nazi book burning in 1933. You're now at the heart of the **⑫ Forum Fridericianum** (➤ 68), home to the Staatsoper (State Opera), the Neue Wache (New Guardhouse), Humboldt University, the Zeughaus (Old Arsenal) and the equestrian statue of Friedrich the Great.

🕓 18:00

Carry on over the **⑯ Schlossbrücke** (Palace Bridge, ➤ 73) with its 8 sculptures by Karl Friedrich Schinkel. The Humboldt-Box has an exhibition on rebuilding the Berliner Stadtschloss (City Palace). The **⑰ Berliner Dom** (Berlin Cathedral, ➤ 73) is also worth a visit.

🕓 20:00

It's approaching dinner time, so stroll down to Bocca di Bacco (➤ 74) on Friedrichstraße or to Borchardt (➤ 74) on the Gendarmenmarkt. It's wise to book ahead. If all you want is some hearty German food, however, head to Augustiner am Gendarmenmarkt (➤ 74).

★Pariser Platz

The square looks almost like it did a century ago. A few years back, however, the Brandenburger Tor stood here alone in the "Death Strip" behind the Wall that had divided Berlin ever since 13 August, 1961. When the Wall came down, the construction workers moved in.

The **Brandenburger Tor** was built in the style of the *Propylaea* (gate) in the Athenian Acropolis by Carl Gotthard Langhans, the city's director of town planning, from 1789–91. It originally served both as the gateway to the historic city and as a monument to the might of Prussia. The double portico sits on 12 Doric columns. The central arch (5.5m/18ft across) was made wide enough for royal carriages, but commoners were forced to walk round the outside. It's the scene of many state occasions today.

The Brandenburger Tor at night

In 1957, the East Berlin Senate had the damaged gate repaired with the same stone from Pirna in Saxony that was used to build it 200 years earlier. After reunification, the monument spent two years under cover while it was thoroughly restored. Cars have been banned from using the gate and the square ever since.

The gate's **Quadriga** (four-horse chariot) was designed by Berlin sculptor Johann Gottfried Schadow (1764–1850) and made by coppersmith Emanuel Jury, whose niece modelled for Eirene, goddess of peace (later known as Viktoria, goddess of victory). She was originally shown nude in true classical style, but the King protested and she was given a robe.

When the French defeated the Prussians at Jena and Auerstedt in 1806, Napoleon I packed the Quadriga into 12 crates and took it to Paris. The Prussian Marshall Blücher arranged for their return in 1814, and the square by the gate became known as Pariser Platz (Parisian Square).

ENOUGH TO MAKE YOU SICK

On 30 January, 1933, some 25,000 of Adolf Hitler's uniformed acolytes celebrated his nomination as Chancellor with a torchlit procession through the Brandenburg Gate. Max Liebermann, the 85-year-old President of the Prussian Academy of Arts, looked on from his window and commented: "I can't eat enough food to be as sick as this makes me feel."

The City's "Reception Room"

From 1850, work was carried out to unify the

square's baroque architecture in a classical style. It became the emblem of bourgeois pride, counter-balancing the palace at the other end of the street. After the Wall came down, town planners sought to recreate the city's destroyed "reception room" in the now empty square. Strict regulations were imposed on the architects' designs: Façades had to be made from natural stone and plans had to echo a 19th-century classical style. The resulting structures include the **American and French Embassies**, the **Academy of Arts**, and the legendary **Adlon Hotel**, all of which were rebuilt on their historic sites. Josef Paul Kleihues' **Haus Sommer** and **Haus Liebermann** could have been designed by Schinkel or Stüler, 19th-century German architects. Despite all this, some of the square's edifices are decidedly contemporary. One example is the ultra-modern DZ Bank building (➤ 54), a futuristic jewel created by star architect Frank O. Gehry. The **Holocaust Memorial** – the central German monument to the Jews murdered in Europe – was designed by New York architect Peter Eisenman.

TAKING A BREAK
Tucher am Tor serves as a coffeehouse, a restaurant and a reading room at different times of day (Pariser Platz 6a).

🗺 200 B2 🚇 Brandenburger Tor 🚌 100

Wandering through the Holocaust Memorial

Holocaust Memorial
🗺 200 B2 🕐 Field of *Stelae* (pillars) open 24 hours a day; Information Centre, 10am–8pm, until 7pm in winter (last entry 7.15pm/6.15pm), closed on Mondays; public tours, Sunday 3pm 💶 Free entry

⭐ The Reichstag

In 1995, conceptual artist Christo and his wife Jeanne Claude covered the Reichstag in a silvery material, creating a monumental sculpture that was seen around the world. Today, it's the seat of the Federal German Parliament. Fascinated visitors flock to see an old building topped with a modern glass dome, and to enjoy the unusual experience of walking right into a national government's headquarters.

The Reichstag, built in 1894, was originally home to a parliament that was as powerless as it was unlucky. They did at least manage to choose a building, settling on erecting this striking structure in the heart of Berlin after 20 years in temporary lodgings. In 1916, Kaiser Wilhelm II had the words *Dem deutschen Volke* ("To the German People") inscribed above the entrance. He had to abdicate soon afterwards. Politician Philipp Scheidemann proclaimed Germany a Republic from one of the building's windows on 9 November, 1918.

On 27 February, 1933, a fire – the cause of which has never been discovered – broke out in the Reichstag, destroying the plenary chamber. An "Emergency Decree" was enacted, suspending civil liberties and giving the National Socialists the chance to persecute their opponents and begin building the Third Reich. At the end of World War II on 30 April, 1945, the Soviet Red Army hoisted their flag over the ruins. Hitler killed himself in his bunker the very same day.

360 mirrors direct daylight into the plenary chamber

The First Parliament of a United Germany

The building, which stood right next to the western side of the Wall, wasn't used as a meeting place again until 1961. The first sitting of a unified German parliament since the fall of the Wall was held here on 4 October, 1990. It was decided to move the Bundestag (German parliament) and the majority of the Federal government from Bonn to Berlin and to renovate the Reichstag so it could be used by parliament once more.

An ultra-modern parliament building was created behind the old façade following plans by architect Sir Norman Foster, who was awarded the *Bundesverdienstkreuz* (Order of Merit) for his work. The structure was inaugurated with a meeting of the Bundestag on 19 April, 1999. Although

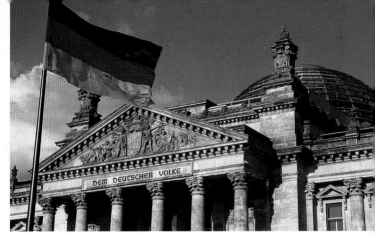

A beautiful combination of old and new

controversy surrounded the creation of the new 23m (75ft)-high dome – as it had with the original over 100 years before – it immediately became a Berlin icon. Two double-helix ramps, each 230m (754ft) with a steady 8° slope, lead you round a mirrored funnel used to direct daylight into the plenary chamber 10m (33ft) below and channel artificial light back out again at night. You can only visit the dome if you register online, by fax (030 22 73 64 36) or by post (Deutscher Bundestag, Besucherdienst, Platz der Republik 1, 11011 Berlin). Appointments are assigned 2 months in advance at the earliest. You can get last-minute tickets up to 2 hours before from the Visitors' Service next to the Berlin Pavilion in Scheidemannstraße.

TAKING A BREAK

Käfer, a roof-garden restaurant next to the dome, boasts an exclusive location with prices to match (9am–4.30pm & 6.30pm–12pm). Book ahead and you won't have to wait to get into the building.

✚ 200 A2

✉ Platz der Republik ☎ For information about tours and events, call 030 22 73 21 52 or visit www.bundestag.de/besuche ⏱ Daily 8am–midnight (last entry 10pm) Ⓤ Brandenburger Tor 🚌 100 💶 Free

INSIDER INFO

- If you want take a **tour**, witness a **parliamentary session** or hear a **speech in the plenary chamber**, you'll still have to register in advance via the online form, by fax or by mail. You can find out if there are any spaces for events open to visitors during your trip to Berlin by ringing 030 22 73 21.
- You might like to borrow one of the free **audio guides** during your visit to the Reichstag dome. These provide you with 20 minutes of information about the building, the surrounding sights and the work carried out by parliament. There's also a special 👶 children's audio guide for kids aged 6–13.
- The basement of the Parliamentary Library houses Ben Wagin's **Mauer-Mahnmal** (Wall Memorial), built from original segments of the Hinterland Wall.

Seat of the German Parliament

Inaugurated in 1894, burned out in 1933, shot at in 1945 and home to unified German parliament since 1990: The Reichstag building has had a rather eventful history. The new dome has become a symbol of Berlin.

❶ **Dome:** The glass dome is 23.5m (77ft) high and 40m (131ft) in diameter at its base. Two double-helix ramps lead up to the viewing platform and back down again. The dome is designed to bring light (via the central mirrored structure) and fresh air down into the plenary chamber below.

❷ **Roof terrace:** The roof-garden restaurant is the perfect place for a break. Book ahead and you won't have to wait to enter the dome (tel: 030 22 62 99 33).

❸ **Plenary chamber:** The number of seats changes to match election results. They're rearranged at the start of each term. Seen from the deputies' point of view, the lectern and the seats for the President and Vice Presidents are in the middle. To their left are the Chancellor and Ministers; Federal Council officials sit to their right.

❹ **Parliamentary Party Rooms:** The President of the Bundestag's office is found below the meeting rooms in the south wing.

❺ **Modern Art:** Various artists' work is displayed in the Reichstag, including Gerhard Richter's interpretation of the colours of the German flag in the entrance hall and a floor sculpture by Ulrich Rückriem in the southern atrium.

❻ **Graffiti:** Some of the inscriptions written on the walls by Soviet soldiers after they took Berlin are preserved in the building.

❼ **Security gates:** Before you're allowed into the dome, you have to pass through security. You're then taken up in the glass visitors' elevator.

The Reichstag

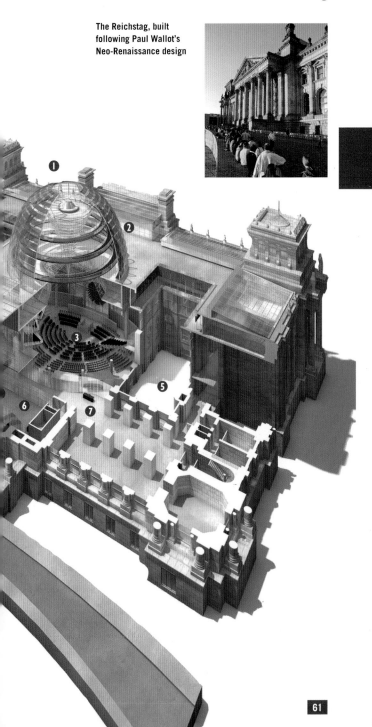

The Reichstag, built following Paul Wallot's Neo-Renaissance design

★❻ Gendarmenmarkt

The Gendarmenmarkt is regarded as the most beautiful square in Berlin and the epitome of Romantic Classicism. When the Classic Open Air concerts are held here in summer, it's transformed into the poshest outdoor stage in the city. You'll sometimes see tired protesters resting on the steps of Schinkel's playhouse. These stairs don't lead up to the entrance to this concert hall – you enter via the doors underneath.

Established in the 17th century as a marketplace for French religious refugees, the square takes its name from the guardhouse and stables set up here for the *Gens d'armes* regiment by "Soldier King" Friedrich Wilhelm I. The square already contained a small replica of the Huguenots' mother church in Charenton (the original was destroyed by Louis XIV) which served as the French church in Friedrichstadt. The Neue Kirche (New Church) was later built for German-speaking Swiss immigrants. To improve the cityscape, Friedrich II commissioned Carl von Gontard to add an identical cupola (*dôme* in French) to each church in 1780, thus unwittingly creating the basis for the names they still bear today: The **Deutscher** and **Französischer Dom** (German and French *dômes*).

A beautiful reflection in the Gendarmenmarkt

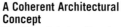
A Coherent Architectural Concept

The Französischer Dom houses the Huguenot Museum. It's also home to a good restaurant in the basement (▶ 75) that boasts the most beautiful terrace to be found in the plaza. If you climb up to the viewing platform, you'll see that the square was designed as a unified whole – none of the buildings stand alone. It's this coherence that gives the square its character. The various phases of construction are documented on wall displays in the Deutscher Dom, and a revamped interactive exhibition shows the development of parliamentary democracy in Germany.

In 1802, a modest French comedy theatre in the middle of the square was replaced by Carl Gotthard Langhans' German National Theatre. It lasted only 15 years, burning down when the curtain caught fire during a rehearsal of Schiller's *Die Räuber* (The Robbers). Its replacement, the most modern theatre in Prussia, was built by Karl Friedrich Schinkel (1818–21) in the classical style in favour at that time. Sculptures by Christian Friedrich Tieck adorn the triangular pediment above the stage area. The SS set fire to the building in 1945 – post-war photos show the square to be nothing more than a field. The GDR decided to renovate the whole square and rebuild the theatre in 1976. As the East already had lots of theatres, it was reopened as the **Konzerthaus** (Concert Hall) in 1984. The classicising interior décor provides a splendid backdrop for various events today.

The Nazis also took down Reinhold Begas' 6m (20ft) **marble statue of Schiller**. It wasn't put back until 1989. The monument shows the great writer with personifications of the Arts at his feet: Lyric Poetry with a harp, Tragedy with a dagger, Philosophy with a scroll that reads *Erkenne dich selbst* ("Know Thyself") and History shown with writing tablets.

Unter den Linden

The Muse of Light Entertainment

The Gendarmenmarkt was a focal point for cuisine and light entertainment in the second half of the 19th century. Johann Strauss, musical director at the Viennese court, taught Berliners how to waltz here, and composer Jacques Offenbach exposed them to lavish Parisian operettas in 1858. Writer E.T.A. Hoffmann lived next to Lutter & Wegner's wine bar, where he was a regular customer. Rahel Varnhagen invited philosophers and scholars to her famous intellectual salons on Jägerstraße where Vau – a gourmet restaurant – now stands. The feel of the square hasn't changed much since then – it's still full of posh eateries and their clientele today.

The square doesn't always live up to its architectural reputation at the edges, where you'll see new builds, pseudo-classical and faux Art Nouveau edifices, and structures made with a pink hue called *Architektenmarzipan* ("Architect's Marzipan").

The Schiller memorial in front of the Konzerthaus

TAKING A BREAK

Insider Tip

Enjoy a hot chocolate made using real cooking chocolate at **Fassbender & Rausch** (Charlottenstr. 60, Mon–Fri 10am–8pm, Sat 10am–5pm), a chocolate house renowned for its sweet-toothed reproductions of famous Berlin landmarks (the Reichstag, the Brandenburger Tor, etc.).

✚ 200 C1/2 🔲 Französische Str.

Huguenot Museum
☎ 030 2 29 17 60 🕓 Tue–Sun noon–5pm 💵 €2

Deutscher Dom
☎ 030 22 73 04 31 🕓 Oct–Apr, daily from 10am–6pm; May–Sept, daily from 10am–7pm; half-hour tours every 30 minutes between 11am and 5pm 💵 Free

INSIDER INFO

- You'll get the best **view of the Gendarmenmarkt** if you climb the 284 steps to the viewing platform in the Französischer Dom (Apr–Oct 10am–7pm, Nov–Mar 10am–6pm, €3).
- Have a sweet tooth? Head to **Ritter Sport Chocoworld** (Französische Str. 24, Mon–Wed 10–7, Thu–Sat 10–8, Sun 10–6) to make your very own chocolate bars.

Ⅱ Friedrichstraße

The magnificent Unter den Linden boulevard stretches from the Brandenburger Tor to the Berliner Dom. It's crossed about halfway along its length by Friedrichstraße. The American military's Checkpoint Charlie – an Allied border crossing point and the site of a US-Soviet tank standoff in October 1961 – is the most famous spot on the street. Today, the 3.3km (2mi)-long Friedrichstraße entices people from all over the world in with its elegant shops and modern buildings designed by famous architects.

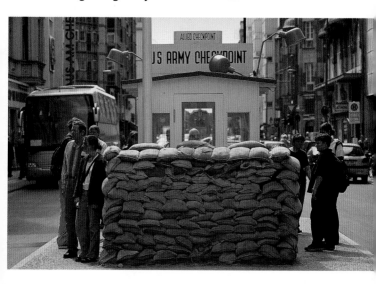

The replica of Checkpoint Charlie

Opened in 1882, **Bahnhof Friedrichstraße** (Friedrichstraße Station) to the north of Unter den Linden used to separate the street into two unequal parts. To the north, it lead through industrial areas which were later built up with tenement blocks. In contrast, the buildings around the station and as far south as Leipziger Straße were splendid and elegant. The tone here was set by luxury restaurants, cellar dives, cabarets, nightclubs and gambling joints and their various clientele. Journalist Franz Hessel wrote of the "narrow pavement [sidewalk] carpeted with light" here "on which dangerous girls moved as if on silk."

There are still a lot of entertainment hotspots to be found along Friedrichstraße today. Elaborately

MAUERMUSEUM
Founded in 1962, the **Haus am Checkpoint Charlie** Wall Museum keeps alive the memory of what life was like during the Cold War. It documents the fear, No Man's Land and the daring escape attempts. Many view it as a modern Cabinet of Curiosities. (Friedrichstr. 43–45, tel: 030 2 53 72 50; www. mauermuseum.de, daily 9am–10pm, U-Bahnhof: Kochstraße; €12.50).

Unter den Linden

staged shows can be seen at **Friedrichstadtpalast**, the largest revue theatre in Europe. You can also spend a fun evening at the Admiralspalast, the Distel Cabaret Theatre and the Quatsch Comedy Club. Highbrow theatrical performances are held at the **Deutsches Theater** and the **Berliner Ensemble**, the latter of which was founded by Bertolt Brecht.

   Bahnhof Friedrichstraße (Friedrichstraße Station), the only link for trains going across the border after the Wall was built, is a normal U-Bahn, S-Bahn and regional train station today. Before **Weidendamm bridge**, you'll see the "**Tränenpalast**" ("Palace of Tears") behind a tower block to the left. It's a reminder of times when people said tearful goodbyes at the frontier. An exhibition with films, first-hand accounts, and such objects as the passport control cabin and a surveillance camera explains what it was like to approach the notorious border crossing at that time. The architecture between the Berliner Ensemble and the Friedrichstadtpalast Palace is chara-

Magnificent: Quartier 206

cterised by 19th-century hotels and apartment blocks.
Turn right to **Museumsinsel** (Museum Island, ➤ 82) before
you reach the bridge.

The Friedrichstadt Passages

Posh shops and hotels line the street to the south. You'll
find the **Galeries Lafayette**, a building with a glass cone at
its centre, at the corner of Französische Straße. It's the
starting point for the "Quartiers 205–207", built in a fine
Berlin "layer-cake" style (with shops below, offices in the
middle and flats on top).

What are the basics you actually need to live a good life?
Taking a stroll through **Quartier 206** with its acute-angled
bay windows and façades like folded cardboard is enough
to drive such questions from your mind. Sat between Jean
Nouvel's glazed Quartier 207 and the stone Quartier 205,
you enter the building via an oval atrium, step onto the
escalator, and rise up into a swirling space of coloured
marble mosaics that's enough to make you dizzy. You'll
catch glimpses of dark suits and expensive furs, breathe
in bold perfumes, and hear snatches of foreign tongues and
a piano tinkling in the distance. Black leather sofas and
armchairs invite you to sit down and take in the spectacle –
it's easy to forget that it's only(?) a shop. Fashion, flowers
and jewellery are bought by a clientele to whom labels
such as Strenesse, Gucci and Moschino are everyday
names. Just when you think it can't get any more exclusive, this store outdoes itself. Dress appropriately: Only the
super-confident would feel at ease here wearing scruffy
shoes and a rucksack. At night, US architect Henry Cobb's
shining strips of light give a hint of the theatre played out
behind the building's façade.

TAKING A BREAK

Friedrichstraße has many snack joints, but the food department with its numerous snack bars in the basement of the
Galeries Lafayette is something rather special.

✚ 200 C1/2 🚇 Friedrichstr., Stadtmitte, Französische Str.

Tränenpalast
✉ Reichstagsufer 17, ☎ 030 4 67 77 79 11; www.hdg.de
🕐 Tue–Fri 9–7, Sat–Sun 10–6 💶 Free

INSIDER INFO

- The **Haus am Checkpoint Charlie** museum often organises special exhibitions, debates
  and film screenings – it's worth taking a look at the **programme of events**.
- Before it reaches Zimmerstraße, Mauerstraße leads to **Bethlehemkirchplatz**, where
  coloured paving shows the outline of the destroyed church of the Bohemian Brethren.
  The sculpture *Houseball* by Claes Oldenburg and Coosje van Bruggen depicts the
  modest, balled-up possessions of refugees.

⑫ Forum Fridericianum

Christian Daniel Rauch's equestrian statue of "Old Fritz" (Friedrich the Great) has stood in the middle of Unter den Linden since 1851. A diverse collection of people is shown grouped around its base. The fact that the poets are depicted standing under the horse's tail gives you an idea of their status at court. Friedrich built the surrounding Forum Fridericianum in his own honour – the result is what you can see in Bebelplatz today.

Friedrich II was 28 years old and said to be as cultured as he was friendly when he took over from his thrifty father, the "Soldier King" Friedrich Wilhelm I. He immediately began modifying Unter den Linden. Almost 50 residential buildings were demolished, and even then it was only just big enough for state visits. Owners of the boulevard's mansions had to provide suites for foreign visitors and were made to help out by lending their best china, silver and tablecloths when banquets were held at the palace.

The Opera

Architect Georg Wenzeslaus von Knobelsdorff only managed to build this Corinthian-style Opera House (1741–43) before he fell from favour. Officially called the *Staatsoper* (State Opera) but known locally as the *Lindenoper*, it's the boulevard's most beautiful building and one of the most popular artistic venues in the city. It's been undergoing extensive renovation work since 2010, but the completion date has been put back many times. Performances are held at Charlottenburg's Schillertheater in the meantime.

Bebelplatz

The only exception to the square's classical architecture is the High Baroque exuberance of the **Alte Bibliothek** (Old Library, 1775–80). Its style has earned it the nickname *Kommode* ("chest of drawers"). It was built because the King wanted a copy of the Michaelertrakt wing in Vienna's Hofburg Palace. Empty subterranean shelves by Israeli sculptor Micha Ullmann stand in memory of the Nazi **Book Burning** of 10 May, 1933, when 20,000 works – including texts by Jewish, Pacifist and Anti-Fascist

"Old Fritz" is accompanied by quite a crowd

writers – were burnt on a pyre. **St Hedwig's Cathedral** (1773) was the only church constructed in the time of Friedrich II. Built as a gesture of religious tolerance toward the Silesian Catholics, it's a poor copy of the Pantheon in Rome. The **Altes Palais** (Old Palace), where Kaiser Wilhelm I died in 1888, is found next to the library.

Humboldt University

Humboldt University (designed by Johann Boumann, 1748–1866), stands opposite Bebelplatz. Originally intended as a palace for Prince Heinrich, Friedrich's brother, it was made available to a newly founded university of 300 students in 1810 on the insistence of Wilhelm von Humboldt. Statues of the scholar and his brother Alexander keep watch over the teaching and research at the institution. Max Planck and Albert Einstein taught here; Karl Marx and Karl Liebknecht were students.

The Neue Wache

The **Neue Wache** (New Guardhouse, 1816–18) next door is regarded as the prototype of Schinkel's classicism. With its enlarged version of Käthe Kollwitz's *Pietà*, it's been the Federal Republic's central War memorial since 1993. The GDR's daily changing of the guard took place here in Prussian goose step before the everlasting flame. The mischievously smiling statue of **Heinrich Heine** – banished to a park by the GDR in 1958 – was returned to the little chestnut wood between the Neue Wache and the **Maxim-Gorki-Theater** in 2003.

Zeughaus

In 1848, enraged Berliners stormed the **Zeughaus** (Arsenal) to seize weapons for a revolution. Originally built in 1730, it served as an arsenal until 1875 and a military

Unter den Linden

museum until 1944. It became a GDR history museum after being rebuilt in 1952. It's now home to the **Deutsches Historisches Museum** (German Historical Museum), whose two floors vividly present around 1,500 years of German history with a great many original exhibition pieces. The upper floor starts with the 5th century and finishes at the end of the First World War. The ground floor then takes over, telling the tale of the Weimar Republic, the Nazi regime, the post-War period and the history of both German states up to the Allied withdrawal in 1994. The spectacular extension, designed by star Chinese-American architect I. M. Pei (also responsible for the Louvre pyramid in Paris), was built in 2003.

The extension of the Historical Museum, designed by I. M. Pei

Kronprinzenpalais and Kronprinzessinnenpalais

The **Kronprinzenpalais** (Crown Princes' Palace, 1663) opposite was a princely residence until c.1840. It later won unexpected fame when the GDR signed the Treaty of Accession to the Federal Republic of Germany in its Red Hall on 31 August, 1990. The nearby **Kronprinzessinnenpalais** (Crown Princesses' Palace), home to the Opera café for many years, has stood empty since 2012.

TAKING A BREAK

The café at the German Historical Museum tempts visitors in with coffee, cake and regional dishes. In good weather you can sit out on the terrace next to the Spree and enjoy the magnificent scenery (tel: 030 2 06 427 44, 10am–6pm).

✚ 200 D2 ▣ 100

Deutsches Historisches Museum in the Zeughaus
✉ Unter den Linden 2 ☎ 030 20 30 40; www.dhm.de
🕐 Daily 10am–6pm 🚉 Hackescher Markt ▣ 100 🎫 €8, under-19s: Free

INSIDER INFO

The **GDR Museum** opposite the Berliner Dom depicts daily life in the GDR. You can see such exhibits as a complete living room, a GDR cinema seat and a kitchen.
🔢 Kids will also enjoy having a drive in the *Trabi* (GDR car) simulator. (On the Spree river promenade by the Liebknechtbrücke bridge, Karl-Liebknecht-Str. 1, tel: 030 8 47 12 37 31; www.ddr-museum.de, Sun–Fri 10–8, Sat till 10; €6).

At Your Leisure

🔟 Regierungsviertel

Completed in 2003, the buildings of the Regierungsviertel (Government District, ► 14) are home to meeting rooms, conference halls and one thousand offices. The **Bundeskanzleramt**, a minimalistic modern edifice by Axel Schultes and Charlotte Frank, is particularly eye-catching. Its circular openings earned it the nickname "the Washing Machine". A sculpture by Eduardo Chillida stands out front. Parliamentary committees gather in the **Paul-Löbe-Haus** opposite. This is where laws are prepared and meetings are held. There's also a restaurant for deputies. You can see into the building from Kronprinzen bridge. Parliamentary members exercise in the Bundestag gymnasium in the **Marie-Elisabeth-Lüders-Haus**. An exemplary, decentralised power supply is provided by biodiesel motors and

> **RELAX TO THE MAX**
> If you're tired from walking round the city, the Tiergarten is the perfect place to relax. You can eat, drink and even rent a boat at the **Café am Neuen See** (► 75).

3,600m² (11,800ft²) of photovoltaic installations.
➕ 200 A/B2 ✉ Otto-von-Bismarck-Allee; www.bundestag.de 🚇 Reichstag

🔟 Tiergarten

At 200 ha (494 acres) in size, this green expanse can be seen from the Reichstag dome. It stretches

down to the Spree on one side, and on to Potsdamer Platz and as far west as Zoologischer Garten station on the other. Once the hunting ground of the Electoral Princes, Berlin's most important park provided the route for the Love Parade for many years. During the reign of Friedrich I in the second half of the 17th century, a lane – known as the Straße des 17. Juni today – was cut through the park to join the city with the newly built Schloss Charlottenburg (► 124). The star-shaped, eight-road **Großer Stern** junction (then called Kurfürstenplatz) was also built at that time. The **Siegessäule** (Victory Column) was moved there from Königsplatz (now Platz der Republik) in 1939. Erected in

The 67m/220ft-high Victory Column

Unter den Linden

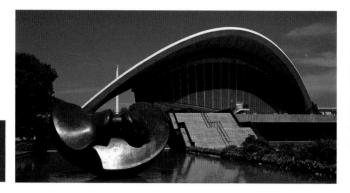

The Haus der Kulturen der Welt, known as the "pregnant oyster"

1873 to celebrate Prussia's victories over Denmark (1864), Austria (1866) and France (1870/71), it's topped by Friedrich Drake's 35 tonne (38.5 ton), 8.3m (27ft)-high statue of Viktoria, the goddess of victory. Climb the 285 spiral steps and you'll reach the 48m (157ft)-high viewing platform below the goddess' bronze skirt.

Today, the Tiergarten shows no sign that its splendours were destroyed during during World War Two. After the conflict, trees and bushes were used for fuel and potatoes and vegetables were grown instead of flowers. Replanting work restored the landscape from 1949.

THE SOVIET WAR MEMORIAL

Built in 1945, the Soviet war memorial – the first erected by the Eastern Power in Berlin – is located near the Brandenburger Tor on the Straße des 17. Juni. The entrance is flanked by two T-34 tanks, the first to enter Berlin in April 1945. The colonnade is made from granite blocks taken from the destroyed Neue Reichskanzlei (New Chancellery). To show that the War is over, the 8m (26ft) bronze of a Red Army soldier has his rifle slung over his shoulder. Some 2,500 soldiers are buried at the back.

The Englischer Garten (English Garden), located between the President's Schloss Bellevue and Altonaer Straße, was also created at that time. It hosts summer jazz concerts today. The trees near the Schloss conceal the black oval form of the President's office.
✚ 203 D4–F5 ⊙ Siegessäule Mon–Fri 9.30am–6.30pm, Sat–Sun till 7 ▣ 100 ▣ €3

⓯ Haus der Kulturen der Welt

This congress hall – a gift from the Americans and nicknamed the *Schwangere Auster* (Pregnant Oyster) – has stood on the riverbank since the International Architectural Exhibition of 1957. The roof, a daringly constructed concrete tent, collapsed in the summer of 1980. The damage was repaired in 1987 to celebrate the city's 750th anniversary. Since 1989, the striking Haus der Kulturen der Welt (House of World Cultures) has held exhibitions, conferences and events related to world culture. There's a jetty for boat trips on the Spree by the terrace, and Henry Moore's sculpture *Large Divided Oval: Butterfly* sits in the pool out front. The 68 bells in the 42m (138ft)-high tower are used for a live classical concert on Sundays (May–Sept, at 3pm). They're also played by a computer at noon and 6pm every day.
✚ 203 F5 ✉ John-Foster-Dulles-Allee ☎ 030 39 78 70; www.hkw.de ▣ 100

16 Schlossbrücke

You can see right away that the name "Marx-Engels Bridge" – its title in GDR times – doesn't suit this structure. At the order of Friedrich Wilhelm III, Karl Friedrich Schinkel designed the Schlossbrücke (Palace Bridge) between 1819 and 1824 to replace the dilapidated "Dog Bridge" – so called because hunters set out from there with their hounds. The new bridge was to be distinguished, decorative and dignified. Schinkel died in 1841, and his statues were not put up until the reign of Friedrich Wilhelm IV. The corner groups of statues depict Nike, goddess of victory, in various roles (from left to right, standing with Friedrich the Great's equestrian statue behind you): Teaching a boy heroic legends; crowning a victor; supporting a wounded soldier; and carrying a fallen hero up to Mount Olympus. The central statues show a young man receiving weapons training, being armed, led into battle, and protected from harm.

➕ 201 D2 🚉 100

17 Berliner Dom

Seelengasometer (the "gasometer of souls") was what Berliners called the ornate cathedral built by Kaiser Wilhelm II to replace its modest, oft-modified predecessor on the banks of the Spree from 1894–1905. The

The cathedral in the centre of Berlin

Imperial client wanted to build something like St Peter's in Rome that would serve as German Protestantism's mother church and the burial place of the Hohenzollern rulers. Julius Raschdorff's design was inspired by the Italian High Renaissance. The massive, richly ornamented Silesian sandstone dome is 74.8m (245ft) high, richly adorned and surrounded by four towers. The war-damaged building was temporarily secured before reconstruction began in 1975. It was reopened with a solemn service in 1993.

The church is home to the sarcophagi of the Great Elector and his wife Dorothea, the first Prussian royal couple (Friedrich I and Sophie Charlotte) and the tomb of Kaiser Friedrich III. The tombs of the Hohenzollern rulers from the 16th to 20th centuries are on show in the Hohenzollern Crypt. The Berliner Dom is the only church in Berlin to charge visitors a fee for admission.

➕ 201 D2 ✉ Lustgarten 🕐 Daily 9–8pm (7pm in winter) 🚉 100 💰 €7

Where to...
Eat and Drink

Prices
A main course without drinks:
€ under 12 euros   €€ 12–25 euros   €€€ over 25 euros

RESTAURANTS

Augustiner am Gendarmenmarkt
€–€€
If you want rustic, down-to-earth cooking, then take a seat at the wooden tables at this Bavarian inn on the Gendarmenmarkt. Grilled sausages and crispy pork knuckle make a good accompaniment to the freshly pulled Augustiner beer. To finish off, try *Kaiserschmarrn* (pancake pieces with raisins) and vanilla ice cream.
🞣 204 C4 ✉ Charlottenstr. 55
☎ 030 20 45 40 20; www.augustiner-braeu-berlin.de 🕙 Daily 10am–1am

Insider Tip

BE-Kantine €
This eatery doesn't have a name – it's actually the canteen for the Berliner Ensemble. It's a good place to sit amidst a smattering of Berlin celebrities and listen in on some theatrical legends. Go down into the back courtyard basement, grab such tasty treats as *Erbsensuppe* (pea soup) or *Bulette* (meatballs), and enjoy a reasonably priced meal. The tables outside are also fantastic for taking a breather while you're strolling round the city.
🞣 200 C3 ✉ Bertolt-Brecht-Platz 1
☎ 030 28 40 80 🕙 Mon–Sat 9am–midnight, Sun from 4pm–midnight

Bocca di Bacco €€€
There's no shortage of eateries around the Gendarmenmarkt or Italian restaurants in Berlin. Nevertheless, Bocca di Bacco (the "Mouth of Bacchus") is one of the area's highlights. This large restaurant is simply but elegantly furnished and serves northern Italian cuisine made with specially selected, outstandingly fresh ingredients. Vegetarians will like the menu, too.
🞣 200 C1 ✉ Friedrichstr. 167–168
☎ 030 20 67 28 28; www.boccadibacco.de
🕙 Daily noon–midnight

Borchardt €€
August Friedrich Wilhelm Borchardt opened his fine wine bar in the 200m² (656ft²) former assembly rooms of the Huguenot community near the Gendarmenmarkt in 1853 to bring a more cosmopolitan flair to the provincial capital. Little did he know that it would become one of the city's most famous, most popular restaurants. Reminiscent of *La Coupole* in Paris, it's long been a favourite of politicans and media types alike. The Wiener Schnitzel is one of the best in town.
🞣 200 C2 ✉ Französische Str. 47
☎ 030 81 88 62 62 🕙 Daily 11.30am–1am

Brasserie am Gendarmenmarkt €€
A truly beautiful brasserie filled with dark wood, chrome and a neo-Art-Deco ambience. If you're in a hurry, the "Quick Lunch" is designed to let you wolf down a full three courses in 30 minutes. Friendly waiters serve freshly prepared Italian, French and German dishes at lunchtime and in the evening. It's not quite as busy in the afternoon – a good time to enjoy the terrace out on the Gendarmenmarkt.

➕ 200 C1 ✉ Taubenstr. 30
☎ 030 20 45 35 01, www. brasserie amgendarmenmarkt.de 🕐 Daily 11.30–midnight, Quick Lunch Mon–Fri 11.30am–4pm

Einstein €–€€

There's a lot to see here. Artistic and political notables come back again and again – some regulars even have their own favourite places laid with white tablecloths. People crowd around the small tables to enjoy tasty cakes and sophisticated Austrian cooking.
➕ 200 C2 ✉ Unter den Linden 42
☎ 030 2 04 36 32; www.einsteinudl.com
🕐 Daily 7am–10pm

Refugium €–€€

Although the best place to sit is out on the Gendarmenmarkt terrace in summer, the baroque vaults of the "French church of Friedrichstadt" are also an ideal place to enjoy *Kalbsbuletten* (veal meatballs) with creamed potatoes or *Welsfilet* (catfish filet) with spinach. The ambience and the courteous staff are worth the price.
➕ 200 C2 ✉ Gendarmenmarkt 5
☎ 030 2 29 16 61; www.restaurant-refugium.de
🕐 Daily from 10am (food from noon)

Soya Cosplay €€

Soya Cosplay uses colourful paper lanterns and sophisticated lights to create a cosy atmosphere without descending into kitsch. The meals are real explosions of taste. Braised pork belly is wonderfully juxtaposed with fresh herbs, and the shrimp balls are given a kick with wasabi mayonnaise.
➕ 204 C5 ✉ Jägerstr. 59–60
☎ 030 20 62 90 93; www.soyacosplay.com
🕐 Mon–Sat noon–midnight, Sun from 5pm

Ständige Vertretung €–€€

This eatery harks back to the glory days of Bonn, the former German capital city on the Rheine. Homesick Rheinlanders come to eat here amidst photos depicting the political history of the nation. They've successfully brought their culture to the banks of the Spree: Berliners happily embrace their customs, sitting very close together and drinking *Kölsch* (a top-fermented speciality beer from Cologne) out of what look like test tubes in comparison with normal glasses. The *Flammkuchen* – wafer-thin pizzas served on wooden boards with various tasty savoury or sweet toppings – is the highlight of the menu.
➕ 200 B3 ✉ Schiffbauerdamm 8
☎ 030 2 82 39 65; www.staev.de
🕐 Daily 10.30am–1am

Vau €€€

TV Chef Kolja Kleeberg's name has been synonymous with quality for many years. He's had a Michelin star since 1997. His recipe for success sounds deceptively simple: Never have more than three ingredients on a plate at any one time.
➕ 200 C2 ✉ Jägerstr. 54–55
☎ 030 2 02 97 30; www.vau-berlin.de
🕐 Mon–Sat noon–2.30pm, 7pm–10.30pm

CAFÉS

Café am Neuen See

Insider Tip

Eat breakfast until 4pm, sit by the water in the beer garden or enjoy the view from the window when it's cold outside. 👫 Kids will love it, too! Whether you want an Italian breakfast with various sausages and cheeses, an Atlantic spread (salmon, halibut) or just some muesli, it's a perfect place to fortify yourself for some more sightseeing. It's packed at weekends, but you'll always find somewhere to sit in the large beer garden in summer. The pizzas smell mouth-watering in the afternoon.
➕ 203 D4 ✉ Lichtensteinallee 2
☎ 030 2 54 49 30 🕐 Mar–Oct, daily, restaurant from 9am, Beer garden 11am–10pm, Winter Sat, Sun 10–10

Where to...
Shop

Unter den Linden isn't a shopping street. You might find picture postcards and chunks of the Wall on the first stretch as you head away from Pariser Platz, but if you really want to shop, you'll be better off in the Friedrichstadt Passages on Friedrichstraße (Galeries Lafayette, ➤ 67).

FRIEDRICHSTRASSE

The southern end of Friedrichstraße down to Leipziger Straße is one uninterrupted shopping strip selling all things posh and expensive, ranging from fountain pens (Mont Blanc) and hand sewn shoes (Budapester) to delicious confectionary. You'll find Da Vinci, Etro, Gant USA, Guess, La Perla, Jil Sander, Joop, Kenzo and Dior in the **Friedrichstadt Passages**. The **Dussmann** Cultural Department Store (Friedrichstr. 90) at the north end of the street has extensive opening hours: Mon–Sat from 10am to midnight. There's an **Antiques Market** under the S-Bahn railway arches to the right of Friedrichstraße station (Georgenstr.) where numerous traders sell wares from various epochs.

TIERGARTEN/ STRASSE DES 17. JUNI

A popular **junk and art market** is held on Straße des 17 Juni starting at the Tiergarten S-Bahn station every Saturday and Sunday (10–5). As well as stands with pricey collector's items, you'll find junk dealers offering bargains galore, including a lot of vinyl and CDs. Head west to the large arts and crafts market to find out what the creative citizenry of Berlin is currently busy dreaming up.

Where to...
Go Out

UNTER DEN LINDEN

The area around Unter den Linden and the Gendarmenmarkt is pretty quiet at night. Anyone out and about here will be on their way to the **Staatsoper** (Unter den Linden 5–7, tel: 030 20 35 45 55), which has become Berlin's leading musical venue under the leadership of Daniel Barenboim (closed for renovation; performances at Schillertheater, Bismarckstr. 110, Charlottenburg), to the **Komische Oper** (Behrenstr. 55–57, tel: 030 47 99 74 00) or to the **Konzerthaus** on the Gendarmenmarkt (tel: 030 2 03 09 21 01). Shermin Langhoff has been staging post-migrant theatre with a multicultural ensemble at the **Maxim-Gorki-Theater** (Am Festungsgraben 2, tel: 030 20 22 11 15) since 2013.

Have a bite to eat at the chic **Club-Restaurant Felix** at the back of the Adlon Hotel before dancing the night away to sought-after DJs (Behrenstr. 72, tel: 030 3 01 11 71 52, Club Thu from 9pm, Mon/Fri/Sat from 11pm).

FRIEDRICHSTRASSE

Behind Friedrichstraße station you'll see a mix of barflies (mostly on their way to the the Spandauer Vorstadt district) and culture vultures hurrying down to the **Berliner Ensemble** (tel: 030 28 40 81 55). The **Admiralspalast** (tel: 030 32 53 31 30) puts on a whole host of events ranging from cabaret to jazz.

Friedrichstadtpalast (tel: 030 23 26 23 26), the largest revue theatre in Europe, has its very own children's ensemble that stages 👫 performances for kids.

Mitte

 **Little Treats**

Creepy Crawlies
The giant beetles by Berlin artists in the 2nd courtyard at Rosenthaler Straße 39 will give you goosebumps.

The City at your Feet
Enjoy the wonderful view of Berlin from up on the **roof of the Park Inn hotel** on Alexanderplatz (entry €3).

A Trabi Trip Above Berlin
Climb into a *Trabi* (GDR car) hung 13m (42ft) in the air at the **Hochseilgarten** by the beach volleyball courts (➤ 96).

Getting Your Bearings

English, French and Spanish are all spoken in Mitte, a meeting place for young people from around the world. They all came seeking chaos, mystery and new opportunities here after the fall of the Wall. It's now a paradise for shoppers and art collectors.

This district is often called the *Scheunenviertel* (Barn Quarter), but this is historically inaccurate: In fact, the actual barn district, which stood outside the city in the 17th century and later provided a home for poor East European Jews, lay where the Volksbühne and Rosenthaler Platz stand today. Perhaps the name stuck because after the Wall came down it was so easy to occupy the dilapidated houses here, set up a secret club in your living room, and test out the market value of your creativity with people from New York, Budapest and Tokyo in the dilapidated Tacheles Art House. All kinds of surprises lay in store in the labyrinth of junk-filled backyards – curiosity here was likely to be rewarded.

A slogan on a wall reads *Das Chaos ist verbraucht* ("The Chaos is Gone"). It's not wrong: Most of the residential buildings have been replastered, the synagogue's dome gleams with gold, and the divey clubs and bars are now elegant. Strolling through the chic courtyards, it's rare to find unused land today. Actors sit next to tourists in restaurants, beloved museums are being restored, and the fringe scene's artists are moving out. Only Alexanderplatz has resisted transformation.

A peaceful residential area

The Nikolaiviertel boasts many riverside cafés

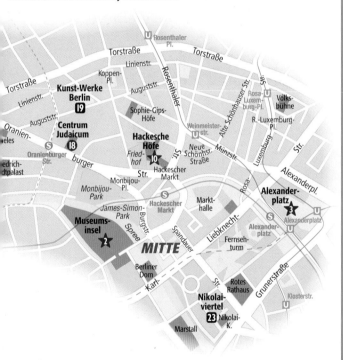

TOP 10

⭐ Museumsinsel ➤ 82
⭐ Alexanderplatz ➤ 88
⭐ Hackesche Höfe ➤ 90

Don't Miss

⓲ Centrum Judaicum ➤ 92

At Your Leisure

⓳ Kunst-Werke Berlin ➤ 94
⓴ Sammlung Boros ➤ 94
㉑ Hamburger Station ➤ 94
㉒ Dorotheenstädtischer Cemetery ➤ 95
㉓ Nikolaiviertel ➤ 95

Mitte

The Perfect Day

It takes a whole day to really explore Berlin's Mitte district. Follow our day's itinerary if you don't want to miss any of the area's highlights. The individual sights are described more closely over the following pages (➤ 82–96).

🌐 10:00

The shops are opening (image above) and you can already get a coffee, but the ⭐Hackesche Höfe courtyards (➤ 90) are still pretty quiet this early on. It's the best time to visit them (apart from in the evening).

🌐 10:30

Five museums are tightly packed onto ⭐Museumsinsel (➤ 82), an island in the river Spree. Your choice of where to go first is made a little easier by the renovation work that's scheduled to close off areas in rotation until 2025.

🌐 13:00

Walk down along the S-Bahn railway arches and find yourself a promising spot to sit and eat lunch in one of the restaurants.

🌐 14:00

Cross Monbijou Park and you'll arrive on Oranienburger Straße. You'll see the shining golden dome of the New Synagogue in the ⓲ Centrum Judaicum (➤ 92) to your left. It's well worth picking up an audio guide. You'll learn more about the district here than anywhere else in the area.

🕓 16:00

Just one U-Bahn stop from the **21** Hamburger Bahnhof (➤ 94), you'll find **19** Kunst-Werke Berlin (➤ 94), a remarkable exhibition space. If you fancy relaxing instead, head to Friedrichbrücke bridge (on Burgstraße) and take a boat trip under the bridges that span the river. 👫 Kids will love it, too.

🕓 17:30

Have a coffee up in the rotating panorama-level café of the 👫 Fernsehturm on ⭐ **Alexanderplatz** (➤ 88) and you'll see the whole city in half an hour. If that's too fast, just enjoy the view from the platform.

🕓 18:30

Walk past the Rotes Rathaus (Red Town Hall, image below left; ➤ 88) down to the **23** Nikolaiviertel (➤ 95), where you'll find the Nikolaikirche, the oldest church in Berlin. Stay here if you want to finish your day in the very spot where Berlin itself began. Head to Le Provençal (➤ 97), an eatery serving hearty French cuisine where you can sit out on the riverside terrace in the summer months. Alternatively, go one stop on the S-Bahn to Hackescher Markt (image below), have a nose through some of the many small shops on Neue Schönhauser Straße and find a nice restaurant for your evening meal.

★2 Museumsinsel

Berlin has around 200 museums, so why visit these ones in particular? Simple! The Altes Museum is one of the finest buildings in the city; the perfectly restored Alte Nationalgalerie has an outstanding painting collection; you'll get an audience with the Egyptian Queen Nefertiti in the Neues Museum; and the Pergamonmuseum boasts treasures from a host of ancient cultures.

If you approach Museumsinsel (Museum Island) from Hackescher Markt, stay on the bridge for a while – there's plenty to see! Tour boats pass by on the Spree – half the passengers will be Berliners, who are always curious to see what has changed in their city. The westbound S-Bahn rattles across the river, and the golden dome of the **Neue Synagoge** (New Synagogue) gleams over on Oranienburger Straße (►92). You might hear the sound of an accordion or saxophone and even the highly skilled stylings of Russian concert musicians who can't find a job back home. Hundreds of starlings gather in the trees by the impressive cathedral every evening. It's also a popular location for floodlit film sets.

The Altes Museum: As noble as the Pantheon

Altes Museum

Approach the Altes Museum (Old Museum, 1824–30) from the Lustgarten (Pleasure Garden) at the front. This was a garden, an exercise ground, a meadow and a parade square before being turfed over again in 1999. In an unusual move for the elitist age, architect Karl Friedrich Schinkel kept Berlin's citizens in mind when designing this

THE ELEVATION OF TASTE

We have the archaeologist Aloys Hirt to thank for the fact that the Altes Museum was built at all. In 1797 he stated that the best of the royal collection should be brought together for the use of artists and the betterment of public taste. Compared with other courtly collections, there wasn't much to assemble, however. In the nick of time, English timber merchant Edward Solly offered up his notable collection for 500,000 silver coins. What's more, the **Giustiniani Collection** in Paris, with its early Italian baroque pieces and works by **Michelangelo da Caravaggio**, also came up for sale. Friedrich Wilhelm III stumped up, and when Schinkel's museum opened on the King's birthday in 1830, there were 1,198 paintings on show.

museum to complement the palace, the cathedral and the Arsenal. A wide staircase leads to an open, columned hall – a temple of the arts in an ancient Greek style. Visitors enter the rotunda, modelled on the Pantheon in Rome, to be "uplifted" (in Schinkel's words) before seeing the collections. The circular gallery of the two-storey domed hall is supported by 20 Corinthian columns. The museum holds antiquities from the Greek, Roman and Etruscan civilisations today. The collection's most important piece is the **Praying Boy**, found in Rhodes in 300BC, which stands in the middle of the North Hall in exactly the same place as when the museum opened in 1830.

Alte Nationalgalerie

The Alte Nationalgalerie (Old National Gallery, 1866–76), designed by Friedrich August Stüler in the style of a Corinthian temple, stands on a high plinth far away from everyday life below. Visitors are greeted by the Prussian King Friedrich Wilhelm IV on his steed. The gallery exists thanks to a resolute patron, the banker Joachim Wagener. He bought Schinkel's **Gothic Church by the Sea** and various smaller genre paintings and bequeathed them to the future Kaiser Wilhelm I on the condition that they be used to found a national gallery for contemporary art in an "appropriate venue". After the bourgeois revolution of

A place to rest near a fighting Amazonian warrior

Mitte

1848, many artists and liberal politicians thought that it was the state's job to care for the collection. In 2001, the gallery was reopened after careful renovation at the grand old age of 125. This former shrine to German national culture has now become an international collection of 19th-century art. You can see works by the great romanticist **Caspar David Friedrich** and Berliners **Adolph Menzel** and **Max Liebermann** alongside pieces by **Renoir**, **Monet** and sculptors ranging from **Reinhold Begas** to **Rodin**.

Neues Museum

The "New Museum", regarded as the most beautiful of them all, suffered the worst damage in the War. Designed by Stüler, the building (1843–55) was a work of art made of cast iron, ceiling papers, integrated oriental objects and new paints and building materials. Famous British architect David Chipperfield gave the ruin a new lease of life by carefully uniting its historic paintings and columns with elements of a modern style. Today, its treasures include the bust of Nefertiti and the papyrus collection in the Egyptian Museum, and the Trojan artefacts in the Museum of Pre-History and Early History.

The Bode Museum juts out over the water like a mighty ship

IT GIRL

Visitors walk round and round her, admiring her beauty – some come to see her and her alone. Her name is **Nefertiti**. She can be found on the first floor of the Neues Museum, where she's been reunited with her entourage from the Egyptian Museum.

Pergamonmuseum

Built following plans by Alfred Messel and Ludwig Hoffmann, the Pergamonmuseum (1909–1930) combines the Middle East Museum, the Museum of Islamic Art and parts of the antiquities collection. Gradual restoration work is planned until 2025, so some sections might be closed when you visit. The north wing and the hall with the museum's eponymous **Pergamon Altar** are shut until 2019, for example. This doesn't make the museum any less worth visiting, however. Its highlights include the magnificent Market Gate of Miletus (165BC) and an Orpheus floor mosaic from a Roman villa (2nd century). As you pass through

The Pergamon Altar tells of heroic deeds

the gate, you'll travel back to Babylon during the days of Nebuchadnezzar II (603–562BC). It's here that you'll find the stunning **Ishtar Gate**, the Processional Way and part of the crown room's façade. Further important monumental pieces of architecture from the Old Middle East include a mosaicked wall (3000BC) and a brick façade (c.1415BC) from the Temple of Eanna in Uruk. The standout exhibits on the upper floor of the **Islamic Museum** are the 8th-century façade from the Mshatta desert palace (found in modern Jordan), and the Aleppo Room, which once served as the reception hall for a Syrian house. Persian miniatures, carpets and carvings, and a prayer niche from the Maidan mosque in Kashan (Iran) are also on display.

Bode Museum

The Bode Museum, which has jutted out over the water like a ship's prow since 1904, houses the Museum for Byzantine Art and a magnificent collection of sculpture that includes works by Tilman Riemenschneider.

TAKING A BREAK

All of the museums provide a café for visitors.

✚ 201 D2/3

✉ Museumsinsel ☎ 030 2 66 42 42 42 🕐 Tue–Sun 10–6pm, Thu till 8pm, Neues Mus. und Pergamonmus. also Mon 10–6pm 🚇 Hackescher Markt, Friedrichstr. 🚌 100 🎟 Tickets for all five museums €18; under 18s, free

INSIDER INFO

The **Museumspass Berlin** (€24, concessions €12) is valid for entry into all of the state museums.

A Refuge for Arts and Antiquities

The Museumsinsel, a UNESCO World Heritage Site, is one of the largest museum complexes in the world. It's a unique cultural landscape that's dedicated to art and archaeology. Don't try to see it all, but don't miss the Pergamon Altar, Nefertiti or the Alte Nationalgalerie either. Bereichskarte tickets are valid for entry into all of the museums. Strange but true: S-Bahn and long-distance trains travel right across the island.

In 2014, the Museumsinsel was visited by 2,390,000 people – 9000,000 of whom went to the Pergamonmuseum. Despite this, the museum isn't one of the world's top 5 most visited museums by a long shot:

- Louvre, Paris: 9,260,000.
- British Museum, London: 6,690,000.
- Metropolitan Museum, New York: 6,410,000.
- National Gallery, London: 6,200,000.
- Tate Modern, London: 5,780,000.

The S-Bahn goes straight over the island. Passengers can even see into the museums' windows.

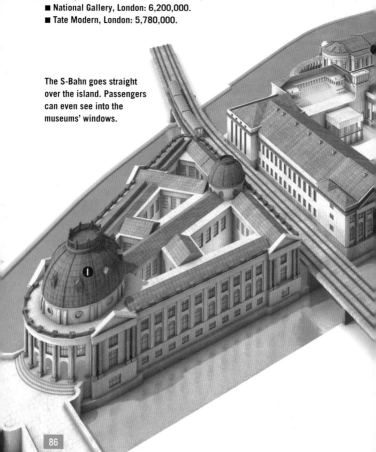

Museumsinsel

❶ The **Bode Museum** was originally known as the Kaiser-Friedrich-Museum when it opened in 1904. The museum was renamed in honour of its founder, Wilhelm von Bode, when it reopened in 1956. It houses the sculpture collection, the Museum of Byzantine Art and the Coin Cabinet.

❷ The **Pergamonmuseum** (1930) consists of three museums: The Antiquities Collection, the Middle East Museum and the Museum for Islamic Art. Parts of the collection are expected to close for renovation until 2019.

❸ The **Alte Nationalgalerie** (1866–1876; designed by Friedrich August Stüler and Johann Heinrich Strack) was originally intended as a hall for lectures and ceremonies related to German art. Sat on a tall base, the building takes the form of a Corinthian temple. After many years of restoration work, the wonderful gallery now houses 19th-century painting and sculpture.

❹ Originally constructed from 1843–1855 following plans by Friedrich August Stüler, the **Neues Museum** has been completely rebuilt. Come here to see the Egyptian Museum and the Trojan Collection at the Museum of Pre-History and Early History.

❺ Designed by Karl Friedrich Schinkel in the style of an Ancient Greek temple, the **Altes Museum** was built from 1824–1830 to serve as a Royal museum.

❻ The foundation stone for the **James Simon Gallery** was laid in October 2013. This building will act as the central reception hall for Museum Island. David Chipperfield's design envisages a 104m (341ft)-long, 18m (60ft)-high structure consisting of a 9m (30ft)-tall base (for the shop, catering and functional spaces, etc.) beneath a 9m (30ft) columnar hall containing the visitor centre.

❼ The **"Archaeological Promenade"** will connect the Bode, Pergamon, Neues and Altes Museums underground, making it possible to visit all the most important exhibits in record time.

★3 Alexanderplatz

East Berliners still call this massive square home. It was the centre of their city in the GDR era, and a hotspot for demonstrations shortly before the Wall came down. The Fernsehturm (TV Tower), Berlin's highest building, can be seen from all over town.

ST WALTER

When the Fernsehturm was completed in 1969, it was discovered that a silvery cross appeared whenever the sun shone on the globe at the top. Not even Walter Ulbricht, head of the atheist GDR, could stop it happening – the tower was nicknamed "St Walter" in his honour.

Locals know it as "Alex" – West Berliners say the name with a more rounded "Ah-lex" sound than people from the East. Whatever you call it, the square is so large and the buildings around it are so far apart that it's difficult to know exactly where it ends. It's a lively place full of department stores, punks with dogs, bored street kids, alcoholics sunning themselves and young people climbing on the roof under the **Fernsehturm**. The tower is the highlight of the square. If the weather's clear, don't miss taking the 40-second trip up to the top.

The Fernsehturm, Germany's tallest building (368m/ 1,207ft), has long been a symbol of the city. While you're up there, look down at the square, a former (cattle) market and parade ground which was renamed in honour of the visiting Tsar Alexander I in 1808. From then on, it slowly developed into a hub for transport. At that time, the **Marienkirche** (Our Lady's Church, begun 1270) still stood in a jumble of small streets. Reinhold Begas' **Neptunbrunnen** (Neptune Fountain, 1891) used to stand in front of the royal palace.

It's reminiscent of Bernini's Fountain of the Four Rivers in Rome, but the women here symbolise the rivers Elbe, Weichsel, Oder and Rhine. The **Rotes Rathaus** (Red Town Hall, 1861–69), the redbrick seat of Berlin's mayor, is modelled on buildings from 15th- and 16th-century Italy and Flanders. A frieze of 36 terracotta tablets tells the history of the city from the 1100s to the Empire's foundation in 1871. On 4 November, 1989, just before the Wall came down, around 500,000 people came to the square for the largest demonstration of the era.

The Neptunbrunnen (Neptune Fountain)

The **Weltzeituhr**, a 1960s creation

Times (on the) Square

People relax in front of the Kaufhaus department store by the **Brunnen der Völkerfreundschaft** (Fountain of the Friendship of Nations), a 1969 work by sculptor Walter Womacka. Erich John's 10m (33ft)-high **Weltzeituhr** (World Time Clock) tells you the time around the globe. It's a popular meeting place, perhaps because it's always 6 o'clock somewhere. Whatever time's on the clock, however, it never seems the right moment to start putting plans to build mighty skyscrapers around the square into action.

TAKING A BREAK

You can get the best view of Alexanderplatz if you head up to the **Dinea-Restaurant** (Alexanderplatz 9, tel: 030 24 74 30, Mon–Wed 9.30–8pm, Thu–Sat 9.30–10pm) on the sixth floor of Galeria Kaufhof. It's a pleasant place to enjoy some coffee and cake and watch the bustling square below. A tip: Your second coffee costs just €1!

Insider Tip

➕ 201 E3 🚇 Alexanderplatz

Fernsehturm

✉ Panoramastr. 1a ⏰ Mar–Oct, daily 9am–midnight, Nov–Feb daily 10am–midnight 🎟 from €13

INSIDER INFO

- ■ A small white **stone cross** stands by the portal of the Marienkirche church. It's a penitence cross paid for by the Berlin congregation in repentance after one of them lynched the Provost of Bernau in 1324.
- ■ Head up into the **Fernsehturm** on a cloudy or misty day when you can't see the tower or the silver globe from below. You'll feel like you've taken off and left the world far behind.

★10 Hackesche Höfe

Escaping noisy streets by diving through a gateway and suddenly finding yourself in a network of quiet courtyards is a common experience in Berlin. The Hackesche Höfe are far from common, however: The scene that awaits you inside is magnificent.

From outside, you'd have no inkling of the reproduction gold, green and blue clinker bricks, high windows, striking patterns and curving rooflines that lie beyond, drawing in curious passersby like magnets. In 1906, renowned Art Deco architect August Endell contrasted the then-common use of Wilhelmine stucco (which used to grace the façades here) with an unusual design expressing his own idea of beauty.

A picture-perfect courtyard

This complex of eight courtyards was built near the City Palace and various department stores at the start of the 20th century, a time when the economy was flourishing and the price of building land in the city was rocketing up. It immediately caused a sensation thanks to its optimised used of space, the way it combined residential and commercial properties, and – of course – the beauty of the first courtyard itself.

OFF THE BEATEN TRACK

A narrow stairway in the courtyard of Rosenthaler Straße 39 next to the Hackesche Höfe leads up to the **Otto Weidt Workshop for the Blind Museum**. Jewish and non-Jewish deaf and blind people survived the Nazi era here by making brooms and brushes – deemed essential to the war effort – under the protection of Otto Weidt (daily 10am–8pm, free).

Insider Tip

Parquet Floors and Indoor Toilets

At a time when flats in Berlin's tenements were home to between six and thirteen people, these apartments were able to boast central heating, parquet flooring, bathrooms, inside toilets and balconies. The occupants came from bourgeois and official circles. Many owned shops and workshops in the courtyards. Producers of textiles, telephones and liquor worked alongside furriers, cobblers and an oilcloth factory. Of the 179 members of the Jewish community who lived and worked here in 1939, not one still appeared in the address book by 1944.

After the Second World War, the courtyards were neglected and used as workshops and storehouses. The stucco façades were removed in 1961. Immediately after the fall of the Wall, a society was founded that has done a great deal to ensure that the Hackesche Höfe remain as beautiful now as the day they were built.

Promoting Urban Living

Following extensive restoration work, a scheme to promote urban living was drawn up by the owners, tenants and the Berlin Senate. This states that all the restaurants and shops here must be run by their proprietors. It also stipulates that the mixed use of the courtyards should continue (flats, offices, culture, workshops, eateries, etc.), with each being charged a different level of rent. The former ballrooms are now used for the Chamäleon variety shows and there's a cinema up in the roof. You can buy creations by fashion designers, watch goldsmiths at work and visit exhibitions at the gallery in the Brunnenhof. Get your hair cut, go dancing, play billiards, listen to music, visit a photo gallery, buy old and new books… or just enjoy having a look around!

TAKING A BREAK

Somewhat hidden in a back courtyard, the Asian eatery **Pan Asia** (Rosenthaler Str. 38, tel: 030 27 90 88 11; www.panasia.de, Sun–Thu noon–midnight, Fri–Sat noon–1am) boasts a great terrace in summer.

➕ 201 D3 ✉ Rosenthaler Str. 40–41 🚇 Hackescher Markt

INSIDER INFO

Exit via Hof (Courtyard) VI to get to Sophienstraße. Turn left and walk till you see the entrance to the **Sophie-Gips-Höfe** on the right (No 21). They're home to a nice café and Erika and Rolf Hoffmann's interesting art collection (Sat 11–4, book ahead for tours, tel: 030 28 49 91 20). Other fine courtyards are found at **Oranienburger Straße 27 and 32**.

⓲ Centrum Judaicum

The golden dome of the Neue Synagoge (New Synagogue) in Oranienburger Straße dominates the skyline in Mitte. Police patrol in front of the building, signalling the ongoing danger to which Jewish institutions are exposed.

The New Synagogue, rebuilt from 1988 to 1995, isn't really very new at all. A small prayer room and some architectural fragments are all that remain in evidence of the original building's former interior beauty. They also stand in memory of its violent destruction. Photographs, original documents and recorded reminiscences are used to bring Berlin's former Jewish culture back to life.

Saved and Destroyed

Schinkel's pupil Eduard Knoblauch had Granada's Alhambra in mind when he designed the original building (completed in 1866). On Kristallnacht (the Night of Broken Glass, 9 November, 1933), a brave policeman stopped right wingers destroying this Moorish-Byzantine masterpiece by saying it was a listed building. Bombs from a British air raid in November 1943 reduced it to ruins, however. All but the dome was torn down in 1958.

Germany's Largest Jewish Community

The synagogue, which used to hold a congregation of 3,200 people, is no longer used today. Although Berlin's

WAITING TO EMIGRATE

There were 173,000 Jews living in Berlin in 1933. By the summer of 1945, there were only 8,000 left. Many of those remaining were awaiting permission to emigrate to the US or Palestine. More than 55,000 of Berlin's Jews were deported and murdered by the Nazis. The rest were forced to emigrate.

The Neue Synagoge in Oranienburger Straße

12,000 Jews make up the largest Jewish community in Germany, the new influx of members – many of whom hail from the former Soviet Union – have not yet enriched the Jewish life of the city as was hoped. The problem is that the newcomers have been distanced from their Jewish traditions and consciousness. The Centrum Judaicum provides them with an archive and rooms for meetings, teaching, study, exhibitions and prayer. Along with the Jewish community hall, the library and the college of further education, it's created a new centre for Jewish life to take root in the city.

The street-side bars along Oranienburger Straße are mainly visited by tourists

Grass and Stone

Turn off Oranienburger Straße into Große Hamburger Straße and you'll find a Jewish memorial on your right. The sculptures (1984) by Willi and Mark Lammert were erected in memory of the fact that the **Jewish Old People's Home** that stood here was the main assembly point for Jews being deported to the death camps. You'll also see the names of former occupants written on the fire-blackened walls of a bombed-out building diagonally opposite.

An inconspicuous area of grass here was once the city's first **Jewish cemetery**. Dating from 1672, it was destroyed and levelled in 1943. Since 1998, a headstone has stood where the grave of Moses Mendelssohn, the philosopher and founder of a creative dynasty, is thought to lie.

TAKING A BREAK

If you fancy a light kosher meal, head to **Beth Café** located on Tucholskystraße.

🕂 200 C3
✉ Synagogue: Oranienburger Str. 28–30 ☎ 030 88 02 83 00
🕐 Sun–Mon 10–8, Tue–Thu 10–6, Fri 10–5
🚇 Hackescher Markt, Oranienburger Tor 🎟 €3.50, Dome €2

INSIDER INFO

- Martin Jander runs regular **Jewish Traces** tours on Berlin's Jewish history (tel: 030 89 06 80 14; www.unwrapping-history.de).
- The **Alte Synagoge** (Old Synagogue, 1714) was found behind the Hakescher Markt in Heidereuter Straße until it was destroyed in World War II. Its foundations can still be seen today.
- Monbijou Park is home to the **Strandbar Mitte** beach bar and the **Monbijou Theatre**, which has an open-air stage in the summer months.

At Your Leisure

🔟 Kunst-Werke Berlin

Head through the gateway of an old rustic house and into the court-yard where you'll see a glazed café on your left. You might even get to walk through a work of art – that's because after the Wall fell, dozens of art lovers occupied the dilapidated properties in this area. In 1991, four artists moved into this former margarine factory, a building that stood alone in a meadow back in the 17th century. They founded the KW Institute for Contemporary Arts, completed makeshift repairs to the structure, and started organising exhibitions. The factory has since been properly renovated, and artists live and work in its wings. In 1998, they organised the 1st Berlin Biennial for Contemporary Art, and their exhibitions are always highly praised by international critics.

➕ 200 C3/4 ✉ Auguststr. 69
☎ 030 2 43 45 90; www.kw-berlin.de
🕐 Wed, Fri–Mon noon–7, Thu till 9
Ⓜ Oranienburger Tor 🎫 €6

🔟 Sammlung Boros

A bunker near the Deutsches Theater – once used by the Red Army to hold war criminals and used to store tropical fruit in the GDR – is where Christian Boros has set up Berlin's most unusual art gallery. This raw concrete structure contains works from Boros' private collection of contemporary art, including pieces by Olafur Eliasson, Ai Weiwei and Wolfgang Tillmans. If you want a tour, you'll have to book online.

➕ 200 B3 ✉ Reinhardtstr. 20
☎ 030 27 59 40 65; www.sammlung-boros.de
🕐 Thu 3pm–8pm, Fri 10–8, Sat–Sun 10–6
Ⓜ Oranienburger Tor 🎫 €12

🔟 Hamburger Bahnhof

Dan Flavin, an artist known for using fluorescent lights, has made this late-classical railway station shine like a blue and green remnant from the Arabian Nights.

The coloured lights prove an irresistible attraction for visitors, particularly at night. The breadth and height of the hall's interior – reminiscent of the Musée d'Orsay in Paris – are pretty astonishing. Hamburger Bahnhof, Berlin's oldest preserved railway station, was used for 40 years until it was replaced by the nearby Lehrter station (now the Hauptbahnhof/Central Station) in 1884. It then became a transport museum. In 1996, after its much-praised conversion by architect Josef Paul Kleihues, it was reborn as the **Museum für Gegenwart** (Museum of Contemporary Art, an offshoot of the Neue Nationalgalerie, ► 110) which contained art owned by Berlin collector **Erich Marx**. The museum's outstanding works in-

---

🦕 REAL DINOSAURS

Berlin has a **Brachiosaurus**, the largest dino on display in the world. This 13m (43ft)-tall, 23m (75ft)-long giant lived in Tanzania 144 million years ago. (Museum für Naturkunde, Invalidenstr. 43, tel: 030 20 93 85 91, Tue–Fri 9.30–6, Sat, Sun 10–6, U-Bahn: Naturkundemuseum, entry €5)

An exhibition in Hamburger Station

clude **Andy Warhol's** *Mao Portrait*, **Cy Twombly's** *Sunset Series*, **Joseph Beuys'** *Tram Stop* and **Robert Rauschenberg's** *Summer Rental +3*. The important **Friedrich Christian Flick Collection** of contemporary art – boasting pieces by the likes of Bruce Nauman and Pipilotti Rist – was added in 2004.

✚ 200 A4 ✉ Invalidenstr. 50–51
☎ 030 2 66 42 42 42 🕐 Tue–Wed 10–6, Thu 10–8, Fri 10–6, Sat–Sun 11–6
🚇 Zinnowitzer Str. 🎫 €10

22 Dorotheenstädtischer Friedhof

The leading lights of Berlin society like to be buried in this cemetery alongside prominent citizens from previous centuries. The notables interred here include: Architect **Karl Friedrich Schinkel**; **August Borsig**, who owned a locomotive factory and was a driving force in the economic and industrial life of Berlin; philosophers **Johann Gottlieb Fichte** and **Georg Friedrich Hegel**; playwright **Bertolt Brecht**, who could almost see this spot from his apartment; Brecht's wife, the actress **Helene Weigel**; sculptors **Johann Gottfried Schadow** and **Christian Daniel Rauch** who created one or two tombs themselves; the writers **Heinrich Mann**, **Anna Seghers** and

Stefan Hermlin; the composer **Hanns Eisler**; and actor **Bernhard Minetti**. Admirers of **Heiner Müller**, playwright and director of the Berliner Ensemble, still leave cigars for him in the ashtray on his grave.

✚ 200 B4 ✉ Chausseestr. 126
🕐 Daily from 8am till sunset, until 8pm in summer 🚇 Oranienburger Tor

23 Nikolaiviertel

There wasn't much left here after WW II until the city's 750th jubilee in 1987, when an "Old Town" was built opposite the Rotes Rathaus (Red Town Hall). It's only old by name: Despite the church's

---

A WALK THROUGH MITTE

Stroll down **Neue Schönhauser Straße** with its rows of shops, cafés and restaurants. Continue on to **Alte Schönhauser Straße**. Turn into Mulackstraße and try to imagine it as it once looked – a murky district full of underworld bars and hoodlums in the former Barn Quarter. If you head down to **Auguststraße** and **Linienstraße**, you might be lucky enough to find an exhibition that no one else has yet seen. Follow people into courtyards – you'll often find a gallery or workplace being set up inside. Discover these hidden spots and you'll begin to understand the attraction of the quarter.

Insider Tip

Mitte

In the Nikolaiviertel

foundation walls dating from c.1200, and although the area was once a Slavic settlement that was turned into a town by Low German merchants, you could only see grass, pigeons and sparrows here by the Nikolaikirche and the Knoblauchhaus until the 1980s. The granite foundation blocks of the 13th-century church tower withstood the War, as did the stone-work of the choir and nave (14th/15th c.). The rest was destroyed, however, and was rebuilt from 1981.

The comprehensively restored **Nikolaikirche** church (daily 10–6, €5) is a museum dealing with such themes as church history, funeral culture and the hymn writer Paul

Gerhardt. It contains decorated epitaphs of prominent Berliners and a hoard of coins from the 16th–18th centuries. Façades made from pre-formed concrete slabs were used along with bow windows and gables, monuments and various other items taken from around the city to construct a brand new Socialist ideal of a historical centre around the church.

The **Ephraimpalais** (Poststraße 16, open Tue, Thu–Sun 10–6, Wed noon–8, entry €5), the most beauti-ful spot in Berlin, is situated between Poststraße and the concrete Spree embankment. It belonged to Veitel Heine Ephraim, financier to Friedrich the Great. Diagonally opposite is the **Knoblauchhaus** (1759–60). Adorned with early-classical filigree decoration, it's the only 18th-century townhouse ex-tant in Berlin today. The 12 rooms trace the history of both the city and the Knoblauch family who lived in the house until 1928 (Poststr. 23, Tue–Sun 10–6, free entry).

The **Zille Museum** has been set up at Propststraße 11 in memory of Heinrich Zille, an illustrator who recorded the lives of Berlin's ordinary citizens in truly impressive style (daily, Apr–Oct 11–7, Nov–Mar 11–6, entry €6).

✚ 201 E2

✉ Nikolaiviertel Ⓤ Alexanderplatz

BEACH VOLLEYBALL

With no fewer than 49 courts, this volleyball complex – one of the largest in Germany – attracts a sporty crowd looking for fun and games. It's floodlit at night, and there's a beach bar for post-game parties. Not a sports fan? Doesn't matter – you'll enjoy the bar anyway! (Caroline-Michaelis-Str./corner of Julie-Wolfthorn-Str., tel: 0177 2 80 68 61; www.beachmitte.de, Apr–Sep daily 10am–midnight, S-Bahn: Nordbahnhof, entry €12–€16)

Where to...
Eat and Drink

Prices
A main course without drinks:
€ under 12 euros   €€ 12–25 euros   €€€ over 25 euros

RESTAURANTS

Ampelmann Restaurant €
Serving up *Ampelmann* (traffic light man) pasta shapes and red-and-green pizza (topped with rocket and tomatoes), this eatery on the banks of the Spree is perfect for families. 🚸 Kids can run riot on the grass before and after the meal while adults relax on *Ampelmann* deckchairs under the shade of the trees.
✚ 201 D3
✉ Am Monbijou-Park
☎ 030 84 71 07 09; ampelmann-restaurant.de
🕙 Daily noon–midnight

District Môt €
Guests are served authentic Vietnamese street food at this hotspot for exotic tasty treats. Well-known favourites are sold alongside things you won't usually see on a menu: Steaming Pho noodles, papaya salad with pig's ear, a grill-it-yourself barbecue, and fried silkworms.
✚ 201 D4
✉ Rosenthaler Str. 62
☎ 030 20 08 92 84; districtmot.com
🕙 Sun–Thu noon–1am, Fri–Sat noon–2am

Hasir €–€€
Despite what you might think, the uniformed doorman isn't there to attract custom: He's employed to greet guests. This typical Turkish hospitality continues after you walk through the door. The numerous staff look after their customers well, and there are nice spots to sit inside and out. You'll be spoilt for choice here, with such treats as lamb dishes and tasting platters served either warm or cold.
✚ 201 D3   ✉ Oranienburger Str. 4
☎ 030 28 04 16 16; www.hasir.de
🕙 Daily noon–1am

Le Provençal €€–€€€
French country cuisine served in a district that's otherwise dominated by hearty German cooking. It smells wonderfully of lavender. Regular guests and Francophiles come to the banks of the Spree for racks of lamb, *confit* of goose and, on Bastille day (14 July), a delicious *bouillabaisse*.
✚ 201 E2   ✉ Spreeufer 3
☎ 030 3 02 75 67; leprovencal.de
🕙 Daily noon–midnight

Restauration Sophien 11 €
A popular spot for new Berliners, workers from around the corner and neighbours getting together for a cup of coffee, a beer or an unpretentious meal. Boasts a beautiful courtyard terrace.
✚ 201 D3   ✉ Sophienstr. 11
☎ 030 2 83 21 36; restauration-sophien11.de
🕙 Daily noon–midnight

Zur letzten Instanz €–€€
Opened as a brandy bar in 1621, this is probably the oldest inn in the city. Many famous guests have sat next to the baroque majolica-tiled stove, amongst them Napoleon, Charlie Chaplin and Jacques Chirac, who's fond of hearty fare. The menu includes meatballs with veg, goulash and *Eisbein* (pork knuckle). The municipal courts are

nearby; the names of the dishes are taken from legal terms.

✚ 201 F2 ✉ Waisenstr. 14–16
☎ 030 2 42 55 28; www.zurletzteninstanz.de
🕐 Daily noon–1am

CAFÉS

Barcomi's Deli

They roast their own coffee and bake their own muffins at this non-smoking café. This treasure trove of American baking culture also serves up bagels, sandwiches and cheesecake.

✚ 201 D3
✉ Sophienstr. 21 (in the Sophie-Gips-Höfe)
☎ 030 28 59 83 63; www.barcomis.de
🕐 Mon–Sat 9–9, Sun 10–9

Café Bravo

Fancy aubergines for breakfast? Or breakfast at night? Or want to drink coffee next to some art? It's all possible at this café, the brainchild of New York artist Dan Graham.

✚ 200 C3 ✉ Auguststr. 69
☎ 030 23 45 77 77
🕐 Mon–Wed, Fri–Sat 9–8, Thu 9–9, Sun 10–8

Cinema Café

A café as narrow as the window outside. Peek through and you'll see a room like a film set, stuffed with cinema memorabilia. Its organic interior stands out in a district where minimalism reigns. A cosy atmosphere that's particularly enticing at night.

✚ 201 D3 ✉ Rosenthaler Str. 39
☎ 030 2 80 64 15 🕐 Daily noon–2am

Oxymoron

A lovely ambience with crystal chandeliers and a coffeehouse feel. A café in the morning, it becomes a restaurant for lunch and dinner. Events (including swing dance parties) are held later on. Sophisticated Mediterranean cooking with local touches.

✚ 201 D3 ✉ Rosenthaler Str. 40–41
☎ 030 28 39 18 86; www.oxymoron-berlin.de
🕐 Daily from 11am

Where to...
Shop

Most of the shops around the Hackesche Höfe don't open until late in the morning. That's because the majority of their hip clients – a lot of whom come to buy retro chic – aren't awake till then. It's a different story on Alexanderplatz with its station, shops and the massive Alexa shopping centre: The shoppers there, many of whom work in the city, are generally in a hurry. The stores in the Nikolaiviertel mainly serve tourists.

HACKESCHE HÖFE

There's a range of unique shops in the Höfe (courtyards). Young people have revived old fashions at the **Trippen** shoe shop, for example. They sell versions of traditional wooden clogs that are both trendy and meant to be good for you.

Many designers display and sell their collections in the Höfe: **Lisa D.**, for instance, sells women's clothes and fun accessories that can be used to make killer combinations. Elegant female urban fashion from four designers is on sale at **quasi moda**. And if you like uncomplicated, simple fashion that borders on purism, head over to **Thatchers**.

An **Ampelmann Shop** is hidden away in Hof V.

ORANIENBURGER STRASSE

Funk Optik (Nr. 87) just sells designer spectacles as far as the eye can see. **Sterling Gold** (Nr. 32, Heckmann-Höfe) doesn't trade in what you might think – they sell ball gowns and cocktail dresses from the 1950s–80s. You'll find exciting items made from felt, ranging from egg cosies to dresses, at **Hut up** (Nr. 32). You can transform yourself into politicians, celebrities and monsters with the masks from **Maskworld** (Nr. 86a).

ROSENTHALER STRASSE

The completely mirrored fitting rooms at the **Hugo Store** (Nr. 49) can be opened and closed with the touch of a button. On the shop's long wall you'll see a relief of Berlin's streets lit up by a scanner. The store carries fresh, younger collections from Hugo Boss.

There's a beautiful array of pearls and jewellery in the shop window at **Tukadu** (Nr. 46/47).

At **Stokx** (Nr. 39) you'll find durable streetwear created by designer Melinda Stokes. The shop is tucked away on the second floor of the rear courtyard.

SOPHIENSTRASSE

Johanna Gräf-Petzold sells handmade nutcrackers, Easter decorations, toy animals and other little works of art from deepest Saxony at **Erzgebirgskunst Original**.

Connoisseurs will love **Whisky & Cigars** (Nr. 8), which has no fewer than 1,600 varieties of the peaty elixir. A bespoke shoemaker makes men's and women's shoes at **Paulinenhof** (Nr. 28/29).

ALTE & NEUE SCHÖNHAUSER STRASSE

The **East Berlin** label (Nr. 33/34) sells cool fashion and accessories. Stumble across your next favourite read at the well-organised **Hundt Hammer Stein** bookshop (Nr. 23/24). Simple, elegant fashion from Denmark is just waiting to be discovered at **Filippa K** (Nr.11). Only the highest quality labels are on sale in the stylishly cosy ambience of **14 oz.** (Neue Schönhauser Straße 13).

Where to…
Go Out

You don't have to look very hard for places to go out between Oranienburger Tor and Alexanderplatz. Many cafés and bars are open here until late into the morning hours. Restaurants become bars at night, and bars become clubs later on. If you can't decide where to go, leaf through tip and zitty events magazines and choose something that suits your musical taste. Alternatively, just go with the flow and follow people going out for a night on the town. With any luck you'll find your way into one of the secret locales called Mittwochsbar or 8mm. You'll only find their addresses and events listings by chance, if you hear of them at all. Only a select few even know of their existence. There's no point going to a club before midnight if you don't want to feel very lonely indeed.

CULTURE

Check out the witty variety events at the **Chamäleon Varieté** (tel: 030 4 00 05 90; Tue–Sun) in the Hackesche Höfe. Climb the stairs at Sophienstraße 6 to reach **Billardsalon KÖH** (Hackesche Höfe, Mon–Sat from 5pm, Sun from 4pm), a very classy club decked out in red and gold with leather sofas, antique furniture and a whisky shelf. It boasts 7 pool tables and a Carom billiards table. You pay by the hour – it's cheaper before 8pm, and cheaper still on Mondays. They hold a tournament every fortnight (there's no need to sign up in advance).

The **Club der polnischen Versager e.V.** (Ackerstr. 168, tel: 030 28 09 37 79, Fri–Sat from

Insider Tip

8pm) holds occasional readings, concerts and film screenings. Go there to see what's on. According to the club statues, it's geared towards "anyone who feels a stranger in their own place and time."

Dancing, readings and recitals are held at the **Roter Salon** and the **Grüner Salon** (www.gruener-salon.de) on both sides of the Volksbühne theatre (Rosa-Luxemburg-Platz 2). There's salsa from 10pm every other Thursday. Live jazz performances (Fri–Sun) take place right next to the window facing onto the street at **b-flat** (Rosenthaler Str. 13, tel: 030 2 83 31 23).

BARS & CLUBS

Ponybar (Alte Schönhauser Str. 44, Mon–Sat from noon, Sun from 6pm) is a good place to kick off your evening. The district's bohemian types come here after work to enjoy beer and cocktails.

If you don't want to go that far north, stay at **Oxymoron** in the first courtyard of the Hackesche Höfe (Rosenthaler Str. 40/41, tel: 030 28 39 18 86). A coffeehouse by day, it's a retro bar where people go dancing in the evening.

If you enjoy a good, classic cocktail or two, head over to **Windhorst** (Dorotheenstr. 65, tel: 030 20 45 00 70, Mon–Fri from 6pm, Sat from 9pm).

Kaffee Burger (Torstr. 60, tel: 030 28 04 64 95, daily from 7pm) has become famous far beyond Berlin's borders. If you didn't know better, you might be put off by the yellow-brown wallpaper and the furnishings that would already have been a long way out of date twenty or thirty years ago. The parties here have become legendary, as have the memorable Sunday readings. At the latter, young men (and some women) recite recent works fresh from the local poetry bars.

They're then mercilessly judged by the audience.

One of the latest cool hangouts is **Bonbon Bar** (tel: 030 24 62 87 18, Torstr. 133, Sun–Wed 7pm–3am, Thu–Sat 7pm–5am), an atmospherically lit, expensively decorated retreat. The small dance floor is rammed full of people when well-known DJs start playing their tunes.

The nearby **G&T Bar** (Friedrichstr. 113, 8pm–3am) is completely dedicated to creating gin-based beverages. Classic gin and tonics are combined with hand-selected tea infusions to produce complex new taste sensations. The Pizzeria Mario next door is ideally placed for grabbing a bite to eat between drinks.

The entrance to **Butcher's** (Torstr. 116, Tue–Sat from 8.30pm) is hidden behind a classic red British telephone box tucked away in a simple sausage stall. The bar itself is found in the slaughterhouse of an old butcher's shop. The drinks – many of which are new in-house creations – are of a very high quality.

Z-Bar (Bergstr. 2, tel: 030 28 38 91 21, daily from 7pm) offers its guests a varied programme that includes readings, films shown in their very own cinema and the occasional karaoke competition. The events are accompanied by cocktails and beer.

One of the newer fashionable nightspots is **Dean** (Rosenthaler Str. 9, Thu from 9pm, Fri–Sat from 10pm), a glamorous venue dedicated to drinking and dancing for grown-ups. The dark slatted walls, golden ceiling and black stone underfoot dominate the design of the long, narrow space that ends in a small dance floor. The music on offer mainly revolves around funk, disco, soul and house.

People dance to indie, club anthems and pop from various decades at the **Sophienclub** (Sophienstr. 6, tel: 030 2 82 45 52, Mon–Sat from 11pm).

Insider Tip

Potsdamer Platz

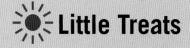 ## Little Treats

The Best Berliner Weiße
The **Lindenbräu** brewery in the Sony Center
(► 106) sells particularly good *Berliner
Weiße* beer with a shot of syrup.

Cost-free Concerts
Outstanding musicians give wonderful free
concerts in the foyer of the **Philharmonie**
(► 111) at 1pm every Thursday.

Homemade Happiness
Take some time out to enjoy the tasty
homemade soups and sandwiches at
Joseph Roth Diele (► 116).

Getting Your Bearings

After the foundation stone was laid in 1994, millions of people came from all around the world to see this new city within a city being built from scratch on Europe's biggest construction site. Today, Potsdamer Platz is a magnet for shoppers and cinema fans alike.

Before the War, Potsdamer Platz was one of Europe's noisiest and most vibrant squares and boasted a number of department stores and cabarets. Germany's first traffic light – imported from New York – had to be installed here in 1925 as traffic police at the centre of the square could no longer make themselves heard over the din. Barely 70 years later, the once war-torn square suddenly became a visionary place where dreams were expressed in glass and stone.

The golden-yellow façade of the Philharmonie gleams to the west of Potsdamer Straße. It's part of the Kulturforum (Cultural Forum), a group of art museums built over several decades along the Wall on the edge of West Berlin. The Diplomatic District, home to numerous modern embassies, is found on the southern edge of the Tiergarten.

Potsdamer Platz in 1925

TOP 10
⭐ Sony Center ➤ 106

Don't Miss
㉔ Kulturforum ➤ 109
㉕ Daimler City ➤ 112

At Your Leisure
㉖ Luiseninsel ➤ 114
㉗ Botschaftsviertel (Diplomatic District) ➤ 114
㉘ Memorial to the German Resistance ➤ 114
㉙ St.-Matthäus-Kirche ➤ 114
㉚ Martin-Gropius-Bau ➤ 115
㉛ Deutsches Technikmuseum ➤ 115
㉜ Topographie des Terrors ➤ 115

Impressive Architecture: The Sony Center by Helmut Jahn

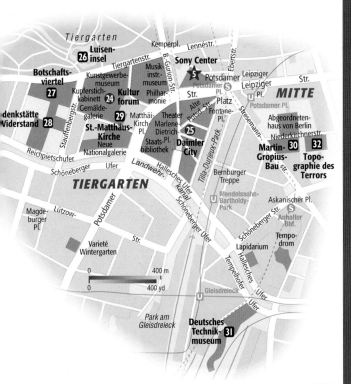

The Perfect Day

The schedule below allows you to visit some of the most interesting sights in and around Potsdamer Platz in the space of just one day. The individual highlights are described in more detail over the following pages (► 106–115).

🕙 10:00

Start the day in **㉕ Daimler City** (image above, ► 104) on Alte Potsdamer Straße by enjoying breakfast in one of the cafés. Many of the trees here are already mature enough to provide some shade.

🕦 11:00

Stroll through the narrow streets and judge for yourself whether international star architect Renzo Piano's grand design has been a success. The **Daimler Kunst Sammlung** (Daimler Art Collection) mainly holds top-class temporary exhibitions of modern art. Book ahead for the Blue Man

Group in the former IMAX Cinema (► 118). Travel in Europe's fastest lift up to the 24th floor of the **Kollhoff-Tower** (► 113) with its panoramic view of the whole of Berlin.

🕛 12:00

Cross Potsdamer Straße to reach the **⭐ Sony Center** (► 106). Pause by the fountain to soak up the atmosphere and admire one of the city's architectural highlights all around you. Prepare to be amazed by the **Museum für Film und Fernsehen** (Museum of Film and TV, image below left, ➤ 107).

🕐 13:00

The former breakfasting hall of the old Grand Hotel Esplanade has been integrated into Café Josty (➤ 107). It's a perfect spot for a quick lunch break – the dishes change every single day.

If you want a breather from all the glass and stone, cross Kemperplatz and follow the path through the Tiergarten to the **26 Luiseninsel** (Luise Island, ➤ 114). It's a great place for 👪 kids to play while adults relax on a bench.

🕐 15:00

Go past the **Philharmonie** (image below) on your way to the **24 Kulturforum** (Culture Forum, ➤ 109). Pay a visit to the **Gemäldegalerie** (Painting Gallery). If that's not to your taste, you might catch an exhibition in the **30 Martin-Gropius-Bau** (➤ 115) instead. If your kids don't fancy seeing any art, head to the **31 Deutsches Technikmuseum** (German Museum of Technology, ➤ 115).

🕐 18:00

Look for a place for dinner – if you're feeling fancy, you could even try **Facil** (➤ 116). Chill out afterwards by enjoying a cocktail in the Viktoria-Bar (➤ 118).

Prefer a trip to the movies? You can see all the latest productions beamed up on a massive screen at the 3D Cinestar cinema in the Sony Center (➤ 117).

Potsdamer Platz

⭐**5** **Sony Center**

A 103m (338ft)-high glazed tower rises over the building complex created by Helmut Jahn. In the middle of it all is a large plaza topped by a tent-like roof of gargantuan sails that's lit up with bright colours in the evening.

The huge tent-like structure over the plaza

When Daimler City was finished, Berliners received it half-heartedly. Their reaction was much more excited when they saw the completed Sony Center in June 2000, however. A small but totally new kind of city had come into being on their doorstep. It's made entirely from glass and steel, but you hardly notice that at all. Everything here reflects everything else, creating an illusion of depth and multiplicity.

The Colourful Tent
The 103m (338ft)-high semi-circular glass building on Potsdamer Straße won architect Helmut Jahn the nickname *Turmvater* ("Tower Father") *Jahn*. The most amazing part of Jahn's design is the tent roof, a structure made of steel sails and rods that's lit up with changing colours at night, creating a sense of magical vitality. Sit by the trickling fountain and watch as it sends occasional illuminated jets of water into the night air. The wind rustles and ruffles the tent above before suddenly blasting down with unexpected speed through the glass ravines, giving the site its very own unique repertoire of sounds.

Floating on Air into the Future
When Sony bought the land here after the Wall came down, it was bordered by the old **Grand Hotel Esplanade**. More grey than

THE KAISER'S KHAZI
The toilets under the *Kaisersaal* (Emperor's Hall) have been restored to all their former glory. The brass doorknobs, wooden toilet seats and marble urinals date from the Imperial German era. It boasts the basin where the Kaiser washed his hands.

grand at that point in time, this luxury hotel (1908) had been badly damaged in the War and its impressive reception spaces were only used for occasional film events and carnivals. Despite standing in the way of the planned enlargement of Potsdamer Straße, the city authorities wanted its rooms to be preserved. Thus began an architectural adventure costing 50 million Marks. The *Kaisersaal* (Emperor's Hall) where Kaiser Wilhelm II once held parties was scooped out of the Esplanade and built into the Sony Center. All 1,300 tonnes of it were moved 75m (246ft) on cushions of air at a top speed of 5m (16ft) a minute. It's home to a café-restaurant today.

Apartments Suspended over the Palm Court

The *Frühstücksraum* (breakfast room) also had to be relocated. Two walls from this neo-rococo room were cut into 500 pieces and reassembled in a glazed case. These two interior surfaces now face outwards behind the glass. The Palmenhof (Palm Court) and the Silbersaal (Silver Hall) stayed put, and provide a grandiose backdrop for private events today. Their decorated façades are elegantly lit at night. An architect has suspended 6 storeys of apartments from an internal bridge construction inside the delicate antique building. They number among Berlin's most expensive residences today.

Just like in the Movies

A room from the old Grand Hotel Esplanade

The Sony Center's next visual treat is the otherworldly wisps of light that flash around the courtyard at dusk. They're best experienced from the lift up to the utterly absorbing **Museum für Film und Fernsehen** (Museum of Film and TV). Take some time to get used to the intensity of the light and

Potsdamer Platz

WINGS OF DESIRE

Potsdamer Platz – which has hosted the Berlin International Film Festival since 2000 – provided the backdrop for Wim Wenders' movie *Wings of Desire* in 1986. The film saw 86-year old actor Curt Bois walking alone over the completely abandoned square, repeating the phrase "I can't find Potsdamer Platz. I can't find Potsdamer Platz." over and over again.

the reflections from the mirrors at the top before taking a trip through the history of German cinema. A separate section on artificial worlds is dedicated to fantasy and sci-fi movies.

Berlinale

The movie world arrives here every February. Ever since the 50th Berlinale film festival in 2000, the red carpets have been rolled out on Potsdamer Platz to cushion the feet

It's hard to see where the cinema starts and reality ends

of film stars from across the globe, cheered on by Berliners and visitors alike. The theatre on Potsdamer Platz hosts important premieres and galas packed with international celebs.

TAKING A BREAK

Billy Wilder's (Potsdamer Str. 2) is a pleasant place to sit for coffee, cake and snacks. The exotic drinks and cocktails are also worth a try.

➕ 200 A1 ✉ Potsdamer Platz
Ⓡ Potsdamer Platz

Museum für Film und Fernsehen
☎ 030 3 00 90 30
🕐 Tue–Sun 10–6, Thu till 8pm
💶 €7

㉔ Kulturforum

The Kulturforum (Culture Forum) was West Berlin's answer to Museum Island. The Neue Nationalgalerie and the Gemäldegalerie house world-famous works of art, and the Berlin Philharmonic Orchestra delights audiences in the Philharmonie. Many students practically live in the Staatsbibliothek (State Library).

The Entrance to the Kulturforum

Philharmonie (Berlin Philharmonic)

When the Philharmonie was opened in 1963, the land around it lay unused. Hans Scharoun, the building's architect and head of the city's planning office, was roundly criticized at first: People claimed that the seats were too narrow and stacked so high as to give you nosebleeds. Berliners quickly named it the "Karajani Circus" after the Berlin Philharmonic's famous director, Herbert von Karajan. Today, however, the Philarmonie is regarded as a world-class concert house and – along with its orchestra – one of the cultural flagships of Berlin. The nearby Kammermusiksaal (Chamber Music Hall), used for more intimate performances, looks a bit like its little brother. The unrivalled architectural ensemble of the Philharmonie, the Kammermusiksaal and the Staatsbibliothek eventually won Hans Scharoun fame around the world.

Staatsbibliothek (State Library)

This, the largest universal academic library anywhere in Germany, provides a treasure trove of knowledge and learning for around 3,500 visitors every day. It's home to over 10 million volumes, oriental and western manuscripts, wills, maps, journals and newspapers. The building displays an obvious architectural affinity with the Philharmonie and the hallmark style of Hans Scharoun. It was opened in 1978, six years after Scharoun's death. After the Wall came down, the Staatsbibliothek was united with its counterpart in the East of the city. It was restyled the "**Modern Research Library**" while its colleague on Unter den Linden boulevard took over the reins for historical research.

Potsdamer Platz

Gemäldegalerie (Painting Gallery)

This gallery, opened in 1998, houses a unique collection of European painting from the 13th to the 18th centuries. You'll need some stamina to navigate the 2km (1.25mi)-long round tour of the 1,400 paintings shared between 72 rooms and cabinets.

The **Rembrandt Room** at the heart of the museum contains a world-famous collection of the artist's work. Particular attention is also given to German, Italian and Dutch painting. Pieces by van Eyck, Brueghel, Dürer, Raphael, Titian, Caravaggio, Rubens and Vermeer are particular crowd-pleasers. The building was designed by Hilmer & Sattler.

DON'T URINATE ON THE MOON...

An exciting picture hangs in room 7 of the Gemäldegalerie. *The Netherlandish Proverbs*, painted in 1559 by **Pieter Brueghel the Elder**, shows a village full of people representing an impressive array of 100 wonderfully rich proverbs from the Low Countries. You'll recognise a couple (is that a man banging his head against a brick wall?), but there are many you won't have heard of, including a man 'urinating on the moon' (i.e. wasting his time on a pointless project), and another who is 'fishing behind his net' (i.e. missing an opportunity).

Musikinstrumenten-Museum

This museum shows around 800 European musical instruments from the 16th to the 21st centuries, including some unique Renaissance and Baroque specimens. The main attraction is the "Mighty Wurlitzer", Europe's largest cinema and theatre organ (played every Saturday at noon).

Insider Tip

Neue Nationalgalerie (New National Gallery)

Architectural luminary **Mies van der Rohe** designed this glass box that houses a collection of famous works of 20th-century art. The gallery is currently being overhauled by David Chipperfield and will remain closed until 2017 at the earliest. The highlights include the work of **George Grosz** (1893–1959) and **Otto Dix** (1891–1969), two important Social Realists active during the 1920s.

The New National Gallery – a Modern Classic

Kunstgewerbemuseum (Museum of Decorative Arts)

The highlights of this museum to the north of the Gemäldegalerie include precious gold and silverwork, baroque costumes, Delft faience and Meissen porcelain. The museum has also been closed for extensive renovation since 2012. At the time of writing this book, no date had yet been set for its reopening.

TAKING A BREAK

There's a cafeteria in the **foyer of the Gemäldegalerie**. If the weather's nice, have a bite to eat outside at the front of the building.

Philharmonie and Kammermusiksaal

✚ 200 A1 ✉ Herbert-von-Karajan-Str. 1 ☎ 030 25 48 83 01. Tickets: 030 24 58 89 99 🎭 Box Office Mon–Fri 3–6pm, Sat, Sun 11am–2pm 🚇 Potsdamer Platz

Staatsbibliothek

✚ 203 F3 ✉ Potsdamer Str. 33 ☎ 030 2 66 43 23 33 🎭 Mon–Fri 9–9, Sat 10–7 (user pass required to access the reading rooms) 🚇 Potsdamer Platz

Gemäldegalerie

✚ 203 F4 ✉ Stauffenbergstr. 40 ☎ 030 2 66 42 42 42 🎭 Tue–Sun 10–6, Thu till 10pm 🚇 Potsdamer Platz 🎟 €10

Neue Nationalgalerie

✚ 203 F3/4 ✉ Potsdamer Str. 50 ☎ 030 2 66 29 51 🎭 currently closed 🚇 Potsdamer Platz

Kunstgewerbemuseum

✚ 203 F4 ✉ Tiergartenstr. 6 ☎ 030 2 66 29 51 🎭 currently closed 🚇 Potsdamer Platz

Musikinstrumenten-Museum

✚ 200 A1 ✉ Tiergartenstr. 1 ☎ 030 2 66 29 51; www.sim.spk-berlin.de/en 🎭 Tue–Fri 9–5, Thu till 8, Sat–Sun 10–5 🚇 Potsdamer Platz 🎟 €6

INSIDER INFO

🚸 Children and young people up to 18 years of age can get into all state museums free of charge.

■ Entry tickets are valid for all Kulturforum buildings and those on the Museumsinsel. The **Museumspass Berlin** (▶ 39) allows you to visit the permanent exhibitions of around 50 museums for 3 consecutive days.

■ Events, themed tours and tours for **people with hearing problems** and disabilities are regularly held in the Gemäldegalerie. You can find out if there are any events suitable for non-German speakers by ringing 030 2 66 42 42 42 (Mon–Fri 9am–4pm). If there's nothing going on during your trip, you can always make use of the English language audio guides that are included in the price of your ticket.

■ Free **chamber concerts** lasting between 40 and 50 minutes are held at 1pm (Tue, Sep–June) in the foyer of the Berlin Philharmonic. Arrive in good time if you want to grab a seat, otherwise you'll have to make yourself comfortable on the staircase.

Insider Tip

㉕ Daimler City

You won't find Daimler City on any maps of Berlin – it's actually just the name for one third of Potsdamer Platz. The architecture here stands in stark contrast to the Sony Center opposite.

This completely new neighbourhood was built on a 7ha (17 acre) site following a master plan by star architect **Renzo Piano**, who also designed the Centre Pompidou in Paris. 14 international architects' firms were invited to compete to design the 19 individual buildings of flats, offices, shops and entertainment facilities. The structures were planned in Tokyo, London, Munich, Milan, Madrid and Berlin.

Boxers, **Keith Haring**'s vivid statue, greets you on Postdamer Straße. The warm terracotta façade of the **Atrium Tower**, the former headquarters of DaimlerChrysler Services, rises into the sky like a cathedral. The ventilation stack from the Tiergarten tunnel can be seen for miles, crowned with the firm's logo, an emerald-green cube made of 100 differently sized rectangles. Korean **Nam June Paik**'s video and neon-tube installation flickers at the entrance. At 82m (269ft) in length and 14m (46ft) wide, the seven-storey atrium is as large as the nave in Notre Dame Cathedral. Blue arcs of light by **François Morellet** draw your gaze upwards. You'll sometimes hear the rattle and squeak of the wheels in **Jean Tinguely**'s sculpture *Méta Maxi* down below, an artistic reminder that time never stands still.

Artificial Water

A casino and a theatre border the stepped, mussel-shaped Marlene-Dietrich-Platz. It's home to Renzo Piano's artificial lake that's filled with harvested rainwater, surrounded by reeds and filled with fish. At 12,000m² (39,400ft²) in size, this body of water was intended to provide a counterbalance to the density of the developments around it. *Galileo*, a sculpture by **Marc di Suvero** representing movement, stands in the middle of the lake.

The Atrium Tower designed by Renzo Piano

The Potsdamer Platz Arcades

The Fastest Lift on the Continent

The **Weinhaus Huth**, the only old building left standing in the area, is now used to display the **Daimler Kunst Sammlung** (Daimler Art Collection). The terrace of the Lutter & Wegner restaurant here is an idyllic place to sit outside under the trees in summer and enjoy some tasty German and Austrian specialities. The 5-star Hyatt Hotel has a fitness centre with a panoramic vantage point and a swimming pool tucked away on the roof. Numerous celebrities and politicians swim there every morning. As you might imagine, the entrance fee is pretty steep. You can look down at it from the neighbouring brick-red, pointy tower block with golden pinnacles designed by Berlin architect **Hans Kollhoff**. It's modelled on New York's sky-scrapers. The fastest lift on the continent carries its passengers smoothly up to the panoramic view on the 24th floor in just 20 seconds. From up there, you'll almost feel like you can step right into the offices of the Deutsche Bank on the other side of the Sony Center (➤ 106).

TAKING A BREAK

If you're hungry and thirsty, go to **Salomon Bagels** on the top floor of the Postdamer Platz Arcades. The selection on offer is impressive.

➕ 204 A3/4 ✉ Potsdamer Platz 🚇 Potsdamer Platz

Panoramic Vantage Point
✉ Potsdamer Str. 1 🕐 Daily 10am–8pm 💶 €6.50

INSIDER INFO

You'll find tasty ice cream at **Caffè e Gelato** (Mon–Sat from 10am, Sun from 10.30am) on the 1st floor of the Potsdamer Platz Arcades. Customers often wait patiently in long lines to taste the legendary sundaes.

At Your Leisure

26 Luiseninsel (Luise Island)

Cross the street behind the Sony Center or the Philharmonie and you'll find yourself in the Tiergarten. A path to the west of Bellevue-Allee leads to Luiseninsel. This part of the park was laid out around a statue of Prussia's popular Queen Luise in the 1800s by one Eduard Neide, the Tiergarten's Royal Director. The princely atmosphere here was restored when the herbaceous borders were replanted to celebrate Berlin's 750th Jubilee.

✚ 203 F4 🚇 Potsdamer Platz

27 Botschaftsviertel (Diplomatic District)

It only takes 5 minutes to walk from Japan to Egypt – or rather from Hiroshimastraße to Stauffenbergstraße. This site on the south edge of the Tiergarten was home to Berlin's Diplomatic District in the 1920s. The area lay unused after the War, however, as only the Italian and Japanese buildings survived. After the Wall came down, many countries moved back in and constructed some spectacular embassies. **South Africa**, for example, represents African culture and tradition via their structure's architectural style and generous roof terrace. The red stone to build the **Indian Embassy** was brought to Berlin from Rajasthan – the inscription on their national emblem

over the entrance reads "Truth Alone Triumphs." **Austria** presents its national interests with a structure made of shimmering green copper on the corner of Stauffenbergstraße. **Egypt**'s ambassadors work in a building composed of strict geometric forms.

✚ 203 E/F4 🚇 Hiroshimastr., Tiergartenstr., Stauffenbergstr. 🚇 Potsdamer Platz

28 Memorial to the German Resistance

The Bendlerblock building complex – home to the German Ministry of Defence – houses an exhibition in memory of the resistance fighters who waged war against the Nazis. Redesigned in 2014, its centrepiece is the failed attempt to assassinate Hitler on 20 July, 1944. The main conspirators, lead by Claus von Stauffenberg, were shot in the building's courtyard that very same night. A memorial has been set up in their honour.

✚ 203 F4 ✉ Stauffenbergstr. 13–14
☎ 030 26 99 50 00
🕐 Mon–Wed & Fri 9–6, Thu 9–8, Sat–Sun 10–6
🚇 Potsdamer Platz 🎫 Free

29 St.-Matthäus-Kirche (Church)

Surrounded by modern buildings, this little church which gave the square its name looks like it was built using the wrong box of bricks. Designed in the 1800s by Friedrich August Stüler – a pupil of Karl Friedrich Schinkel – it was due to be demolished in the 20th century along with all the neighbouring structures because it didn't fit in with plans to create a "Germanic World Capital" dreamt up by Hitler's architect, Albert Speer. He didn't get his way, however, and the church was rebuilt from 1959–60 after being damaged in the War. The church, much praised for its acoustics, has regained its three

The Deutsches Technikmuseum (German Museum of Technology)

parallel gabled roofs. Groups of slender windows break up the long, brick-built side walls. *Antlitz* ("Face"), a two-faced sculpture made from a dented bucket by Vadim Sidur, one of the most significant members of Moscow's alternative art scene, hangs on the gallery wall in front of the organ. The church is regularly used for exhibitions, concerts and theatrical performances.

✚ 203 F4 ☒ Matthäikirchplatz ⏰ Tue–Sun 11–6; organ recital Tue–Sat 12.30–12.50 🚇 Potsdamer Platz 🎟 Free

30 Martin-Gropius-Bau

This structure, named after the architect who designed it, was built from 1877–81 as a museum where students at the Arts and Crafts school could study the exhibits. Reliefs and mosaics turned the façade into a showcase for artistic handiwork. The war-damaged building stood in the way of a proposed urban motorway and was threatened with demolition until the 1970s. Now regarded as Berlin's finest exhibition building, it was restored from 1977–81 and later converted in 1999 to allow to it host large, prestigious exhibitions.

✚ 204 B3 ☒ Niederkirchnerstr. 7 ☎ 030 25 48 60 ⏰ Wed–Mon 10–8 🚇 Anhalter Bahnhof

31 Deutsches Technikmuseum

The *C-47 Skytrain* – once used to airlift supplies into West Berlin during the Soviet blockade of 1948–49 – looks like it's about to land right in the middle of Potsdamer Platz. In fact, it's found its final resting place up on the roof of the Deutsches Technikmuseum (German Museum of Technology), from where it gives visitors a taste of the extraordinary collection of aircraft housed inside the new museum building. Two exhibitions show the development of air travel from its beginnings right up to the 1950s via the First World War. You can also see a historic brewery, classic cars, locomotives and trains. The most fascinating area for many people – and 👫 kids in particular – is the **Science Center Spectrum**, a science complex where visitors can carry out their own experiments.

✚ 204 B2 ☒ Trebbiner Str. 9, Science Center Spectrum, Möckernstr. 26 ☎ 030 90 25 42 84; www.sdtb.de ⏰ Tue–Fri 9–5.30, Sat–Sun 10–6 🚇 Gleisdreieck 🎟 €6

32 Topographie des Terrors (Topography of Terror)

The most feared institutions of the Third Reich, including the headquarters of the SS and the Gestapo (Secret Police), once stood to the south of Niederkirchnerstraße on the former site of the Prince Albrecht Palace. Today, a simple cube structure houses an extremely informative modern exhibition about this hub of Nazi criminality. A further exhibition located in front of the former Gestapo prison cells tells the tale of the special role Berlin played in the machinations of the Third Reich. A 200m (656ft)-long stretch of the Berlin Wall still stands along Niederkirchnerstraße.

✚ 204 B3 ☒ Niederkirchnerstr. 8 ☎ 030 25 45 09 50 ⏰ Daily 10am–8pm, Exterior area open until dusk (8pm at the latest) 🚇 U/S Potsdamer Platz or Kochstraße 🎟 Free

Where to...
Eat and Drink

Prices
A main course without drinks:
€ under 12 euros   €€ 12–25 euros   €€€ over 25 euros

RESTAURANTS

Café Einstein Stammhaus €€

A truly stylish classic Viennese coffeehouse in a villa once owned by German actress Henny Porten. It's a must for connoisseurs who know the difference between a *Melange* (Mix) and a *Kleines Braunes* (Small Brown). But be warned: If you don't, you might get disapproving stares from the waiters! The floors are marble and the chairs are covered in velvet. Although too small to really tuck into a *Wiener Schnitzel*, the tables are perfect for a *Sachertorte* (chocolate cake). The beautiful garden is a great place to relax with a newspaper.

➕ 203 E3 ✉ Kurfürstenstr. 58
☎ 030 2 61 50 96 ⏰ Daily 8am–midnight, Plat du jour Mon–Fri 11–3

5 – Cinco €€€

5 – Cinco at the Hotel Stue is Catalan Master Chef Paco Pérez's first restaurant project outside Spain. Guests sit under artfully arranged copper pots with a view of the kitchen and enjoy avant-garde gourmet creations that excite all five senses. A set menu here consists of around two dozen 'courses' that are brought to your table and presented like tiny culinary jewels.

➕ 203 D4 ✉ Drakestr. 1 ☎ 030 3 11 72 20; www.5-cinco.com ⏰ Tue–Sat 7pm–10.30pm

Facil €€€

This two Michelin star restaurant on the 5th floor of The Mandala Hotel in Postdamer Platz uses its reasonably priced lunches to give people the gourmet bug in the hope they'll later come back to experience the superb evening meals. The food bears Mediterranean influences. Dress code: Relaxed.

➕ 200 A1 ✉ Potsdamer Str. 3
☎ 030 5 90 05 12 34; www.facil.de
⏰ Mon–Fri noon–3pm & 7pm–11pm

Joseph Roth Diele €

Unusually, the selection here, written up on a board behind the bar, never extends beyond two *plats du jour*, one soup and one simple set menu. The décor – complete with wooden benches, Thonet chairs, divans from Morocco and well-lit spots for reading – also differs from other eateries. It used to be a patisserie whose owners found a beautiful stone floor and old pastry recipes when they were clearing out what had previously been used as a warehouse. They also discovered that the Austrian writer Joseph Roth lived next door in the 1920s and had started a novel in the café. The sausage sandwiches and stews are home-made, and the images of saints are a discrete reminder that Ave Maria, a shop selling devotional objects, can be found next door.

➕ 203 F3 ✉ Potsdamer Str. 75
☎ 030 26 36 98 84
⏰ Mon–Fri 10am–midnight

Tizian €€–€€€

This elegant eatery in the Hyatt Hotel is one of the best in Potsdamer Platz. The food is excellent, the décor cool and uncluttered. Choose with abandon: Everything from the *hors d'oeuvres* to the *tiramisu* is superb.

➕ 204 A4 ✉ Marlene-Dietrich-Platz 2
☎ 030 25 53 15 27; www.tizian-restaurant.de
🕐 Daily 8am–11pm

Where to...
Shop

POTSDAMER STRASSE

Potsdamer Straße runs over the Landwehr canal down to Schöneberg. It's still a bit grungy and full of cheap shops in places, but it's also been lifted over the last couple of years by renowned **galleries** from the likes of Isabella Bortolozzi, Arratia Beer and Guido Baudach. The **Andreas Murkudis** design emporium and hat maker **Fiona Bennett** have also set up shop in the area.

Ave Maria (Potsdamer Str. 75, Mon–Fri noon–6pm, Sat till 3pm) has a hint of Lourdes about it. Not only does it stock forty types of incense, there are also Madonnas with flashing eyes and crucifixes shining with pseudo-baroque splendour that are perfect for your car or handbag. Looking for a votive offering? You'll find them between various silver arms and legs. Pilgrims offer them up in the hope of being cured of all sorts of ills. They also sell candles of every size and state of consecration.

SHOPPING CENTRES

The **Potsdamer Platz Arcades** at the heart of Daimler City invite you in for a spot of shopping over three storeys. You'll find everything here, ranging from a supermarket and well-known fashion retailers to a large TK Maxx, which sells designer fashion at low prices. There are row upon row of snack stands in the basement, and tasty ice cream is sold on the 1st floor.

The **LP12 – Mall of Berlin** has recently been set up on Leipziger Platz to compete with the Arcades. Nearly 300 retailers – including many notable designer labels – have set up shop there.

Where to...
Go Out

If you've got tickets for the **Philharmonie** (▶ 109) or want to see a movie, then you'll have no problems at all. If you'd like to go drinking or dancing, however, you'll begin to realise that the options are scarce in Potsdamer Platz – it isn't yet a fully developed district.

The **Blue Man Group** (Marlene-Dietrich-Platz 4; tickets from €70, tel: 01805 44 44) has been thrilling audiences on Potsdamer Platz since 2004. Over 2 million people have seen the Canadian artistes' polished acrobatic and artistic performance to date, and there's no sign of their popularity letting up. For the time being, the blue baldies have taken up residence in the former IMAX cinema on Marlene-Dietrich-Platz.

CINEMAS

Visitors to Potsdamer Platz can choose between nearly two dozen films every day at the **Cinemaxx Multiplex** in Daimler City (Potsdamer Platz 1–19) and at **Cinestar** in the Sony Center (Potsdamer Str. 4). Some are shown in their original languages.

Potsdamer Platz

The **IMAX Cinema** in Cinestar offers a totally different kind of cinematic experience. The giant screen (588m²/1,930ft²) makes you feel like you're right in the centre of the action – in a lava field with volcanic boulders flying around your head, for example. The selection on offer includes nature documentaries and 3D Hollywood flicks.

The programme at **Arsenal** (➤ 108) caters to lovers of art-house cinema.

THEATER AM POTSDAMER PLATZ

This elegant, 1,800-seater theatre (Marlene-Dietrich-Platz 1; tickets, tel: 01805 44 44) draws in international crowds with its constantly changing selection of musicals. It's turned into a large cinema during the film festival in February.

SPIELBANK BERLIN (CASINO)

Already spent all of your holiday money? The Spielbank Berlin Casino (Marlene-Dietrich-Platz 1, tel: 030 25 59 90) gives you the chance to win it back by playing Roulette, Baccarat and Black Jack. If you head down the staircase, you'll find one-armed bandits and other contraptions in the slot-machine room (daily 11am–3am, some machines till 5am).

It's usually already pretty full in the morning. More experienced players who enjoy classic casino games will find posher rooms at their disposal (open 3pm–3am). You no longer have to wear a tie, but they do ask that you wear appropriate clothing (men: Long trousers and no open-toed shoes).

BARS

"Caroshi" is the Japanese word for "death by overwork". The **Caroshi Bar** (Linkstr. 4, tel: 030 25 29 33 52, Mon–Fri from 10am, Sat–Sun from 6pm) does its utmost to help you avoid this terrible fate by getting you to relax with sushi and colourful cocktails. The tower with a view is a particularly cosy place to sit. Italian architectural luminary Renzo Piano designed the bar, which looks a bit like a spaceship.

The fashionable **Victoria Bar** (Potsdamer Str. 102, tel: 030 25 75 99 77, Sun–Thu 6.30pm–3am, Fri–Sat 6.30pm–4am) is a true Berlin institution. It's particularly popular for its professionally mixed cocktails. Light snacks are also served until late at night. Order before 9.30pm to benefit from the discount Happy Hour prices.

If you haven't been to **Kumpelnest 3000** (Lützowstr. 23, tel: 030 2 61 69 18, daily from 7pm) you haven't truly experienced nightlife in Berlin. It's very easy to spend far too long there – you'll wonder which film was playing when you lost track of time. Kumpelnest sweeps up office parties, survivors from dwindling events, insatiable night owls migrating from bars that have already closed, and people who want to know who's still out and about... It's a place where age isn't a problem if you like Abba and don't particularly care what you listen to.

Solar (Stresemannstr. 76, tel: 0163 7 65 27 00, daily from 6pm) is particularly popular with lovers and romantics at sunset thanks to its wonderful views enjoyed from a height of 70m (30ft).

The **Vox Bar** at the Grand Hyatt Hotel (Marlene-Dietrich-Platz 2, tel: 030 25 53 17 72, daily from 6pm, live music from 10pm) is decked out all in red and black. Dry martinis are served with a piece of ginger instead of the usual olives. You can also choose from the 240 varieties of whisky for which the bar is renowned. Music from jazz and soul legends creates an atmospheric nightclub ambience.

Around the Kurfürstendamm

 **Little Treats**

Scented Souvenirs

The **Berliner Kaffeerösterei** (Uhlandstr. 173/4) has the city's largest selection of coffee. Treat yourself!

Top-class Currywurst

Wittys opposite KaDeWe (➤ 129) sell tasty organic *Currywurst* (sausage with curry sauce). Simply order and enjoy!

A Pool with a View

The **Pool der Therme** on the 6th floor next to the Europa-Center (➤ 129) has fantastic views out over Berlin.

Getting Your Bearings

"Ich hab' so Heimweh nach dem Kurfürstendamm"... (I'm so homesick for the Kurfürstendamm...). This one song line was enough to win singer Hildegard Knef a place in West Berliners' hearts. After the city was divided up, this street, known locally as the "Ku'damm", became their new city centre. It's long been Berlin's answer to the Champs-Elysées, and it remains the city's best-loved shopping street to this day.

After the Wall came down, no one really talked about the Ku'damm for 20 years or so. "Berlin" meant Unter den Linden, Mitte and Potsdamer Platz, and there was little interest in the West. Things have changed today, however, and people now come here again to stroll down the avenue, visit the new Bikinihaus, wander down the side streets and enjoy the unique atmosphere. The Kurfürstendamm has a rich, established charm thanks to its lively streets where people live out their daily lives and enjoy their free time. Not much new happens here, which makes it all the more relaxing. And if someone does innovate, they quickly fit in just fine. (Well... usually).

Schloss Charlottenburg and its parks provide calm oases that are used by locals and visitors alike.

Café Kranzler and the Neues Kranzler Eck

Baroque Magnificence in Schloss Charlottenburg

The Perfect Day

You'll need a whole day to to visit all the sights around the Kurfürstendamm. Follow our one-day itinerary and we'll make sure you don't miss any of the highlights. The individual attractions are described in more detail in the pages below (► 124–132).

🕙 10:00

Start the day with a visit inside the ⭐**Kaiser-Wilhelm-Gedächtniskirche** (Kaiser Wilhelm Memorial Church, ► 127). This new, shimmering church stands beside the ruined tower that's been left as a memorial to peace and reconciliation.

🕚 11:00

If you've never visited the **34 Kaufhaus des Westens** (image left; ► 131), the largest department store to be found anywhere in Europe, cross the road and walk the short way back down Tauentzienstraße. The selection of goods on offer is quite simply overwhelming. If you're out and about with 🧒 kids who might not be very interested in a shopping experience, head to the **35 Zoo** (► 131) instead.

🕐 13:00

Now go and experience the magnificent architecture of the **Bikinihaus** (image below; ► 135) with its collection of unusual shops. Treat yourself to a break in one of the numerous cafés.

🕑 14:00

Take bus 309 or M45 to ⭐**Schloss Charlottenburg** (Charlottenburg Palace, image right; ➤ 124). Be sure to take a walk through the park after visiting the palace.

🕑 16:00

The **36 Berggruen Collection** opposite boasts works by Picasso and his contemporaries (➤ 132). Grab a snack in the Kleine Orangerie (Small Orangery, ➤ 126) afterwards and ready yourself for another stroll along the **33 Ku'damm** (➤ 129).

🕑 17:30

Take the bus back. Walk along the Ku'damm, explore its side streets (try Bleibtreustraße and Schlüterstraße, for example) and have a peek in at the beautifully elegant doorways. You can find out a great deal about the city by visiting **38 The Story of Berlin** (➤ 132), an impressive multimedia exhibition.

🕑 19:30

Your stomach will no doubt be rumbling after such a busy day. It's a sure sign that it's time to find somewhere good for your evening meal! If it's summer and you fancy sitting outside, follow the crowds and walk to **40 Savignyplatz** (➤ 132). It's advisable to book somewhere well in advance – perhaps try the Zwölf Aposteln ("Twelve Apostles", ➤ 134). Alternatively, head to Bar jeder Vernunft (➤ 136) where you can enjoy good food while watching the stars of the variety scene (including the likes of Desirée Nick). Have a look at the programme of events before you go.

Schloss Charlottenburg

Spandauer Damm

36 Sammlung Berggruen
37 Sammlung Scharf-Gersten-berg

Rathaus
R.-Wagner-Pl.
Suhr. Str.
Otto. Allee
Ernst-Reuter-Pl.

Deutsche Oper Berlin
Bismarckstr.
Schiller-theater
Hardenbergstr.

Museum für Fotografie **39**

Leibniz.

Savignyplatz
40 Kant-str.

Zoologischer Garten **35**

Budapester Str.

CHARLOTTEN-BURG

Savignpl.

Kurfürsten-damm

Kaiser-Wilh.-Gedächtnisk.

Kurfürstenstr.

Kurfürstendamm **33**

Uhlandstr.
Kurfürsten-

Witten-bergpl.

34 KaDeWe

Adenauer-platz
38 The Story of Berlin

Augsburger Str.

0   400 m
0   400 yd

☆ Schloss Charlottenburg

Sophie Charlotte was just 16 years old when she married Elector Friedrich von Brandenburg in 1684. He had a palace built for her (1695–99) following designs by Arnold Nering. It's the largest and most beautiful palace in the city today.

Nine feudal residences still exist in Berlin. Most look in need of some repair, and Schloss Charlottenburg is no exception. Nevertheless, the structure was trusted enough in 2007 to move the statues from their temporary home by the Orangerie back to their rightful place up on the roof.

Modelled on Versailles

This historically important structure in the west of the city was originally built as the small **Lietzenburg** summer palace in rural surroundings in the 17th century. It was much more modest than the palace you see today, consisting of just the central section of the building. Friedrich's mounting prestige was responsible for the first in a series of additions that saw the palace grow to its present size. He had himself crowned King Friedrich I of Prussia in 1701 and wanted his new status to be reflected in exquisite stone. Taking the

The former master of the house: Friedrich II

Palace of Versailles as a model, architect Eosander von Göthe was commissioned to extend the existing main building and add side wings to form a ceremonial courtyard.

A 505m (1657ft) Palace

The Große Orangerie (Great Orangery) was added to the west wing (a. k. a. the Eosander Wing) between 1709–12, and a tower was built to crown the baroque central section in 1710. Georg Wenzeslaus von Knobelsdorff constructed the simple, two-storey Neuer Flügel (New Wing) from 1740–46. Finally – nearly 100 years after work began – Carl Gotthard Langhans built the palace theatre on the Orangery Wing (1787–1791). The palace was now 505m (1,657ft) long. Sophie Charlotte had passed away long before (1705). The structure was renamed Schloss Charlottenburg in her memory.

Alter Flügel (Old Wing)

Start your visit in the Altes Schloss (Old Palace), the oldest part of the complex. It's where you'll find Friedrich I and Sophie Charlotte's private chambers and some other impressive rooms. The latter include the Porcelain Cabinet (with East Asian porcelain from the 17th and 18th centuries), the Palace Chapel and the Tapestry Rooms. The Crown Prince's Silver is on show in Friedrich Wilhelm IV's living quarters on the 1st floor.

Neuer Flügel (New Wing)

This wing, built under Friedrich the Great, is home to the most beautiful rooms in the palace: The **Weißer Saal** (White Hall), decorated with pink stucco marble, and the **Goldene Galerie** (Golden Gallery), a 42m (138ft)-long ballroom lavishly decorated with gilt stucco work. Behind that are the King's private chambers which hold such masterpieces of French painting as works by Antoine Watteau.

Between Belvedere and the Mausoleum

The extensive palace park is a relaxing place to be. Originally laid out in a formal French baroque style, it was transformed into a landscape garden at the end of the 18th century. Although now largely returned to its former layout, the carp pond breaks up the formality, and the English landscape garden is full of flying balls and boomerangs, sun-worshippers and kids at play. Queen Luise's **Mausoleum**, designed in the form of a little Doric temple by Karl Friedrich Schinkel, is hidden at the end of an avenue of pines. The **Belvedere**, a teahouse built by Langhans, is home to a significant collection of porcelain from Berlin's Royal Porcelain Factory (KPM). Schinkel's

Around the Kurfürstendamm

Neuer Pavillon (New Pavilion) will make you dream of Italy. Friedrich Wilhelm III commissioned it as a simple residence in 1824. It's used to house 19th-century furniture, pictures and sculpture today.

TAKING A BREAK

The **Kleine Orangerie** (Small Orangery) at the park's entrance is a delightful place for an extended break. You can sit amongst old kitchen appliances on one side or get a view of the surrounding greenery on the other. The best spot to rest in summer is under the old trees in the garden. Musicians play discrete coffeehouse music and sausages sizzle on the grill at weekends.

> ### 🛝 LET OFF STEAM
> Behind the carp pond and the Belvedere in the palace park is a kids' playground by the river Spree. River cruises set out from a jetty outside the park (across the Schlossbrücke bridge).

➕ 202, west of A5
✉ Luisenplatz
☎ 030 3 22 20 21
🚌 109, 145

Altes Schloss
🕐 Tue–Sun 10am–5pm, open till 6pm in summer; tours and audio guides available 🎫 €12

Neuer Flügel (Knobelsdorff Wing)
🕐 Daily 10am–5pm;
reopened in December 2014

Neuer Pavillon
🕐 Apr–Oct, Tue–Sun 10–6;
Nov–Mar, Tue–Sun 10–5 🎫 €4

Belvedere
🕐 Apr–Oct, Tue–Sun, 10–6 🎫 €3

Mausoleum
🕐 Apr–Oct, Tue–Sun 10–6 🎫 €2

Park
🕐 6am until dusk
🎫 Free entry

Welcome to the Palace

INSIDER INFO

- Find out if any **Palace Concerts** are taking place – they're a great way to experience a slice of courtly splendour.
- Stroll up Schlossstraße to Number 69b on the left side of the road. The **Abgusssammlung antiker Plastik** (Greek & Roman Plaster Cast Collection) doesn't just contain what its name suggests – the ancient statues usually serve as an exciting backdrop for modern art (Thu–Sun 2pm–5pm, free).

⭐9 Kaiser-Wilhelm-Gedächtniskirche

On Sunday 22 November, 1943, the day when the dead are commemorated in Germany, a sermon was preached on the text "All things shall pass". A few hours later, bombs fell on the church, creating the famous ruin that would become an icon of West Berlin.

The old, ruined tower and the new building

Religion and the Crown

You might think it would be difficult to top all that symbolism – but wait, there's more: The church was consecrated on 1 September, 1895, a day memorialising the 25th anniversary of the French surrender after the battle of Sedan in the Franco-Prussian War. Wilhelm II had begun an intensive church-building programme, and this five-towered place of worship – built in honour of his grandfather Wilhelm I who died in 1888 at the age of 91 – was intended to be the focal point of a new city centre in west Berlin. It was also meant to represent the unity of religion and the crown, just like his grandfather would have wanted. A frieze of Hohenzollern rulers – from Elector Friedrich I through to the last Crown Prince Friedrich Wilhelm and his wife Cäcilie – immortalises the noble family.

The Beloved "Hollow Tooth"

The west tower, reduced from 113m to 63m (370 to 260ft) during the War, soon became known as the *Hohler Zahn* ("Hollow Tooth") by locals. It's dangerous to confuse such typical Berlin flippancy with indifference, however: When architect **Egon Eiermann**'s plans for a new church proposed to demolish the iconic ruin, a storm of protest broke out and waves of letters from outraged readers flooded the offices of the city's newspapers.

A Vision in Blue and Grey

You can see the result of their outrage: The Senate didn't ignore the people, and the ruined tower was kept as a memorial. In 1961, a new church – an ascetic, grey, flat-roofed octagonal edifice – was put up next to the late 19th-century building. It glows blue in the evening, attracting the attention of passersby. Its colour comes from 33,000 stained glass blocks made in Chartres in France, most of which are a deep, warm blue (a few are red, green and yellow).

The effect inside the building is stunning. The architect clad the church's 2.5cm (1")-thick walls with a second internal octagonal wall. The space between the two dampens the noise from outside and houses the lights that illuminate the glass blocks at night.

Your Cities are Burned with Fire

Six bells hang in the new, 53m (174ft)-tall hexagonal church tower. The largest bears a German inscription from the prophet Isaiah: "Your cities are burned with fire. But my salvation remains for ever, and my justice shall know no end."

TAKING A BREAK

You can enjoy some healthy salads, wraps and soups at **Dean & David** in the Neues Kranzler Eck.

✚ 202 C3 ✉ Breitscheidplatz
🕓 Church daily 9–7, Memorial Hall Mon–Fri 10–6, Sat 10–5.30, Sun 12–5.30
🚇 Zoologischer Garten 💶 Free entry

INSIDER INFO

The church offers some English-language guided **tours** alongside its regular German programme. Enquire to find out details and times.

㉝ The Kurfürstendamm

What's a boulevard? A wide, straight road with enough room to stroll around? An urban highway shaded by trees and bordered with fine houses and shops? For a more precise definition, just take a look at the 53m (134ft)-wide, 3.5km (2mi)-long Kurfürstendamm.

Stroll around or watch the passersby

It's hard to say exactly where it begins. Perhaps at KaDeWe, the **Kaufhaus des Westens** department store (▶ 131), Europe's largest temple to consumerism? It's worth a visit, but its address says it's on Tauentzienstraße… In that case it must start at **Breitscheidplatz**, where Kaiser Wilhelm's ruined church soars skywards, where street vendors, pavement artists, performers and beggars ply their trades, where Christmas markets are held, and where Joachim Schmettaus' **Weltkugelbrunnen** (World Globe Fountain) – a popular meeting point – serves as a reminder that the globe is divided into two hemispheres.

THE NEW WEST

Bismarck had the Parisian Champs-Elysées in mind when he transformed the existing road – which had linked the Stadtschloss with the Grunewald hunting lodge since the 16th century – into a boulevard. The emancipated middle-class moved into this new west side of the city at the end of the 19th century and built large houses with elaborate façades.

Western Self-Confidence

Standing at 22 storeys and 86m (282ft) high, the **Europa-Center** was regarded as a giant when it opened in 1965. You wouldn't think so today. Topped with a revolving, 14m (46ft)-high Mercedes star, it was built to show East Berlin how much the West loved their independence. The Center was the showcase of the West, with shops, restaurants, theatres, offices and a 13m (43ft)-high 🕐 water clock. Helmut Jahn's **Neues Kranzler Eck**, a gigantic glass gateau of a building on the corner of Joachimstaler Straße, juts out above the road. A red and white-striped awning is the only reminder of the famous Café Kranzler that once stood here.

Around the Kurfürstendamm

Stunning Side Streets
The side streets with their lush trees and cosmopolitan flair are the best thing about the Kurfürstendamm. **Meinekestraße** has good restaurants and **Fasanenstraße** boasts the Wintergartenensemble, a group of Berlin's most beautiful Neo-Renaissance villas that includes the **Literaturhaus** with its delightful garden café-restaurant (➤ 133) and steps leading down to a small bookshop. These buildings were due to be torn down in the late 1960s to make way for an urban motorway; determined resistance saved them. You can't leave without having a look in at the marble entranceways on **Uhlandstraße** and strolling round the shops on **Bleibtreustraße**.

Boutiques and Cafés in Bleibtreustraße

Going Up-market
Explore **The Story of Berlin** (➤ 132), a multimedia exhibition in the Kurfürstendamm-Karree buildings between Uhlandstraße and Knesebeckstraße. **Savignyplatz** (➤ 132) with its fashion stores, small restaurants and specialist shops lies to the north. Schlüterstraße boasts chic little fashion boutiques. The further you go, the classier and pricier the Kurfürstendamm gets (there are no price tags to help you here!). Further west beyond **Olivaer Platz** and **Adenauer Platz**, the Kurfürstendamm becomes a residential street with greengrocers, bakers and food shops. The **Schaubühne** (➤ 136) theatre is the predominant cultural force on the west of the boulevard. Its modern plays give the Volksbühne theatre in East Berlin a run for its money.

TAKING A BREAK

Einhorn ("Unicorn", Wittenbergplatz 5/6) is a self-service vegetarian bistro with a delicious selection.

➕ 202 A3–C3

INSIDER INFO

- The **Käthe-Kollwitz-Museum** shows socio-critical and political drawings by Kollwitz (1867–1945) along with the Berlin artist's complete sculptural oeuvre (Fasanenstr. 24, tel: 030 8 82 52 10, daily 11am–6pm, entry €6).
- There are **art galleries** in Fasanenstraße, on the corner of Uhlandstraße/ Kurfürstendamm, in Mommsenstraße and in Niebuhrstraße.
- For a particularly classy **haircut**, pay a visit to Berlin's celebrity stylist Udo Walz on Kempinski-Plaza (Uhlandstr. 181, tel: 030 8 82 74 57).

At Your Leisure

34 KaDeWe

Whether you're after saucepans or caviar, pins or high-fashion dresses, you can get it all – and in many different varieties – at the KaDeWe (Kaufhaus des Westens) department store which opened in 1907. The highlight is the legendary fine foods floor, a gourmet's paradise and a favourite with the public. You need to be extraordinarily decisive to choose between the 1,300 cheeses, 1,200 speciality sausages and hams and 60 kinds of bread and rolls on offer. The only greater challenge is the one confronting wine lovers faced with 3,400 labels from every continent. The fish department bears comparison with many an aquarium: Depending on the season, the tanks hold swarms of sturgeon, pike, catfish, carp, perch and trout along with sea urchins and various types of crab. After visiting the 7,000m² (23,000ft²) food hall – the largest in Europe – you can enjoy the work of chefs and patissiers: International representatives of fine dining from Bocuse to Cipriani have branches here serving wonderful concoctions at 30 counter restaurants.

🚩 202 C3 ✉ Tauentzienstr. 21–24
☎ 030 2 12 10
🕐 Mon–Thu 10–8, Fri till 9, Sat 9.30–8
Ⓜ Wittenbergplatz

35 Zoologischer Garten

You can smell the camels from Zoologischer Garten station – even if thick foliage is blocking the view from the car park (parking lot) in summer, you'll know you've come to the right place! There's always a line of people waiting to get in at the **Löwentor** (Lion Gate) entrance to the 🦁 Zoo. Berliners love it, going in droves to sympathise with an elephant's two-year pregnancy, rejoice at the birth of the 80kg (176lb) infant, and wonder how long it will take to grow to its full size of 3m (10ft)

Schloss
Charlottenburg

Spandauer Damm
36 37 Otto- Wagner-Pl.
Sammlung Sammlung Suhr-
Berggruen Scharf- Allee Ernst-
Gersten- Reuter-Pl.
berg
Bismarckstr. Museum für
CHARLOTTEN- Fotografie
BURG Hardenbergstr. 39
Savignyplatz Zoolo-
Kant- 40 str. 35 gischer
Garten
Kurfürstendamm 33 Kaiser-Wilhelm-
Kurfürstendamm Gedächtnisk.
38 34
Adenauer- 0 400 m
platz **The Story** 0 400 yd
of Berlin **KaDeWe**

tall and 6 tonnes (6.6 tons) in weight (15 to 18 years). Hundreds of thousands mourned the death of Knautschke, a legendary hippopotamus who had survived the war.

Opened in 1844 at the suggestion of Alexander von Humboldt and landscape architect Peter Joseph Lenné, Berlin Zoo was the first zoo in Germany. Its initial stock came from Emperor Friedrich Wilhelm IV's menagerie on the Pfaueninsel (Peacock Island). Boasting more than 10,000 creatures, the **Aquarium** was founded and directed by zoologist Alfred Brehm. It's semi-dark inside, so you'll feel like you're underwater. As well as the fish department with its reef tank full of blacktip sharks, you'll also find areas dedicated to the lower animals, reptiles, amphibians and arthropods.

🚩 202 C4 ✉ Hardenbergplatz 8 (Löwentor), Budapester Str. 34 (Aquarium, Elefantentor)
☎ 030 25 40 10 🕐 Apr–Aug 9–7pm, Sep–Oct 9–6.30pm, Nov–Mar 9–5pm; Aquarium 9–6pm Ⓜ Zoologischer Garten
💶 Zoo or Aquarium €13, combined ticket €20

Around the Kurfürstendamm

36 Sammlung Berggruen

An exhibition of works by Picasso and his contemporaries Paul Klee, Georges Braque and Giacometti. It was originally owned by returned emigrant Heinz Berggruen, an art collector and friend of Picasso who first loaned and finally donated his collection to his native city. That's how Berlin came by the priceless **Picasso Museum** which boasts paintings, drawings and sculptures by the artist. It includes *Le chandail jaune (Dora)*, a portrait of Dora Maar, the artist's mistress. Works of African tribal art accompany the Cubist and Classic Modern paintings.

✚ 202, west of A5 ✉ Schlossstr. 1
☎ 030 32 69 58 15 🕓 Tue–Fri 10–6, Sat–Sun 11–6 🚋 309, M45 🎟 €10

37 Sammlung Scharf-Gerstenberg

The East Stüler Building opposite Schloss Charlottenburg houses a collection of over 200 works by the Surrealists and their forerunners. The exhibition includes works by Goya, Paul Klee, Max Ernst and Hans Bellmer.

✚ 202, west of A5 ✉ Schlossstr. 70
☎ 030 2 66 42 42 42; www.smb.museum
🕓 Tue–Fri 10–6, Sat–Sun 11–6
🚉 Richard-Wagner-Platz 🎟 €10

38 The Story of Berlin

A fully functional nuclear bunker under the Kurfürstendamm forms part of "The Story of Berlin" museum. Luckily, it's only ever been used by visitors to date. The museum deals with the development of the capital city from its origins to the present day. Multimedia and light installations make visiting the 23 themed rooms a real experience.

✚ 202 A3
✉ Kurfürstendamm 207–208,
☎ 030 88 72 01 00; www.story-of-berlin.de
🚉 Uhlandstraße 🕓 Daily 10am–8pm 🎟 €12

39 Museum für Fotografie

The Museum of Photography in a former Officers' Mess behind Zoo Station is where the Helmut Newton Foundation shows the work of the Berlin-born fashion photographer and his contemporaries. Temporary exhibitions from the Art Library's archives are held in the impressive setting of the Kaiser Hall on the 2nd floor.

✚ 202 B4 ✉ Jebensstr. 2
☎ 030 2 66 42 42 42; www.smb.museum
🕓 Tue, Wed, Fri 10–6, Thu 10–8, Sat–Sun 11–6
🚉 Zoologischer Garten 🎟 €10

40 Savignyplatz

At first glance, Savignyplatz just looks like a small patch of green on either side of the wide Kantstraße. In actual fact, it's the true urban

centre of Berlin's west end, consisting of all the narrow streets that converge at this point. Indeed, West Berliners consider the whole district with its exquisite small shops, beautiful residential buildings and dozens of restaurants and bars to be part of Savignyplatz itself. Stroll around here on a summer's evening and you'll see what they mean. The restaurants spread their tables out onto the street and people laugh and chat under ancient trees.

✚ 202 A3 🚉 Savignyplatz

25

Where to...
Eat and Drink

Prices
A main course without drinks:
€ under 12 euros   €€ 12–25 euros   €€€ over 25 euros

RESTAURANTS

Café im Literaturhaus €€
Grab a place in the garden of this Literaturhaus ("House of Literature"). If you can't, try to get a table above the stairs near the entrance. This idyllic spot, just 2 minutes away from the Ku'damm (Kurfürstendamm), was once a well-kept secret that got let out of the bag – it's still lovely, but the pale poets who used to frequent the café have since been driven away. The kitchens use organic ingredients.
🚩 202 B3 ✉ Fasanenstr. 23
☎ 030 8 82 54 14 🕓 Daily 9am–midnight

Diekmann €€
The history of this former general store shows through in the beautiful floor-to-ceiling shelves of goods and some of the old-fashioned ingredients they serve. The snow-white tablecloths and pointed napkins also hark back to a bygone age. The food here is perfect. There's a reasonably priced lunch around midday. *Insider Tip*
🚩 202 B3 ✉ Meinekestr. 7
☎ 030 8 83 33 21; diekmann-restaurants.de
🕓 Mon–Sat noon–1am, Sun 6pm–1am

Florian €–€€
You used to see celebs here when the film festival was held in West Berlin. Some stars have stayed faithful to this German eatery on Savignyplatz. They still serve *Rostbratwürste* (grilled sausages) on *Sauerkraut* after 11pm.
🚩 202 A4 ✉ Grolmanstr. 52 030 3 13 91 84;
www.restaurant-florian.de 🕓 Daily 6pm–3am

Hard Rock Café €
Music fans come here to eat fast food, listen to rock and admire a *Trabi* car once belonging to U2, a shirt from German punks *Die Toten Hosen* and a suit worn by Elton John. The tables on the balcony with a view of the Ku'damm are particularly popular.
🚩 202 B3 ✉ Kurfürstendamm 224
☎ 030 88 46 20 🕓 Sun–Thu 11.30–11.30,
Fri–Sat 11.30am–half past midnight

Hugos €€€
Chef Thomas Kammeier proves day in, day out that this restaurant – located above the rooftops of Berlin on the 13th floor of the InterContinental Hotel – is one of the best in the city. It's expensive, but the superb views of the West of the City are included.
🚩 203 D3 ✉ Budapester Str. 2
☎ 030 2 60 20; www.hugos-restaurant.de
🕓 Tue–Sat 6.30pm–10.30pm

Kabir €€
Vegetarians in particular will love the powerfully spiced Indian cuisine served here.
🚩 202 B4 ✉ Carmerstr. 17
☎ 030 3 12 81 57; restaurant-kabir.de
🕓 Mon–Sat 12–12, Sun from 4pm

Kuchi €€
A marvellous, inexpensive Japanese lunch menu with fish balls, yakitori dishes and other delicacies. It's absolutely packed in the evenings.
🚩 202 A3 ✉ Kantstr. 30 ☎ 030 31 50 78 15;
www.kuchi.de 🕓 Daily noon–midnight; lunch,
Mon–Sat noon–5pm

Around the Kurfürstendamm

La Mano Verde €€

Vegans will be spoilt for choice with such delicious dishes as ravioli made using white beet and filled with a tomato and cashew crème.

✚ 202 B3 ✉ Uhlandstr. 181
☎ 030 82 70 31 20; lamanoverdeberlin.com
🕐 Mon–Sat noon–5pm, 6pm–11pm

Lubitsch €–€€

The stucco on the ceiling, the mirrors on the walls (which make the space look bigger) and the modern cuisine make this eatery one of the most popular in the area. There's always a vegetarian option, pasta and a meat dish at lunch.

✚ 202 A3 ✉ Bleibtreustr. 47
☎ 030 8 82 37 56; www.restaurant-lubitsch.de
🕐 Mon–Sat 10am–1am, Sun 6pm–1am; lunch Mon–Sat noon–6pm

Manzini €€

Marble floors and Murano glass ceilings – that's the sort of elegance media types go for in old West Berlin. It's a look that's been done particularly well here. The bistro-style cooking is excellent (finally, a perfect risotto!). Enjoyable evenings guaranteed.

✚ 202 A2 ✉ Ludwigkirchstr. 11
☎ 030 8 85 78 20; www.manzini.de
🕐 Daily 8am–2am, food until 1am; lunchtime plat du jour Mon–Fri 11.30am–5pm

Namaskar €€

A beautiful gourmet Indian restaurant whose refined, aromatic food has been praised by the Gault et Millau restaurant guide. Couples serve themselves from luxurious copper cauldrons. They also offer Indian wine.

✚ 202 B2 ✉ Pariser Str. 56/57
☎ 030 88 68 06 48; restaurantnamaskar.de
🕐 Tue–Sun noon–midnight, Mon from 5

Opera Italiana €

At this restaurant opposite Schloss Charlottenburg you can eat surrounded by plenty of images of saints and little houses in Italian streets with washing hanging on the line. It's a perfect backdrop for the fresh, homemade pasta, the enormous pizzas and the *Saltimbocca* in a white wine sauce.

✚ 202, west of A5 ✉ Spandauer Damm 5
☎ 030 34 70 36 26; www.opera-italiana.com
🕐 Daily 11am–midnight; lunch, 11.30am–4pm

Zwölf Apostel €€

The excellent pizzas are named after the *Zwölf Apostel* ("12 Apostles"), whose images you'll see on the ceiling. They also serve pasta, meat and fish.

✚ 202 A3 ✉ Bleibtreustr. 49 (Passage)
☎ 030 3 12 14 33; www.12-apostel.de
🕐 Daily 8am–1am

CAFÉS

Brel

This French-inspired café-restaurant right on Savignyplatz serves breakfast right up till 6pm.

✚ 202 A3 ✉ Savignyplatz 1
☎ 030 31 80 00 20; www.cafebrel.de
🕐 Daily from 9am

Café Hardenberg

This student café not far from the Technical University is often full and usually noisy. Anyone tired out by the city can daydream here undisturbed.

✚ 202 B4 ✉ Hardenbergstr. 10
☎ 030 3 12 26 44
🕐 Daily 9am–1am

Schwarzes Café

It used to be totally black inside, and some prospective customers were reluctant to leave the sunlight to enter such a dark box. That's now changed. Nevertheless, it still has a reputation as a legendary place for breakfasts, lunches, beers and several cocktails. *Insider Tip*

✚ 202 B3 ✉ Kantstr. 148
☎ 030 3 13 80 38;
www.schwarzescafe-berlin.de
🕐 Tue 3am–10am, otherwise 24 hours

Where to...
Shop

IN AND AROUND THE KURFÜRSTENDAMM

When the **Europa-Center** (Tauentzienstr. 9) was built back in 1965, it was one of the first shopping centres in West Germany. It still boasts a wide selection of goods for all budgets. Germany's first "Concept Mall" was opened directly opposite in the fully reno-vated **Bikinihaus** in April 2014. Independent boutiques are its mainstay, making a nice change from the usual big chains. As well as selling fashion, shoes and de-sign, the 60 speciality shops also include sports and technology stores, cafés and restaurants. Unusually, it also has two dozen "Pop-up Stores" which can be rented for 3 to 12 months to test out new product ideas. You can get a great view into the monkey enclosure of Berlin Zoo from the panoramic window on the ground floor and up on the roof terrace.

Helmut Jahn's **Neues Kranzler Eck** also stands out thanks to its extravagant architecture. It's mainly home to fashion stores ranging from Gerry Weber to Mango.

You can buy everything you need to make your own personal-ised jewellery at the **Perlen-Bar** (Uhlandstr. 156). 🛍 **Paint Your Style** (Bleibtreustr. 46) also inspires creativity in its customers by getting them to paint their own plates and mugs. Fans of old books will love the selection in **Düwal** (Schlüterstr. 17), where precious tomes are piled right up to the ceiling. A small shop by Sabine Dubbenkropp called **Confiserie Melanie** (Goethestr. 4) is crammed full with over 4,000 tasty treats from spicy mustard and Italian milk liqueur to handmade pralines. They're just waiting to be discovered by a cult following.

Secondo (Mommsenstr. 61) sells second-hand designer fashion. You can buy beautiful lingerie at **Roserosa** (Bleibtreustr. 48), avant-garde shoes at **Bleibgrün** (Bleibtreustr. 29–30) and eco-friendly footwear at **Gangart** (Mommsenstr. 45).

Classy shops like **Jil Sander** (Kurfürstendamm 185) can be found near Olivaer Platz. **Moda Mo** (Giesebrechtstr. 17) will dress you up for a glamorous evening out. Berlin designer **Nanna Kuckuck** presents her glittering haute couture at Bleibtreustr. 52.

AROUND SAVIGNYPLATZ

Stilwerk, a designer department store (Kantstr. 17), has everything imaginable to make your home more beautiful: Bang & Olufsen hifi systems, antiques, wooden furniture and ethnic knickknacks. Bargain hunters won't find anything to suit them here!

Olbrish (Kurfürstendamm 210) has bags designed in-house, while **Riccardo Cartillone** (Savignyplatz 4) sells Italian shoes. Check out his cut-price footwear outlet diagonally opposite.

Berliner Zinnfiguren (Knesebeckstr. 88) sells pewter models of numer-ous famous figures.

Bücherbogen right on Savignyplatz (S-Bahnbogen 593) is a treasure trove of reading on architecture, art, design and photography. *Insider Tip*

Fans of good poetry should head to the **Autorenbuchhandlung** (Else-Ury-Bogen 599–601) which has the largest selection of verse in the German-speaking world and holds regular readings.

Prinz Eisenherz (Motzstr. 23) contains a collection of gay and lesbian books.

Manufactum (Hardenbergstr. 4–5) sells a whole range of beauti-fully made products.

Where to…
Go Out

THEATRE AND MUSIC

Lovers of good acting and choreography are well catered for at the **Schaubühne** (Kurfürstendamm 153, tel: 030 89 00 23). Modern plays are staged at the **Renaissance-Theater** (Knesebeckstr. 100, tel: 030 3 12 42 02), a thoroughly beautiful Art Nouveau edifice.

The performances held in the circus tent at **Bar jeder Vernunft** (Schaperstr. 24, tel: 030 8 83 15 82) provide some of the very best entertainment around. **Stachelschweine** (Europa-Center, tel: 030 2 61 47 95) has lost some of its old fiery cabaret bite over the years. The **Theater und Komödie am Kurfürstendamm** (Kurfürstendamm 206–209, tel: 030 88 59 11 88) are devoted to performing light comedy, farce and popular theatre.

Built in 1961, the **Deutsche Oper** (German Opera; Bismarckstr. 35, tel: 030 34 38 43 43) might look sober and utilitarian from the outside, but its acoustics are exceptional. The **Staatsoper Berlin** (Berlin State Opera) is found at the Schillertheater (Bismarckstr. 110, tel: 030 20 35 45 55) while its east Berlin home is being renovated.

Quasimodo next to the **Theater des Westens** (Kantstr. 12a, tel: 01805 44 44) is a legend of the Berlin jazz scene. Come to listen to live jazz and blues and some surprising jam sessions. **A-Trane** (Bleibtreustr. 1, tel: 030 3 13 25 50) has modern jazz and swing almost every evening.

BARS

If you like to finish off your evening at a bar, you'll have several establishments to choose from around the Kurfürstendamm. All of them have had time to establish their own individual character.

Monkey Bar in the 25Hours Hotel (Budapester Str. 40, tel: 030 1 20 22 12 10, Mon–Fri 3pm–1am, Sat–Sun 3pm–2am) on the 10th floor of the newly renovated Bikinihaus offers a large selection of gin and tiki cocktails along with a great view of the city and the zoo. You can also get good cocktails at **Gainsbourg** (Jeanne-Mammen-Bogen 576–77, tel: 030 3 13 74 64; www.gainsbourg.de, daily from 5pm, from 4pm in summer) with its beautiful terrace. It's where the area's bohemian types meet up. The landlord sometimes sings some songs on his guitar.

People come out of performances at the Schaubühne theatre to to discuss the the evening's dramatics over a drink at the **Universum Lounge** (Kurfürstendamm 153, tel: 030 32 76 47 93; www.universum lounge.com, every day from 6pm).

Actors and wannabes find an "audience" for their thespian ways every night at **Diener** (Grolmanstr. 47, tel: 030 8 81 53 29; www.diener-tattersall.de, daily from 6pm), an inn left over from the "Tattersall des Westens", a two-storey horse riding hall from 1893. The walls haven't seen a single lick of paint for the last 50 years – something the place is famous for.

More of a pub than a bar, **Zwiebelfisch** at Savignyplatz 7–8 (tel: 030 3 12 73 63, zwiebelfisch-berlin.de, daily noon–6am) is a hangout for student activists from 1968 and their sympathisers.

Cigar smokers will feel right at home at the **Times Bar** in the Savoy Hotel (Fasanenstr. 9, tel: 030 31 10 30, daily from 11am). This classic bar set up a Casa del Habano lounge for stogie lovers many years ago. There's a walk-in humidor (for keeping cigars moist) and expert advice is on hand.

Kreuzberg

Splashing down the Spree

Enjoy discovering the river Spree by **canoe**.
They're available for rental next to Café
Freischwimmer (➤ 145).

Bargain Hunters

Bergmannstraße (➤ 149) between
Marheinekeplatz and the Mehringdamm
boasts the highest density of second-hand
stores in the city.

Döner Delights

Try an *Obstdöner* (fruit döner kebab) from
Wonder Waffles at Adalbertstr. 88 round the
corner from Oranienstraße (➤ 147).

Kreuzberg

Getting Your Bearings

West Berliners used to think of Kreuzberg as a multicultural melting pot where all-night parties and riots were held in the GDR era. When the Wall fell, this poor "alternative" area where young people longed to live suddenly found itself in the middle of the city. It's recently become cool once again.

Kreuzberg is one half of the Kreuzberg-Friedrichshain district which used to be divided into East and West by the river Spree. The Oberbaum bridge joins them up again today. Refrigeration plants and warehouses are being converted into media factories and lofts here, and Schlesische Straße, Skalitzer Straße und Oranienstraße are full of countless cool bars, clubs and cafés. The streets are busier at night than during the day.

All this new development doesn't mean that the old Kreuzberg has disappeared, however. The largest Turkish community outside Turkey has settled here, building its own banks and jewellers alongside alternative bars and pierced punks. Oranienstraße is still the alternative scene's answer to the Ku'damm, even though the squatters have become homeowners and good restaurants now welcome visitors from other areas. There's a place for everyone here: Artists still love moving in despite the increasing rent, and it's the perfect setting for Daniel Libeskind's extravagant Jewish Museum. Kreuzberg's expanded population seem to beam with happiness and a sense of belonging around Bergmannstraße.

Map labels: Checkpoint Charlie, Koch-str., Kochstr., R.-Dutschke-Str., Oranien-, Bundes-druckerei, Wald-eckpark, Wilhelm-, Streesemann-, Ritter-, Jüdisches Museum, Berlinische Galerie, Th.-Wolff-Park, Alte Jakob-, str., KREUZ, Mehringplatz, Patentamt, Prinz, Hallesches, Tempelhofer Ufer, Ufer, Hallesches Tor, Gitschiner Str., Gitschiner, Prinzen-, Waterlooufer, Blücher-pl., Blücher-, Mehring-damm, damm, Friedhof, str., Hornstr., Rathaus, Blücher-, Urban-, Yorck-, str., Gneisenau-, Gneisenaustr., 46 Riehmers Hofgarten, Bergmann-straße, Zossener, Baer-, str., Südstern, Kreuzberg-, str., Bergmann-, 43 str., Marheineke-pl., Bergmannstr., Südstern, Viktoria-park, Chamisso-pl., Friesen-, Friedhöfe, 45, Wasser-turm

Friends come to meet and eat: Bergmannstraße boasts lots of restaurants and street cafés

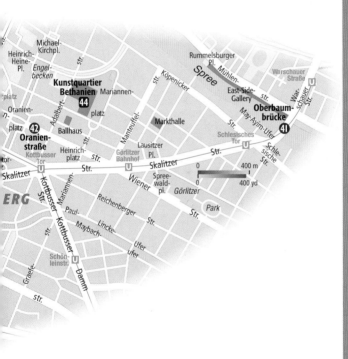

TOP 10
⭐ Jüdisches Museum ➤ 142

The Perfect Day

The following route is one option for seeing some of Kreuzberg's most interesting sights in the space of a single day. The individual highlights are described in more detail over the following pages (➤ 142–151).

🕐 10:00

Start at the **41 Oberbaumbrücke** (image below ➤ 144), the most beautiful bridge in Berlin. Pop into porcelain artist Paul Reimert's shop/studio (➤ 145) and admire his model of Kaiser Friedrich II made from old teapots and fragments of grandmotherly crockery. You should also spend some time dreaming of moving to May-Ayim-Ufer. Sadly, you don't have a chance: The architects have built the houses for themselves. Move away from the noisy Skalitzer Straße and turn into the friendly Muskauer Straße which leads on down to Mariannenplatz – scene of the legendary May Day riots – and the **44 Kunstquartier Bethanien** cultural complex (➤ 151).

🕐 12:00

Stroll on to Heinrichplatz. If you fancy, take the opportunity to have a break in the Rote Harfe (➤ 147), a former hub for revolutionary groups planning their anti-establishment protests.

🕐 13:00

There's a lot to see in **42 Oranienstraße** (➤ 147): You'll find little shops and bars for punks, skateboarders and people of all sexualities. Don't be put off by these apparent divisions – everyone's welcome everywhere.

🕐 14:00

Take the U-Bahn to Hallesches Tor from Kottbusser Tor (*Tor* means 'gate'). Then catch a bus (240) or walk to Lindenstraße and the ⭐ **Jüdisches Museum** (Jewish Museum, image right; ➤ 142). The building's ground plan looks like a flash of lightning has hit the district.

🕧 16:30

Take U-Bahn train No. 6 one stop to the Mehringdamm, then change onto the No. 7. Get out at Gneisenaustraße just one stop further on. Zossener Straße leads directly to Marheinekeplatz and **43 Bergmannstraße** (➤ 149) which boasts various shops, cafés and restaurants.

🕧 18:00

If you'd like to see some greenery, go to **45 Viktoriapark** (➤ 141), one of Berlin's most beautiful parks. Sat atop Kreuzberg hill, it starts just behind the Mehringdamm. You can also check out the elegant rear courtyard at **46 Riehmers Hofgarten** (➤ 151) in Yorckstraße.

🕧 20:00

Hungry and exhausted? If you're here in summer, reserve a place at Osteria No. 1 (➤ 152), an eatery where you'll feel like you've been transported to Italy. Afterwards, you might be in the mood to have a dance at Golgatha (➤ 156) at the foot of Kreuzberg hill. Stay awhile and discover just how long the nights in Kreuzberg really are…

★⑧Jüdisches Museum

Is it an exploded Star of David or just a metallic zigzag? Daniel Libeskind's Jüdisches Museum (Jewish Museum) has caused quite a stir ever since it was opened in September 2001. It's already been visited by over 9 million people.

A pomegranate tree made from plastic and silk stands at the entrance to the exhibition. That could throw you off your guard – most visitors to a Jewish Museum might expect it to start off by discussing the Holocaust. Not so here: The pomegranate tree is a sign of fertility, showing that this museum is designed to document a full 2,000 years of Jewish history.

Light enters the silver building through the mysterious symbols

Mysterious Walls

You won't be sure what to expect at first. The building's zinc exterior reflects the sun. The slits and wedges in the almost windowless walls could be signs from a secret code. There's no direct entrance – you enter through the basement of the Baroque law court which housed the Berlin Museum until 1993. Even when you've made it into the building itself, you won't have reached the exhibition space proper just yet.

The bold shapes of the rooms, the empty ravines and the sloping floors are best understood as components of an historical aesthetic: The whole structure stands as a memorial to the Holocaust. The empty spaces that extend through every floor (referred to as "voids" by the architect) are intended to symbolise a vanished culture. Once the door has closed in the tall Holocaust tower, you'll experience nothing but darkness and a sense of emptiness. The narrow slits which can be seen from the outside represent hope: They alone let light into the building.

A walk through Jewish daily life

Documents and Biographies

Visitors learn about German-Jewish history in a variety of different ways. You can accompany Hamburg business-woman Bertha Pappenheim through her life in the 17th century, for example, and see the briefcase which Gerd W. Ehrlich took with him in 1943 when he escaped across the frontier into Switzerland. His wife gave the briefcase to the museum on permanent loan, as did the many others who have contributed personal mementos to help visitors get to grips with Jewish life in Germany during both the good times and the bad. You'll see books which gave comfort and solace when on the run; cutlery which helped to maintain a link with family life; and photos, coins, weapons and documents that take you on a trip through history. You can even see a modern Jewish children's nursery – you'll be surprised to see a Barbie doll wearing a kippah between Hebrew colouring books.

Everything Seems Fine

Wild olive trees grow out of 49 concrete pillars in the **E.T.A. Hoffmann garden**. The slanting structures in this stony copse not only serve as a memorial to the poet who worked in the courts in the old building next door – they're also meant to convey a feeling of an emigrant's life in exile: Everything seems fine, but the system isn't totally trans-parent and you never feel as if you're on solid ground.

TAKING A BREAK

Enjoy some snacks and Jewish specialities in **Café Schmus**.

☩ 205 D3 ✉ Lindenstr. 9–14 ☎ 030 25 99 33 00 🕐 Tue–Sun 10–8, Mon till 10pm, except on Jewish holidays (Rosh Hashanah, Yom Kippur) and Christmas Eve 🎟 €8 🚇 Hallesches Tor

INSIDER INFO

- 👫 **Young visitors** can follow **children's paths** through the museum, build synagogues and taste some kosher gummy bears.
- The **Berlinische Galerie** (Alte Jakobstr. 124–128, tel: 030 78 90 26 00, Wed–Mon 10–6) right around the corner shows Berlin art from 1870 to the present day.

㊶ Oberbaumbrücke

A lively art, café and nightlife scene has established itself around Oberbaum bridge. That's no great surprise: The structure connects the hip districts of Friedrichshain and Kreuzberg.

Traversed by the yellow U-Bahn and colourful cars, this striking red-brick bridge with its two towers gives the impression of being playful yet defiant. Boats, pleasure steamers and barges sail past on the Spree below. The bridge was built in 1896 following designs by chief government architect Otto Stahn. It was partially destroyed in the War and could only be used by pedestrians until its restoration in the mid-1990s. The bricks conceal a massive reinforced concrete structure beneath. The elegant steel arch, used to replace the missing central arcades, was designed by Portuguese architect Santiago Calatrava in

The Oberbaum bridge is a particularly atmospheric sight at night

1992. The two pointed towers, inspired by Prenzlau's city gate, hark back to the bridge's original function as a toll station. A tree trunk – the *Oberbaum* ("upper tree") – used to bar access to the city at night.

Nightlife
There's usually a whole load of people out and about on the twin-towered bridge at night. Around 2 or 3am, partygoers head between the river's north and south banks to continue their revelries on the other side. In Kreuzberg, they'll call in at bars, pubs and the cool Club Watergate (► 156) with its fantastic views of the Spree. Night owls on the northern side have fun in Matrix, Busche and Cassiopeia – clubs for different crowds with varying musical tastes. The old commercial buildings on the Kreuzberg riverbank are home to such trendy club-restaurants as Spindler & Klatt (► 153), which is housed in a former bakery.

Not far from here you'll find the Tresor Club, an authentic early techno joint housed in a former heating plant. It was moved here from its original home in the vaults of a department store on Leipziger Platz in 1991.

ABC: Artists, Bars, Cafés
Bars such as the San Remo Upflamör (► 156) by the Oberbaum bridge are transformed into cafés every morning. Students, mums with toddlers and other early risers sit down to a caffè latte and treat themselves to a lavish breakfast.

Every morning at 10am, artist **Paul Reimert** (Falckensteinerstr. 45; www.paul-reimert.com) opens his workshop and looks to see what people from the neighbourhood have left by his door that night. Some days he gets boxes and boxes of old porcelain – that's because everyone knows that Reimert can use their

The *Molecule Men*, three giants on the Spree, symbolise three city districts

Kreuzberg

unwanted items to create fantastic things. Take his mosaic of Kaiser Friedrich II wearing nothing but scarlet boots, for example. Reimert's work is now renowned enough that he can also make a living from commissions.

Refashioned

Cool **Schlesische Straße** with its numerous bars and pubs is now home to Killerbeast (Schlesische Str. 31; www.killerbeast. de), where treasured garments are altered to make brand new clothes (their motto? "Turn something old into something new"). Each piece is unique, but they're not that expensive. Their very own *Schnullerbiest* label also has fashion for kids, including babygros made from old band t-shirts and cargo pants with a lollipop pocket. It's a unique place that perfectly encapsulates the character of the city.

The Schlesisches Tor U-Bahn station is no longer the end of Line 1

Insider Tip

TAKING A BREAK

Freischwimmer (▶ 145), an idyllic bar in an old boathouse on a peaceful Spree canal, is a perfect place to take some time out. You can sit right next to the water in summer, enjoy food from their lava stone grill, try their refined seasonal meals and taste crispy *Flammkuchen* (a thin, pizza-like dish). Lots of guests come for a coffee, a beer or an aperitif during the day. Their lavish Sunday brunch buffet is also very popular.

✚ 206 C3
Ⓜ Schlesisches Tor

INSIDER INFO

The **Arena-Badeschiff** (bathing boat) actually lies across the district border in Treptow. This old container ship boasts a pool complete with a jetty and a sandy beach. The whole thing is covered over in winter and used as a sauna – it's cool and cosy at the same time! There's a beautiful view of the *Molecule Men*, Jonathan Borofsky's gigantic sculpture. (Eichenstr. 4, tel: 030 5 33 20 30, May–Sep, daily 8am–midnight, Oct–Apr, daily 10am–midnight, €5).

㊷ Oranienstraße

For many years, people moving to Berlin from places ranging from Anatolia to Swabia had one destination in mind – Kreuzberg's S036 postcode (zip code). This area in the south of the district between the Wall, the Spree and the Landwehr canal was cheap, cheerful and lively. O-Straße – as the street is known by locals – lies at its centre.

S036 still exists – it's the name of a club at Oranienstraße 190 where partygoers throng after dark (►156). Rock and Punk concerts take place here several times a week alongside such regular events as the "Café Fatal" tea dance on Sundays and the monthly Roller Disco. Such festivities are only a part of what multi-cultural Oranienstraße has to offer – the courtyard next door leads through to a mosque.

Headscarves and Piercings

There's a particularly vibrant mix of people on the streets and in the cafés and shops

Oranienstraße is always bustling

here. Turkish women – some fashionably dressed, others in long robes and headscarves – mingle with hip young things with tattoos and piercings. They're joined by tourists from all over the world who love seeing the area's exotic cultural mishmash.

The area is home to tailors, delicatessens, bars, fashion boutiques and galleries that have resisted the temptation to move down to Mitte. People cure heartache with cake on Paul-Lincke-Ufer, and cheap lunches are served in the Familiengarten community café. Shops advertising their services in Turkish and Arabic let you phone anywhere in the world for very little money indeed. The banks and jewellers seem mainly geared towards the Turkish people who make up a third of the area's inhabitants.

The End of the Line for the Revolutionaries

Heinrichplatz, the strategic centre of the street, boasts such famous bars as **Zum Elefanten** and **Rote Harfe**. It was here in the 1970s that plans were hatched to thwart the Senate's proposal to clean up the district and clear out

Kreuzberg

KREUZKÖLLN

This area south of the Maybachufer where the famous twice-weekly **Türkenmarkt** (Turkish Market) takes place is actually part of the Neukölln district. So many bars, cafés, designer stores and studios have set up here over the last few years, however, that it almost feels like Kreuzberg. The locals certainly think so – that's why they've named the area *Kreuzkölln*, a mix of *Kreuz*berg and Neu*kölln*. It's bustling with young party animals at night, particularly around Weserstraße. You can still get beer and cocktails at very low prices, but landlords have scented blood, and the days of cheap rent and *Pilsner* for €2 are slowly coming to an end.

its rear courtyards. At that time, half of all Berlin's squats were found in Kreuzberg, and the enraged occupiers set up barricades and bombarded tourist buses with stones. Eventually, a programme of cautious urban renewal could begin with the aim of developing the area while retaining its essential historical character.

TAKING A BREAK

The **Bateau Ivre** (Oranienstr. 18) on Heinrichplatz serves good cakes and a delicious deli breakfast accompanied with traditional French *chansons*. You can also sit outside.

➕ 202 E3–F3 🚇 Görlitzer Bahnhof

INSIDER INFO

- You'll find **Stolpersteine** (literally "stumble stones") – brass cobblestones engraved with names and embedded in the pavement – all over Berlin. You can spot some on the corner of Oranienstraße and Skalitzer Straße. They're part of a project by artist Gunter Deming that shows where Jewish people once lived and tells of their fate at the hands of the Nazis.
- Rows of small **cafés and restaurants** with beautiful gardens are found on the Paul-Lincke-Ufer next to the Landwehr canal.
- Every Tuesday and Friday from noon till 6pm, the **Turkish Market** on the Maybachufer sells fresh fish, baked goods, fruit and vegetables, materials, tea glasses and much, much more.
- **DIM**, the "Imaginary Manufactory", uses brushes from the blind people's workshop to make everyday design (Oranienstr. 26).
- Women of all nationalities meet up at the Turkish **Hamam** in the chocolate factory. It's a man-free zone. An eastern ambience reigns (Mariannenstr. 6, tel: 030 6 15 14 64, Mon 3pm–11pm, Tue–Sun noon–11pm).

Insider Tip

㊽ Bergmannstraße

The houses and streets in west Kreuzberg are popular movie locations. The area's an interesting mix: You'll see New Yorker readers, organic wine drinkers, and Polish producers meeting with Turkish directors in the market hall on Saturdays.

You could be forgiven for thinking you've been transported back to the end of the 19th century. A collection of historic façades lines Bergmannstraße, Heimstraße and the Mehringdamm almost without a gap. This unusual architectural collection owes its survival to Tempelhof Airport: The Allies are said to have wanted it as a landing place for their own planes and thus spared the surrounding area in their bombing raids.

As a result, the area boasts wide streets, old trees, developed neighbourhoods and a great number of shops, bars and theatres. It also doesn't have any empty apartments: Bergmannstraße and Chamissoplatz are chic places to live, and no one has wanted to move out for quite some time. Many students who moved into the cheap rear-courtyard lodgings here in the 1980s now hold down well-paid jobs and have simply decided to buy up and stay in their (freshly renovated) apartments.

Marheinekeplatz

A row of eateries and bars in Bergmannstraße

On Saturdays, dogs bark at the entrance to the pretty market hall in Marheinekeplatz while their owners dawdle inside. They're presumably standing at the cheese stall exchanging views on the organic wares or passing on wine recommendations from the weekend papers before trying them out for themselves at the Enoteca (wine shop).

Kreuzberg

The large pots in the square aren't for flowers – they're part of a fountain installation by Paul Pfarr. The Passionskirche at the end of the square only acts as a church on Sundays – it's otherwise used for concerts and debates.

Chamissoplatz

On the corner of Chamissoplatz you'll see a green "Café Achteck" (literally: "Octagonal Café") – that's what Berliners call these old eight-sided urinals that are found all over the city.

The **water tower** on the corner of Fidicinstraße provided the district with water from 1888. It was lived in until the 1950s before being renovated and turned into a youth centre and concert hall.

Artist Kurt Mühlenhaupt bought a former metalwork factory at Fidicinstraße 40 in 1991 and transformed it into an arts centre. The **English Theatre**, the only English-speaking theatre in the city, has taken up residence here (tel: 030 91 12 11). Staging shows from around the world, it's popular with English native speakers and internationals alike.

"Café Achteck"

TAKING A BREAK

Whether you want Swabian, Mexican, Arabic or Italian cuisine, there's something for everyone in Bergmannstraße.

➕ 205 D1
🚇 Gneisenaustr.

INSIDER INFO

There are four **historic cemeteries** between Heimstraße and the Südstern: Dreifaltigkeitskirchhof, Friedrichwerderscher Kirchhof, Kirchhof Jerusalems- und Neue Kirchengemeinde, and Kirchhof Luisenstadt I. They contain the impressive monuments, mausoleums and tombs of prominent personalities (including Chancellor Gustav Stresemann and architect Martin Gropius).

At Your Leisure

44 Kunstquartier Bethanien

This gargantuan building on Mariannenplatz and the edifices behind it are home to around two dozen youth clubs, social societies and cultural associations.

Designed by Schinkel's pupil Ludwig Persius, the building complex was built in 1847 as the Bethanien Deaconesses' Hospital. The hospital was shut down in 1970. It entered the history books in 1971 as the first squat in Berlin when 150 young people forced their way into the empty structure and named it after Georg von Rauch, a supporter of the *Rote Armee Fraktion* (Red Army Faction, a.k.a. Baader-Meinhof group) who was shot dead by a West Berlin policeman.

➕ 206 A3 ✉ Mariannenplatz 2
☎ 030 9 02 98 14 55 🕐 Daily noon–7pm
🚇 Görlitzer Bahnhof 🎫 Free

45 Viktoriapark

The land rises from Großbeerenstraße up 66m (217ft) to this, the highest point in the city. The park's waterfall is a great place to cool your feet and for 👫 kids and dogs to play. Paths of varying steepness wind up to Schinkel's 20m (72ft)-high National Memorial (1818–21). Topped with an iron

In Riehmers Hofgarten

cross, it stands in memory of a campaign against Napoleon. The buildings of the former Schultheiss brewery below have been turned into a city within a city with lovely

apartments and working spaces. Golgatha (► 156) is hidden amongst the trees.

➕ 204 B1 ✉ Kreuzbergstr. 🚇 Mehringdamm

46 Riehmers Hofgarten

Two muscular figures at the entrance invite visitors into Riehmers Hofgarten, an exclusive model apartment block from the reign of Wilhelm II (late 19th century). Twenty 4 and 5-storey buildings are grouped around landscaped courtyards linked by an internal road. The flats were generously sized when they were built in 1881. It's home to a peaceful hotel on a noisy street today.

➕ 204 B1 ✉ Yorckstr. 83–86
🚇 Mehringdamm

Where to...
Eat and Drink

Prices
A main course without drinks:
€ under 12 euros   €€ 12–25 euros   €€€ over 25 euros

RESTAURANTS

Defne €
A Turkish eatery on the Landwehr canal with decent cooking, tasty grilled dishes and a beer garden. Ideal for vegetarians.
➕ 205 F2 ✉ Planufer 92c
☎ 030 81 79 71 11; www.defne-restaurant.de
🕐 Daily from 5pm, from 4pm in summer

E.T.A. Hoffmann €€
Gourmet cuisine made with fresh local produce. Game and asparagus are served in season. They also have more exotic dishes, including confit of *Skrei* (Norwegian cod) with creamed *sauerkraut* and chive purée. A beautiful ambience in the listed Riehmers Hofgarten.
➕ 204 B1 ✉ Yorckstr. 83 ☎ 030 78 09 88 09; www.restaurant-e-t-a-hoffmann.de
🕐 Wed–Mon from 5pm

Henne €
Punks and celebs are amongst the regulars at this old Berlin inn. Serves the crispiest *Milchmasthähnchen* (milk-fed roast capon).
➕ 205 F3 ✉ Leuschnerdamm 25
☎ 030 6 14 77 30; www.henne-berlin.de
🕐 Tue–Sat from 6pm, Sun from 5pm

Horváth €€€
Sebastian Frank serves the finest Austrian cuisine at one of the classiest restaurants on the Landwehr canal. Guests are asked to choose how many courses they'd like from the set tasting menus.
➕ 206 A2 ✉ Paul-Lincke-Ufer 44a
☎ 030 61 28 99 92; www.restaurant-horvath.de
🕐 Wed–Sun 6pm–11pm

Café Jacques €
The menu includes two platters: The oriental house special, and another with couscous of your choice, fish, meat or vegetables that's only available on Wed and Sun.
➕ 206 A1 ✉ Maybachufer 14
☎ 030 6 94 10 48 🕐 Daily from 6pm

Jolesch €–€€
A beautiful space with parquet flooring and a chandelier. It looks wonderfully old fashioned, but the imaginative Austrian cuisine is decidedly modern. It's also worth coming just to try the cakes.
➕ 206 B3 ✉ Muskauer Str. 1
☎ 030 6 12 35 81; www.jolesch.de
🕐 Mon–Fri 11.30–midnight, Sat–Sun from 10

Le Cochon Bourgeois €€
Good rural French cooking served at a rather plain little bistro with a small garden out front in a lovely part of Kreuzberg.
➕ 205 F1 ✉ Fichtestr. 24 ☎ 030 6 93 01 01; www.lecochon.de 🕐 Tue–Sat 6pm–1am

Osteria No. 1 €€
Palm trees and natural stone, the smell of garlic and fresh fish, wailing toddlers and quick-fire Italian sentences… it's an extremely attractive combination that's perfect for dining out on a summer's evening between Bergmannstraße and the Viktoriapark. The *tageszeitung*, an alternative newspaper, was supposedly founded here.
➕ 204 B1 ✉ Kreuzbergstr. 71
☎ 030 7 86 91 62; www.osteria-uno.de
🕐 Daily noon–midnight

Pagode €

Lots of people wait in line for the Thai food here (collect it from the counter). A wide selection, good cooking and generous portions.

✚ 204 C1 ✉ Bergmannstr. 88
☎ 030 6 91 26 40; www.pagode.berlinasia.de
🕐 Daily noon–midnight

Sale e Tabacchi €–€€

A classy Italian restaurant with views of the Wall Museum. You can eat out in the idyllic walled garden in summer.

✚ 204 C3 ✉ Rudi-Dutschke-Str. 25
☎ 030 25 29 50 03; www.sale-e-tabacchi.de
🕐 Mon–Sun 10am–1am

Spindler & Klatt €€

A trendy club-restaurant in the factory building of a former bakery. A beautiful Spree terrace and pan-Asian cuisine await you early in the evening. The dancing kicks off later on.

✚ 206 B3 ✉ Köpenicker Str. 16–17
☎ 030 3 19 88 18 60; spindlerklatt.com
🕐 Sun–Thu from 6pm, Fri–Sat from 8pm, Club Fri–Sat from 11pm

Van Loon €–€€

This restaurant housed on a Dutch sailing barge dating from 1914 is moored on a jetty in the Landwehr canal. It also has a terrace on the river bank. You can order from a small standard menu or choose seasonal specialities.

✚ 205 E2 ✉ Urbanhafen, Carl-Herz-Ufer 5 (near Baerwaldbrücke bridge)
☎ 030 6 92 62 93; vanloon.de 🕐 9am–1am

Weltrestaurant Markthalle €–€€

This local institution serves as a kitchen, living room and workspace for many people. Unpretentious cooking in traditional surroundings with oak tables. Their *Sauerbraten* (pot roast) won fame through the film adaptation of Sven Regener's bestseller, *Berlin Blues*.

✚ 206 B3 ✉ Pücklerstr. 34
☎ 030 6 17 55 02; www.weltrestaurant-markthalle.de 🕐 Daily 10am–1am

Snacks from all over the world are sold in Kreuzberg. They're popular as a faster, cheaper alternative.

Mo's Kleiner Imbiss

The "King of Falafel" always serves his fare freshly made – be prepared to wait a little while for your food

✚ 205 F1 ✉ Graefestr. 9 🕐 Daily 1pm–11pm

Curry 36

Insider Tip

Loyal Kreuzberg sausage fans like to claim that this is the very best *Currywurst* to be found anywhere in Berlin.

✚ 204 C1 ✉ Mehringdamm 36
🕐 Daily 9am–5pm

Seerose

A very good selection for vegetarians in a hurry. Serves everything from salad to spinach lasagne.

✚ 205 E1 ✉ Körtestr. 38 🕐 Mon–Sat 10am-midnight, Sun noon–11pm

Where to...
Shop

If you take a stroll around Oranienstraße, you'll notice that it's home to a host of little specialist shops. You'll also find countless unusual stores selling a wealth of interesting goods between the Südstern and the Mehringdamm. Have an explore around Bergmannstraße and simply go wherever the wind takes you.

AROUND ORANIENSTRASSE

You can buy books, toys and gifts in **Lilofee** (Spreewaldplatz 4). **Groove Records** (Pücklerstr. 36) sells independent records along with world music and music of Black origin.

Kreuzberg

Ölkampagne (Leuschnerdamm 15) sells a range of top-quality olive oils. **Luzifer Now** (Oranienstr. 38) deals in clothing made from hemp and linen.

You can get your hair beautified until 8pm in the evening at **Basecut** (Oranienplatz 1), an apartment-style salon.

Alimentari i Vini (Skalitzer Str. 23) serves Italian cheese and sausages to peckish clients.

Weinhandlung Suff (Oranienstr. 200) sells wine and spirits. **Mondlicht** (Oranienstr. 14) has a variety of esoteric books. The women's collective **Kraut und Rüben** (Oranienstr. 15) stocks natural cosmetics alongside fruit, vegetables and dairy products.

Knofi (Oranienstr. 79) sells Mediterranean specialities; **Verrutschi** (Oranienstr. 180) carries Kreuzberg fashion; and **DIM** (Oranienstr. 26) offers attractive design – brushes from the workshop for the blind are their mainstay.

Kisch & Co (Oranienstr. 25) sells new and reduced-price books (out-of-print titles, misprints, etc.) and newspapers. **Kalligramm** (Oranienstr. 28) stocks antique books.

You can buy fresh rolls and eastern patisserie 24/7 at **Melek Pastanesi** (Oranienstr. 28).

Check out the jewellery at **Schmuck Fritz** (Dresdner Str. 20), the ceramics at **O-ton** (Oranienstr. 165a), and the literature (not all of it in Italian!) at **Dante Connection** (Oranienstr. 165).

AROUND BERGMANNSTRASSE

Kadó – authentic flavours (Graefestr. 20) sells special varieties of liquorice sourced from all over the world. They also make some themselves.

Games for babies, children and adults are piled high at **Spielbrett** (Körtestr. 27). You can try out hybrid bikes free of charge diagonally opposite at **Räderwerk** (Körtestr. 14).

British foods are sold at **Broken English** (Körtestr. 10).

Otherland (Bergmannstr. 25) stocks Science Fiction, Fantasy and Horror books. **Hammet** (Friesenstr. 27) only sells crime stories – they give great advice about what to read next.

Insider Tip

The **market hall** on Marheinekeplatz (Mon–Fri 8–8, Sat 8–6) sells French cheese, organic German bread, sophisticated wines, fresh juices, newspapers, etc.

Zeitlos! (Zossener Str. 36) is a shoe shop that crams a large selection into a small space.

Grober Unfug (Zossener Str. 33) sells German and international comics along with a large selection of posters, t-shirts and figurines. The shop stocks all the German comics available in print and a large selection from the UK, France and the USA. They also hold some temporary exhibitions.

Knopf-Paul (Zossener Str. 10) has become quite the tourist attraction in recent times with its vast selection of buttons, buckles, studs, eyelets, etc.

bagAge (Bergmannstr. 13) sells the last word in luggage. **Ararat** (Bergmannstr. 99) is a cult shop that stocks postcards, paper and various trendy gifts.

You'll find eastern-inspired fashion and home accessories at **Chapati-Design** (Bergmannstr. 99).

The attractively decorated **Knofi** (Bergmannstr. 99) sells antipasti and other Mediterranean delicacies. Their homemade cheese paste is particularly popular.

Logo (Nostizstr. 32) sells a whole range of second-hand records.

Belladonna (Bergmannstr. 101) stocks natural cosmetics.

Faster Pussycat! (Mehringdamm 57) has labels from Berlin and international designers.

Where to...
Go Out

THEATRE AND MUSIC

Ballhaus Naunynstraße (Naunynstr. 27, tel: 030 75 45 37 25 for programme information and tickets) is an authentic old Berlin Ball house dating from the nineteenth century. Today it provides a stage for migrant and post-migrant dance and musical theatre, concerts of modern and classical music, and intercultural events.

Set above the roofs of Kreuzberg, **BKA**, the "Berlin Cabaret Institute" is a renowned fringe theatre for all kinds of cabaret (Mehringdamm 34, tel: 030 2 02 20 07).

Die **C-Halle** (Columbiadamm 13–21, tel: 030 6 98 09 80) is *the* place for high-profile events in the city. This gigantic site on the border between Kreuzberg, Tempelhof and Neukölln used to boast a sports hall and a cinema for US forces. Since the army isn't there any more, it hosts big rock, pop and jazz concerts, festivals and techno parties today.

HAU – Hebbel am Ufer (Stresemannstr. 29, tel: 030 2 59 00 40) becomes a place of pilgrimage for dance lovers every year during its annual autumn festival. The art deco theatre is *the* stage for the experimental arts in the city. It predominantly hosts dance, music and performance art.

The **Passionskirche** church (1905–08) is often used for world music and jazz concerts (Marheinekeplatz, tel: 030 69 40 12 41). Abdullah Ibrahim and Ricky Lee Jones both performed here.

In 1980, nurse Irene Moessinger used her inheritance to buy a circus tent which was put up in the Tiergarten and called the

Tempodrom. Many well-known performers appeared there. The original tent has now given way to the Federal Chancellery, but the new Tempodrom, a cathedral of high-tech, puts on a varied programme (cabaret, concerts, art, major events) behind Anhalter station today.

If you feel like a swim at night, go to the saltwater **Liquidrom**. Musical accompaniment from classical to electro and jazz is provided in the evenings. Harp concerts sometimes take place on the edge of the pool (Möckernstr. 10, tel: 030 2 58 00 78 20, swimming Sun–Thu 10am–midnight, Fri–Sat 10am–1am).

The **Mehringhof Theater** (Gneisenaustr. 2a, tel: 030 6 91 50 99; www.mehringhoftheater.de) is known for its political cabaret evenings. Comedy and musical cabaret have also made their way onto the programme.

The **Ratibortheater** (Cuvrystr. 20a, tel: 030 6 18 61 99; www. ratibortheater.de) has been a successful improv theatre for a number of years.

Wild at Heart (Wiener Str. 20, 030 61 07 47 01; www.wildatheart berlin.de, daily from 8pm) is already a Kreuzberg legend. Hosts indie and punk concerts. DJs lay down their beats at the weekends.

CINEMAS

Film buffs will also find something to their taste in Kreuzberg. The **Eiszeitkino** (Zeughofstr. 20, tel: 030 61 16 01 60; www.eiszeitkino. de) has films for 🔧 kids and young people, movies in their original languages, an Israel film festival and Turkish cinema. They also put on sneak previews. The **fsk** (Segitzdamm 2, on Oranienplatz, tel: 030 6 14 24 64; www.home. snafu.de/fsk-kino) is another paradise for fans of the silver screen. This art house cinema has premieres, French and English movies and documentaries.

Kreuzberg

BARS AND PUBS

Insider Tip

Try to find a spot on the balcony over the Landwehr canal at **Ankerklause** (Kottbusser Damm 104, tel: 030 6 93 56 49, Tue–Sun 10am–4am, Mon from 4pm). You'll get some fresh air while hearing the tunes from the well-stocked juke-box inside. This neighbourhood bar was once a well-kept secret – it's now popular with visitors from all four corners of the world.

You can't miss **Möbel Olfe** (Dresdener Str., right by the pas-sage to Adalbertstr., tel: 030 61 65 96 12, Tue–Sun from 6pm) – it's lit up just as it used to be back in the days when it was a furniture shop. It's now a haunt of hard-drinking Kreuzbergers who enjoy vodka and Polish draught beer.

Located in an old Post Office, the **Privatclub** (Skalitzer Str. 85–86, tel: 030 61 67 59 62, Fri–Sat from 11pm, concerts from 7 or 8pm) is a relaxed hangout for concerts and parties.

Decorated all in red and gold, **Würgeengel** (Dresdener Str. 122, tel: 030 6 15 55 60, every day from 7pm) takes its name from a film by director Luis Buñuel. It's famous thanks to its range of fantastic cocktails.

Konrad Tönz (Falckensteinstr. 30, tel: 030 6 12 32 52) is a living room-style bar named after a presenter from a famous interactive crime-fighting TV show called "Aktenzeichen XY" ("Case Number XY") that first aired back in 1967. The show used to begin at 8.15pm, and that's when the evening kicks off here too (Tue–Sun) with music from an old record player.

Bar Nou (Bergmannstr. 104, tel: 030 74 07 30 50, daily from 8pm) is buzzing – cocktails have recently been accepted as part of the tra-ditionally beery Kreuzberg scene. The people here seem completely at ease with a sophisticated Daiquiri in their hand, anyway.

Madonna (Wiener Str. 22, tel: 030 6 11 69 43, daily from 3pm), is a true Kreuzberg legend. You can choose from 250 kinds of whisky under a ceiling decorated with the seven deadly sins.

Yorckschlösschen (Yorckstr. 15, tel: 030 2 15 80 70, Mon–Sat from 5pm, Sun from 11am) remains steadfastly the same as it always was: A jazz bar for old Kreuzbergers with a summer garden, down-to-earth cooking and a jazz brunch on Sundays.

Time has also forgotten **Junction Bar** (Gneisenaustr. 18, tel: 030 6 94 66 02, Sun–Thu from 9pm, Fri–Sat from 10pm) where you can hear live music in the cellar.

The **San Remo Upflamör** (Falckensteinstr. 46, tel: 030 74 07 30 88, daily from 2pm) changes from a café into a bar during the course of the day.

DANCING

SO36 (Oranienstr. 190, tel: 030 61 40 13 06) has an enticing and var-ied programme of bingo, karaoke, concerts, readings, discos, parties, panel discussions, benefit events and much, much more. Regular events include Café Fatal (a tea dance, Sun 7pm–1am), Kiez Bingo (every 2nd Tue, 7pm–1am), and Gayhane (a gay/lesbian party with a Turkish feel, 4th Sat of the month, 10pm).

Golgatha (Dudenstr. 40/entrance on Katzbachstr., tel: 030 7 85 24 53, Apr–Sep, daily from 9am) is a beer garden with a grill and cocktail bar hidden in Viktoriapark. DJs start spinning their discs from 10pm and play everything but hip hop.

The Spree almost laps onto the dance floor in **Watergate** (Falckensteinstr. 49a, tel: 030 61 28 03 94, Wed, Fri, Sat from mid-night). There are two bars over two floors. Only the best international DJs come here, mainly playing house, electro and techno.

Prenzlauer Berg & Friedrichshain

 **Little Treats**

The Cult of Karaoke
People love to belt out the hits every Sunday on the **Open Air Stage in the Mauerpark** (► 167).

An Artistic Dream
Wonderful **sound and light installations** in storerooms under the water tower enchant visitors in summer (www.singuhr.de).

An Enticing Beach Bar Across the Wall
Relax in a deck chair on the banks of the Spree after visiting the East Side Gallery (► 169).

Prenzlauer Berg & Friedrichshain

Getting Your Bearings

While Prenzlauer Berg is predominantly populated by well-off academics, Friedrichshain is full of students and young professionals living a subculture lifestyle with rising rents and lively nightlife. The density of bars, clubs and restaurants here must surely break some records. Despite their differences, the inhabitants of these two districts have a lot in common: They're all pursuing an alternative way of life. It's been that way here since the days of the GDR.

Schönhauser Allee

Gethsemane- **53**
kirche

Max-
Schmeling-
Halle

Schönhauser

Pappelallee

52 Mauerpark

Eberswalder Str.

Ebers-
walder
Str.

Dar

Kulturbrauerei

Kastanienallee
50

Kulturbrauerei
51

Kollwitz-
platz
47

Chodowiecki Str.

Allee

Jüdischer **49**
Friedhof

Senefelder-
platz

Kollwitz

Wasser
turm

Metzer Str.

The typical resident of Prenzlauer Berg works at one of the Federal agencies, designs successful wallpaper, lamps and fashion, or runs their own restaurant. By contrast, the average inhabitant of Friedrichshain gets up at 11am, treks over to uni, studies till 10 at night, and then heads off on a tour of the bars and clubs of their choice. The majority of the occupants of both districts have only recently moved in: Since the Wall came down, over half of the previous tenants have packed their bags, left their hometown and gone to settle down in terraced houses in the Berlin hinterland. The districts' new denizens have been busy procreating, however, so the play parks are full once again – for a few years, the birth rate in Prenzlauer Berg was one of the highest in Europe. Parents like to sit in the cafés round Kollwitzplatz while their offspring lay siege to the playground in the middle.

Exciting diversity: A market scene in Kollwitzplatz

Getting Your Bearings

The organic and flea markets on Boxhagener Platz regularly draw in crowds. That's when Berlin's young, stylish legions come out in force. Bold combinations of colourful skirts, pink sunglasses and parkas are ten a penny here, and fashion scouts will find inspiration by the bucket load. Even during the GDR era, Prenzlauer Berg was a haven of individualism and opposition. Gethsemane church was a meeting point for dissidents, and many of the district's formerly dilapidated houses were full of squatters making cool t-shirts and trousers that they sold illegally – even to people in the West.

Don't Miss

At Your Leisure

Ernst-Thälmann-Park

Str.

walder Str.

Arnswalder Platz

PRENZLAUER BERG

Knaackstr.

Kniprode-str.

Am Friedrichshain

Volkspark 54 Friedrichshain

Friedenstr.

Landsberger Allee

Platz der Vereinten Nationen

Friedenstr.

Friedhof der St.Georgen-Gemeinde

Petersburger Str.

Strausberger Platz

Weber-wiese

Karl-Marx-Allee

Bersarinplatz

Karl-Blumenstr.

Marx- **55** Allee

Frankfurter Tor

Petersburger Str.

Frankfurter Allee

FRIEDRICHSHAIN

Pariser Kommune

Boxhagener Str.

Samariterstr.

Wedekindstr.

Grün-

berger Str.

Str.

Boxhagener Platz 48

Ostbahnhof

Kopernikusstr.

Wühlischstr.

0 ___ 500 m
0 ___ 500 yd

Str. der

Mühlenstr.

56 East Side Gallery

Warschauer Str.

Warschauer Str.

Mediaspree 57

Rudolfplatz

Stralauer Allee

Spree

Prenzlauer Berg & Friedrichshain

The Perfect Day

You'll need to spend a whole day if you want to stroll through Prenzlauer Berg and Friedrichshain. Follow our itinerary and you won't miss any of the highlights. The individual sights are described in more detail in the following pages (► 162–169).

🕙 10:00

The wide selection selection of cafés round **47 Kollwitzplatz** (image above; ► 162) will mean you're spoilt for choice. If you want to visit a true Berlin institution, order your morning coffee at Anita Wronski (► 171). The cafés' terraces overlap each other here. Whole families gather in the square from 10am at weekends to enjoy a leisurely brunch.

🕦 11:30

Take a walk through the **49 Jewish Cemetery** (► 166) around ten minutes away on foot. It's the final resting place of painter Max Liebermann and the book and newspaper publisher Leopold Ullstein.

🕧 12:30

Now it's time for a stroll down **50 Kastanienallee** (image right; ► 166). Head over to Luxus International (► 173) and marvel at their outrageous hot water bottles and placemats adorned with images of the Fernsehturm. Then go to Thatchers (► 173) and try on some Berlin fashion.

🕐 13:30

Have a break in Café Manolo (▶ 171) and try one of their delicious fruit salads. Look out of the window and enjoy the fantastic view of one of the liveliest intersections in Berlin. A CD player on the wall equipped with headphones lets you to listen to tales of the city by Berlin authors.

🕐 14:00

The M10 tram will take you over to **54 Volkspark Friedrichshain** (▶ 168). Someone might invite you to join them for a spot of beach volleyball. Whatever happens, don't miss climbing up Trümmerberg hill. The pavilion with a beer garden in the middle of the park is a great spot for a refreshing drink.

🕐 15:00

Hop back on the M10 tram to Frankfurter Tor. That's where you'll find **55 Karl-Marx-Allee** (▶ 168), the most beautiful boulevard in east Berlin. Adorned with Moscow-style architecture, it measures in at 90m across! Walk on to **48 Boxhagener Platz** (▶ 164) and enjoy the lively, bustling streets boasting lots of little shops and cheap cafés.

🕐 17:00

It's now not far to the **56 East Side Gallery** (image above; ▶ 169). Ride the M10 tram to the last stop at Warschauer Brücke bridge and walk the last 500m or so on foot. The original, 1.3km (0.8mi)-long stretch of Wall here was was decorated after the fall of the Communist regime.

The grass behind the Wall is a great place to relax and wait for the sun to sink below the horizon.

If you fancy partying all night long, you'll find a whole load of bars and clubs at the RAW complex and on Revaler Straße.

⓸⓻ Kollwitzplatz

Perhaps it's the architectural unity here that makes this square so attractive to so many people. It doesn't take many rays of sun to entice folk out of the surrounding buildings and onto the terraces of cafés. Kollwitzplatz is the beating heart of Prenzlauer Berg.

The *Autonome Republik Utopia* ("Autonomous Republic of Utopia") was announced in Café Westphal at midnight on 2 October, 1990. It was, according to its founding declaration, "to become a home for all those who look reality in the eye and nevertheless refuse to give up hope for the future of humanity". This new form of citizenship was christened with kirsch-whisky, an invention from the GDR.

Lots of fancy shops have moved into Kollwitzplatz

Café Westphal no longer exists and the grungy chic of yesteryear has been ousted by western firms on behalf of wealthy clients. The shops now sell things to beautify the home, and pricey rents have driven sculptors, painters and photographers out of their studios. If you look up, you'll see that people have planted gardens on the new roof terraces. The only fixed point are the 🧗 kids climbing on the memorial to Käthe Kollwitz (1867–1945) as they have since 1959. The artist wouldn't have minded them scaling Gustav Seitz's bronze that's based on a self portrait from 1938.

KULTURINSEL

During the days of the GDR, anyone who was able left the ramshackle buildings of this densely populated workers' district and moved into modern prefab blocks of flats. Young people from all over the GDR were drawn here by the empty houses, however: They moved to the GDR capital without official permission and simply stayed. An unconventional counterculture gradually began to develop, with private concerts and readings held in apartments and backyards. Actors, painters, songwriters and students felt at home here and sympathised with the peace movement in the West.

KÄTHE KOLLWITZ

Wörther Platz was renamed in honour of the sculptor and artist Käthe Kollwitz back in 1947. She lived with her husband Karl – a doctor who cared for the poor – on the corner of Knaackstraße from 1892 to 1943. It was here that she found her inspiration. Kaiser Wilhelm II publicly denounced her work, and the Nazis forced her to resign from the Prussian Academy of Arts. Her house was bombed in 1943, and the couple moved to Moritzburg near Dresden, where Käthe died shortly before the end of the War.

The Kulturbrauerei (Culture Brewery)

Look through the arches of the four-storey brick house at Rykestraße 53 and you'll see a **synagogue** (1903–04) in the courtyard beyond. Only fear of the fire spreading to the neighbouring houses saved this place of worship from flames and fascist fury on "Kristallnacht" (9 November, 1938). It was used as a stable instead. Restored in 1953 and then reconsecrated, it's now Germany's largest synagogue.

The **water tower** on Windmühlenberg ("Windmill Hill") is the symbol of the district. Dozens of windmills were in operation here in the 18th and 19th centuries. Construction of the water tower – the first in the city – began in 1855. It started working in 1877, was shut down in 1952 and has been lived in ever since. The cellar of the tower's engine room was transformed into a notorious torture chamber by the Nazi SA in 1933.

TAKING A BREAK

There's no shortage of places to sit, eat and drink in and around Kollwitzplatz. You won't find any great difference between the various cafés.

✚ 201 F5 🚇 Senefelder Platz

INSIDER INFO

Every Saturday, the Kantinelesen ("Canteen Readings") are held in the **Alte Kantine** (Old Canteen) of the Kulturbrauerei (► 166). The stars of Berlin's many *Lesebühne* (reading stages) flock to perform their trendy texts (www.kantinenlesen.de).

48 Boxhagener Platz

Prenzlauer Berg has long been completely gentrified, and even Friedrichshain has also developed from being a lower income, studenty quarter into a neighbourhood for families and higher earners. Nevertheless, you can still party pretty hard here – check out Boxhagener Platz, Simon-Dach-Straße, Revaler Straße and the Ostkreuz.

The district's inhabitants gather for the weekly markets on Boxhagener Platz. Artists, young families, students and a growing number of well-to-do shoppers come to buy organic vegetables, chat with the cheese merchants and give a bit of change to the bottle-wielding tramps and alcoholics. Boxhagener Platz, lovingly known as "Boxi" to locals, is the heart of Friedrichshain. It's almost like a village square, where everyone's nice to each other, enjoys the sun on the terrace of one of the many cafés, and spends a bit of time with their neighbours. It's rare to see anyone in a hurry, and many residents have carved out a daily routine that starts at 10am at the very earliest and seldom finishes before 2 in the morning. More and more families are moving into the area, and the streets

Simon-Dach-Straße is a popular place to hang out

RURAL IDYLL

Boxhagen was still a village on the outskirts of Berlin 120 years ago. A country lane – today's Boxhagener Straße – passed through a collection of little houses. When industrialisation came to the area, more and more workers moved here to slave away in the nearby factories. Their houses, most of which still stand today, were built between 1900 and 1905. They were furnished simply to make them halfway affordable for the poor of the city. Boxhagener Platz was inaugurated in 1903. Boxhagen was part of the town of Lichtenberg until it was incorporated into Berlin in 1920.

HELENENHOF

Helenenhof, a housing complex for civil servants built between Holteistraße and Gryphiusstraße in 1904, is a nicely restored island in a sea of Imperial-era tenements. There's an almost park-like feel here between the magnificent buildings. It's named after Helene von Budde, wife of the Prussian President of DWM (German Weapons and Munitions). The shops, the day-care centre and the inhabitants of the 440 apartments lend it its own special flair today.

around the square are now home to a number of 🧸 toy shops.

Squatter's Row

The beautifully renovated buildings in Mainzer Straße might exude a friendly atmosphere today, but in 1990 they were the stage for one of the worst housing riots seen in Germany since the end of the Second World War. 4,000 police officers were mobilised to return the property to its original owners. The battle for the houses was fought brutally on both sides. At the height of the violent clashes, three warning shots were fired by a Berlin policeman while the 13 residential buildings were being evacuated.

Boxhagener Platz is a great place to relax in summer

TAKING A BREAK

Check out the lively **Szimpla Kaffeehaus Budapest** (► 172) which serves as a bar, a restaurant, a meeting place and a living room.

✚ 206, east of C4 🚇 Samariterstr.

INSIDER INFO

Torsten Schulz's exciting novel *A Square in East Berlin* tells the story of a childhood spent in this neighbourhood in the days of the GDR. It was made into a movie in 2009.

At Your Leisure

49 Jewish Cemetery

When it opened in 1828, this cemetery was located in an open field outside the city. The funeral corteges caused annoyance by delaying royal carriages making their way from the city palace to the regal summer residence. For that reason, a track known as the *Judengang* ("Jewish Path") was created round the back. It's barely visible today. More than five thousand people are buried here, including musician Giacomo Meyerbeer, publisher Leopold Ullstein and painter Max Liebermann, whose 1935 funeral was poorly attended because he had been outlawed by the National Socialists. Some pacifists hid here in late 1944, but they were caught and hanged shortly before the end of the war.

➕ 201, east of F4 ✉ Schönhauser Allee 22
🕐 Mon–Thu 8am–4pm, Fri till 1pm
🚇 Senefelder Platz

Gravestones covered in greenery

50 Kastanienallee

This hip boulevard draws in people from all over the city and all over the world. You'll be spoilt for choice here if you're on the hunt for Berlin fashion. Thatchers and Eisdieler (► 173) are just two of the labels that helped Berlin win the title of UNESCO City of Design. The countless cafés and bars between the clothes shops are perfectly placed for a break. The designer scene has long crept into neighbouring streets (e.g. Oderberger Straße).

There's a lively ambiance in the area's many watering holes at night.
➕ 201 E5
🚇 Rosenthaler Platz

51 Kulturbrauerei

This 25ha (6 acre) brick-built brewery complex between Schönhauser Allee and Knaackstraße is a city within a city. Designed by Franz Schwechten, Head of the Royal Planning Department and architect of the Kaiser-Wilhelm Memorial Church, it was built from 1890–1910 as the headquarters of the Schultheiss Brewery, which ran until 1967 (although they only did bottling for the last 20 years). The names of the brewery's astonishing array of departments are written

A section of Wall thick with spray paint

over the doors and gateways:
Heuboden (hayloft), *Sattlerei*
(saddlery), *Flaschenbier* (bottled
beer), *Böttcherwerkstatt* (coopers),
Stellmacherei (carriage works) and
Schlosserei (metalworkers).

The listed buildings started to
play host to cultural events in 1999.
Since then, the Kulturbrauerei has
become one of the best-loved venues in Berlin, boasting stages, a
multiplex cinema, restaurants and
a museum whose permanent exhibition is dedicated to "Daily Life
in the GDR". A great number of
documents and exhibits here deal
with various aspects of life in the
GDR, including the "economy of
scarcity", the Socialist regime's
mechanisms of power, collectivisa-
tion, and people's search for freedom by withdrawing into private life.

🚹 201 E/F5

✉ Knaackstr. 75–97/Schönhauser Allee 36–39

☎ 030 44 31 50; www.hdg.de

🏛 Museum in the Kulturbrauerei Tue–Sun
10–6pm (Thu till 8pm)

Ⓜ Eberswalder Str. 🎫 Free

52 Mauerpark

Oderberger Straße was long one
of the most neglected roads in the
city. After the Wall came down,
it was painfully obvious that it was
a dead end street in more ways
than one. In 2000, the Mauerpark
(Wall Park) was opened at the end
of the road on the site of the former
freight station through which the
Wall ran from 1961. A piece of
Hinterland Wall – an officially des-
ignated surface for graffiti artists –
still stands by the Friedrich-Ludwig-
Jahn Stadium as a reminder of
those times.

An ecological garden and a
🐷 children's farm have been
set up in the area to give it
some much-needed greenery.
A well-loved karaoke show   *Insider*
and a popular flea market   *Tip*
attract a lively crowd on Sundays.
You can buy wares by Berlin
designers alongside a whole host
of junk from private sellers. Plans
are afoot to build new residences
along park's edge over the next
few years.

🚹 201, north of E5 Ⓜ Eberswalder Str.

53 Gethsemanekirche

In the autumn of 1989, this evan-
gelical church became known
far beyond its parish borders.
Like the Nikolai Church in Leipzig,
it was Berlin's meeting place for

opponents of the regime. Built in 1893, the church – one of the largest places of worship in the city – was well-suited to large assemblies. In the weeks before the fall of the Wall, civil rights broadsheets were posted up on the walls, services of exhortation were held and prayers of intercession were said. Singer-songwriters who were forbidden from performing elsewhere found an audience here. Candles were lit in front of the entrance to show everyone the way. On the evening of 7 October, 1989, a brutal police operation put an end to the opposition's gatherings. It was here, however, that the Wall was first broken down just a month later (Bornholmer Straße, 9 November).

🕇 201, north of E5
✉ Stargarder Str.
🕑 Wed, Thu 5pm–7pm
🚇 Schönhauser Allee

54 Volkspark Friedrichshain

The oldest park in Berlin has been a local recreational area for the densely populated districts of Prenzlauer Berg and Friedrichshain since 1848. Adults and kids will never be bored with more than 40 beach volleyball courts, a public skate park and tennis facilities, and various 👫 playgrounds at their disposal. Lovers and pensioners meet at the Märchenbrunnen ("fairy-tale fountain") by the park's western entrance.

Its Grimm fairy-tale figures and balustrades covered in animal statues are pretty but kitschy. No visitor to the park should go without climbing through the thick trees to the top of the 78m (256ft)-high Trümmerberg hill. You won't see much up there, however – the trees are too high. The hospital in the south east of the park was opened in 1874. Run by famous doctor Rudolf Virchow, it was the first municipal infirmary in Berlin.

🕇 201, east of E4   🚋 Tram M5, 6, 8, 10

55 Karl-Marx-Allee

Measuring it at 90m (295ft) wide and lined with 9-storey buildings in a Moscow style, Karl-Marx-Allee is a great example of socialist architecture. Get out of the U-Bahn at Frankfurter Tor and walk

A close-up of the Märchenbrunnen

**Magnificent architecture in
Karl-Marx-Allee**

westwards to Strausberger Platz,
where two Art Deco Deco high-
rises frame the boulevard like
an old city gate. The domed towers on the buildings at Frankfurter
Tor were modelled on the
Gendarmenmarkt's cathedrals –
they're just as imposing as the
originals. The magnificent boulevard was built from 1952–60 by
labourers from the east of the city
in their spare time after work. To
thank them, many volunteers were
given apartments in these so-called
"Workers' Palaces". The East
German Uprising flared up near
the Weberwiese U-Bahn station in
1953, but was violently supressed
on 17 June of the same year.
➕ 206, A5–C5 🚇 Frankfurter Tor

56 East Side Gallery
In the autumn of 1990, 110 artists
from 24 countries turned this
1.3km (0.8mi) stretch of Wall –
which blocks the view of the river

Spree from Mühlenstraße on the
eastern bank – into an open-air
gallery. The East Side Gallery
still proudly displays the artists'
euphoric, international post-Wall
outpourings. Some images have
been freshened up and others have
been painted anew. The most
famous are the *Fraternal Kiss* by
Dimitri Vrubel, depicting Brezhnev
and Honecker locking lips, and
Birgit Kinder's *Trabi*, a car shown
smashing through the Wall.
➕ 206 B3–C3
🚇 Warschauer Str.

57 Mediaspree
If you look out east from
Oberbaumbrücke Bridge you'll
see what's known as "Mediaspree",
a controversial settlement of
media and communication companies (including MTV and the
Universal Music Group) located
on the banks of the Spree. The
extravagant architecture of the
nHow Hotel is also a remarkable
sight. Behind that is Oberbaum-City,
a place where light bulbs were
produced by OSRAM before the
war and by VEB Narva in the days
of the GDR. You'll find a business
district there today.
➕ 206 C3
🚇 Warschauer Str.

**The East Side Gallery: Adding colour
since the Wall came down**

Where to...
Eat and Drink

Prices
A main course without drinks:
€ under 12 euros   €€ 12–25 euros   €€€ over 25 euros

PRENZLAUER BERG: RESTAURANTS

Fleischerei €–€€

The honest home-style cooking here stands in contrast to the cool ambience of this former *Fleischerei* (butcher's shop). You'll be left smiling by such classic dishes as Berlin-style calf's liver, Brandenburg Pork Schnitzel and Beef Stroganoff. Customers sit on benches at bare tables or at countertops in the window with a view of Schönhauser Allee (perfect for single diners). No credit cards.

➕ 201 E4 ✉ Schönhauser Allee 8
☎ 030 50 18 21 17; www.fleischerei-berlin.com
🕙 Mon–Fri noon–3pm & 6.30pm–midnight, Sat–Sun 6.30pm–midnight

Gugelhof €€

Serves such hearty Alsatian specialities as *Flammkuchen* (a sort of thin pizza), *Käsefondue* (cheese fondue) and *Choucroute* (sausages with pickled cabbage). There's a terrace with a view of Kollwitzplatz in summer. Politicians often pop by – Clinton and Schröder ate here in 2000.

➕ 201 F5 ✉ Knaackstr. 37
☎ 030 4 42 92 29; www.gugelhof.de
🕙 Mon–Fri 4–11pm, Sat–Sun 10am–midnight

La Muse Gueule €–€€

François Delaunay has made down-to-earth French cooking a firm fixture of Prenzlauer Berg at this small, friendly bistro. He serves a daily selection of differing seasonal specialities. The cheese platter filled with warm goat's cheese is big enough for two.

➕ 201 F5 ✉ Sredzkistr. 14
☎ 030 43 20 65 96
🕙 Daily from 5.30pm; no credit cards

La Soupe Populaire €€–€€€   *Inside Tip*

For a change, Michelin-starred chef Tim Raue sometimes serves up such German classics as *Königsberger Klopse* (meatballs), *Eisbein vom Spanferkel* (pork knuckle) and *Brathering* (fried herring). Guests to the former Bötzow Brewery eat while admiring a gallery full of contemporary art.

➕ 201 F4 ✉ Prenzlauer Allee 242
☎ 030 44 31 96 80; www.lasoupepopulaire.de
🕙 Thu–Sat noon–midnight

Lucky Leek €€

Who said vegan restaurants can't be gourmet hotspots? Alongside the *plats du jour* fresh from the market, Lucky Leek also serves up a different menu every week and Sunday brunch.

➕ 201 F5 ✉ Kollwitzstr. 54
☎ 030 66 44 87 10; www.lucky-leek.de
🕙 Wed–Sun 6pm–11pm

Prater €

In 1862, a long way outside the city, there was a popular little inn called the Café Chantant. When the horse-tram came to the area in 1875, it suddenly became an attractive place to live and was quickly developed. In 1880, the inn grew to include a theatre, a concert hall and a buffet room. It also adopted its present name. Berliners came here with the whole family in their free time. It was also perfect for rousing speeches from

Trade Union leaders. Rosa Luxemburg spoke here, as did August Bebel. An open-air theatre was constructed in the garden in 1960, and the local cultural centre held dances here on Sundays. It all came to an end in 1991, but when an offshoot of the Volksbühne theatre later moved in, the inn and beer garden came to life once more. Sit down at the simple old tables and chairs and feast on good honest cooking. The beer garden is self-service.

➕ 201 E5 ✉ Kastanienallee 7–9
☎ 030 4 48 56 88 🕔 Inn, Mon–Sat from 6pm, Sun from noon; garden, Apr–Sept, daily from noon; no credit cards

Restauration 1900 €€

Although this eatery's name exaggerates its age, you wouldn't guess it from the furnishings. It's been a Kollwitzplatz institution since 1986, remaining unchanged while many others have come and gone all around. They serve lavish breakfasts and regional specialities. It's worth a visit any time of day.

➕ 201 F5 ✉ Husemannstr. 1
☎ 030 4 42 24 94; www.restauration-1900.de
🕔 Daily from 10am

The Bird €–€€

This mother of all burger joints looks like it's been airdropped into Berlin straight from New York City. The burgers here come fresh out of the meat grinder and are accompanied with homemade sauces. The menu also includes some juicy steaks.

➕ 201, north of E5 ✉ Am Falkplatz 5
☎ 030 51 05 32 83; www.thebirdinberlin.com
🕔 Mon–Thu 6pm–midnight, Fri 5pm–midnight, Sat–Sun noon–midnight; no credit cards

Weinstein €€

500 varieties of wine are the main attraction served at the benches of this very sociable eatery. The menu features classic and seasonal dishes, and many ingredients are locally sourced.

➕ 201, north of F5 ✉ Lychener Str. 33
☎ 030 4 41 18 42; www.weinstein.eu
🕔 Mon–Sat 5pm–2am, Sun from 6pm

PRENZLAUER BERG: SNACKS

Konnopke's Imbiss

Max Konnopke used to sell *Kartoffelpuffer* (potato fritters), fish fillets and sausages from 4.30am till 6.30pm at this stand that's been a Berlin institution since 1930. His granddaughter, Waltraud Ziervogel, is now a third-generation fryer. Try a *Currywurst* (curry sausage), the house speciality – they'll ask *"mit oder ohne?"* (with or without skin?). *"Ohne"* (without) is the most popular choice. The recipe is a family secret. Early risers can enjoy a *Bauernomelett* ("peasant" omelette).

Insider Tip

➕ 201, north of E5 ✉ Schönhauser Allee 44a/ under the overhead railway
🕔 Mon–Fri 9am–8pm, Sat 11.30am–8pm

PRENZLAUER BERG: CAFÉS

Anita Wronski

This café on Kollwitzplatz has gained a great many faithful friends with its famously large, inexpensive breakfasts. It's also worth checking out after 5pm, however. They serve a large selection of teas.

➕ 201 F5 ✉ Knaackstr. 26
☎ 030 4 42 84 83
🕔 Daily 9am–1am

Manolo

This French-style corner café uses its speciality coffees and WiFi connection to draw in people who like to do their work in public spaces.

➕ 201, north of E5
✉ Schönhauser Allee 45
☎ 030 24 62 79 58
🕔 Daily from 7am

Pasternak

Once you've deciphered the Cyrillic script, you'll see that they serve such typical Russian dishes as caviar, pancakes with curd cheese and *solyanka* (spicy ragout). You can also order a "Doctor Zhivago".

✚ 201 F5 ✉ Knaackstr. 22/24
☎ 030 4 41 33 99; www.restaurant-pasternak.de
🕐 Daily 9am–1am

FRIEDRICHSHAIN: RESTAURANTS

Papaya €

Thai cooking with a good reputation. You can watch them preparing the dishes – dominated by fresh spices and vegetables – at the open kitchen.

✚ 206, east of C4 ✉ Krossener Str. 11
☎ 030 29 77 12 31 🕐 Daily noon–11pm

Szimpla Kaffeehaus Budapest €

This cosy café decorated with old-fashioned furniture is a great place to relax with a cappuccino and a slice of cake. The substantial breakfasts are particularly popular at the weekend.

✚ 206, east of C4 ✉ Gärtnerstr. 15
☎ 030 66 30 85 23; www.szimpla.de
🕐 Sun–Mon 9am–midnight, Tue–Wed 9am–1am, Thu–Sat 9am–2am

Schneeweiß

Alpine cooking with crispy Wiener Schitzel, *Spätzle* (egg noodles) and goat's cheese. The totally white décor shows the veg and golden potatoes off to their fullest advantage.

✚ 206, east of C4 ✉ Simplonstr. 16
☎ 030 29 04 97 04; www.schneeweiss-berlin.de
🕐 Mon–Fri 6pm–1am, Sat–Sun 10am–1am

Vöner €

Run as a collective, Vöner is a popular spot to order vegan Döner kebabs, burgers and organic fries accompanied with tasty homemade garlic sauce.

✚ 206, east of C4 ✉ Boxhagener Str. 56
☎ 030 99 26 54 23 🕐 Daily noon–11pm

FRIEDRICHSHAIN: SNACKS

Frittiersalon

The large selection here includes hamburgers with cheese, chilli or bacon and a whole range of veggie burgers. The fries are hand made using organic potatoes.

✚ 206, east of C4 ✉ Boxhagener Str. 104
☎ 030 25 93 39 06 🕐 Daily 1pm–midnight

Nil Imbiss

Although this small Sudanese joint can't compete with its namesake river in terms of size (*Nil* means Nile in German), its central African cooking tastes wonderful. Treats include halloumi, Sudanese falafel and kofta.

✚ 206, east of C4 ✉ Grünbergerstr. 52
☎ 030 29 04 77 13; www.nil-imbiss.de
🕐 Daily 11am–midnight

FRIEDRICHSHAIN: CAFÉS

Café Sybille

A bright café on Berlin's most beautiful boulevard. The good selection of newspapers and cakes mean it's always full. There's a permanent exhibition with pictures of the construction of Karl-Marx-Allee.

✚ 206 B5 ✉ Karl-Marx-Allee 72
☎ 030 29 35 22 03 🕐 Mon–Fri 10am–8pm, Sat–Sun 11am–8pm

Café Übereck

One of the oldest neighbourhood cafés. People come for breakfasts and working lunches. The midday menu changes daily. There's a breakfast buffet from 9.30am–4pm on Sundays and holidays. Cocktails are served in the evening.

✚ 206, east of C4 ✉ Lenbachstr. 8
☎ 030 2 91 27 92 🕐 Daily 10am–2am

Kaufbar

Everything's for sale here – including the chairs! Don't miss out on enjoying one of their lattes, but be quick and drink up before someone buys the retro stool from under you or snaffles the cups. The bread rolls come from an organic bakery.

✚ 206, east of C4 ✉ Gärtnerstr. 4
☎ 030 29 77 88 25; www.kaufbar-berlin.de
🕐 Daily 10am–midnight

Where to...
Shop

Go shopping here after noon – or better still between 2pm and 7pm. Even if you find a notice saying *Bin gleich wieder da* ("Back Soon") on the door, try your luck all the same – some of the signs are never taken down.

PRENZLAUER BERG

Thatchers (Kastanienallee 21) sells avant-garde women's clothes. Young his and hers fashion from Scandinavia and Berlin is on sale next door at **Crème Fresh** (Kastanienallee 21). You can also buy shoes at reasonable prices.

Tabea Design (Schönhauser Allee 152) sell playfully erotic dresses, skirts and corsets. **JAAP** (Stargarder Str. 68) is known for its elegant made-to-measure evening and bridal wear. The shop's design, with its silver birches and a swing, should win an award.

Tausche Taschen (Raumerstr. 8) uses truck tarpaulins to make various types of bag. The "Schutzbefohlene" (family) model is perfect for parents – it even has space for nappies/diapers.

Fashion designer **Mane Lange** (Hagenauer Straße 13) makes corsets from velvet, silk, brocade and lace. You can buy club wear at **Le Gang** (Kastanienallee 65) and **Eisdieler** (Kastanienallee 12). Younger football fans will find outlandish t-shirts and team strips at **Jugendmode Fuck Fashion** (Schönhauser Allee 72b).

Meldestelle (Danziger Str. 1) sells the latest fashions – there are usually a lot of bargains.

Black Dog (Rodenbergstraße 9) sells nothing but American comic books.

Goldhahn & Sampson, a delicatessen on Helmholtzplatz (Dunkerstr. 9), holds cooking courses in the evening. Subjects include Turkish and Vietnamese cuisine. Find out more at www.goldhahnundsampson.de.

Luxus International (Kastanienallee 84) sells products by over 120 Berlin designers, ranging from funky bed sheets to old fashioned bicycle horns.

FRIEDRICHSHAIN

You can buy Berlin fashion at **Prachtmädchen** (Wühlischstr. 28) – check out the humorous cat collection by Emily the Strange.

Stiefelknecht (Wühlischstr. 27) next door will entice you in with its wide selection of good value shoes.

Olivia (Wühlischstr. 30) sells the very finest chocolates, biscuits and cakes. Take a break and enjoy them on the street terrace.

If you want something savoury, head to **Proviant** (Wühlischstr. 32) next door, where you can buy a Corsican ham or a good bottle of Mediterranean wine.

dazu (Kopernikusstr. 14) sells bags from the "IchIchIch" label's collection. They also have a selection of outrageous hats for men and women.

Such new and well-known Berlin fashion labels as mio animo, nikkes, and fux, the shop's own brand, are the centre of attention at **Heimspiel** (Niederbarnimstr. 8). Scandinavian labels like Modström also often feature on the clothes racks.

Tea's all the rage, and it's always worth paying a visit to the **Bohea Teehandlung** (Niederbarnimstr. 3). They sell a selection of over 300 varieties of yellow, green, black and white tea from all over the world. If you can't make up your mind, the friendly, competent staff are happy to help.

Where to...
Go Out

PRENZLAUER BERG

You can dance to Ostblock Rock and Singapore Sling at **8mm-Bar** (Schönhauser Allee 177b, tel: 030 40 50 06 24, Mon–Thu from 7pm, Fri from 8pm, Sat from 9pm).

August Fengler (Lychener Str. 11, tel: 030 44 35 66 40, daily from 7pm, events from 10pm, free entry) is a cosy neighbourhood bar with a small dance floor. The music ranges from New Wave to soul.

Bassy (Schönhauser Allee 176a, tel: 030 37 44 80 20; www.bassy-club.de, from 9pm) exclusively plays music from the 1960s – that means pretty much everything ranging from jazz and swing to rock and soul. A somewhat older crowd enjoys attending the venue's DJ parties and live concerts.

Tuesday is Hippy-Shake night at **Duncker** (Dunckerstr. 64, 030 4 45 95 09; www.dunckerclub.de, Mon from 9pm, Thu, Sun from 10pm, Fri–Sat from 11pm). This former GDR youth club presents bands and DJs with free entry every Thursday. A Dark Wave scene takes over on Mondays.

The Franz Club in the Kulturbrauerei has been kitted out in leather and given new name: **frannz** (Schönhauser Allee 36, tel: 030 72 62 79 30; www.frannz.com, party from 10pm).

If you want to play table tennis at midnight, head to **Dr. Pong** (Eberswalder Str. 21; www.drpong. net, Mon–Sat from 8pm, Sun from 6pm). DJs play their tracks while guests knock small white balls around the room. It's cool!

Le Croco Bleu (Prenzlauer Allee 242, tel: 0177 4 43 23 59, Thu–Sat from 6pm), a cocktail bar located in the engine room of the former Bötzow Brewery, serves elegant drinks in fairy-tale surroundings.

FRIEDRICHSHAIN

Techno fans will love going to **Berghain** (Am Wriezener Bahnhof, Fri–Sat from midnight), a great venue in a former power station with 18m (60ft)-high ceilings.

Classic cocktails and such daring new creations as the Jägermeister-based "Hubertus & Jade" are prepared and served beneath a gigantic chandelier in the **Chapel Bar** (Sonntagstr. 30; www.chapelberlin.com, every day from 6pm).

Located in a former Reich Railway Repair Works, the **RAW Tempel** (Revaler Str. 99, tel: 030 2 92 46 95, Tue, Thu from 8pm, Wed, Fri–Sun from 10pm) has regular readings as well as various themed parties at the weekends.

The grungily charming **Cassiopeia** (Revaler Str. 99; www.cassiopeia-berlin.de, tel: 030 47 38 59 49), an important part of the Berlin subculture, can also be found in the RAW complex. A relaxed, mixed crowd come here to enjoy parties and live acts playing a whole host of musical styles (events throughout the week).

Cool cocktails are served in **CSA** (Karl-Marx-Allee 96, tel: 030 29 04 47 41; www.csa-bar.de, daily from 8pm), a bar with a GDR architectural ambience. It meets the very highest of expectations – and not just in terms of its interior décor.

Salsa and Latin pop get guests on their feet at the **Cueva Buena Vista** restaurant (Andreasstr. 66, tel: 030 24 08 59 51, daily from 5pm, disco Fri–Sat from 10pm).

Lauschangriff (Rigaer Str. 103, tel: 030 42 21 96 26, Mon–Sat 9pm–6am) has two floors of booming electro beats at the weekend. Monday is reggae day.

Excursions

Excursions

All of these three locations are linked by the romance of the fabled "Sands of the Brandenburg March". For centuries, these idyllic natural and manmade areas were some of the ruling classes' favourite retreats. They've long been popular day trip destinations for people looking to escape the cold stone of the city.

Potsdam: Sanssouci

The name Sanssouci – which means "without a care" – conjures up the image of a Prince longing to put a bit of distance between himself and the burdens of ruling life. Potsdam is just 30km (18.5mi) away from the centre of Berlin, and few tourists miss the chance to visit this idyllic spot next to the river Havel. The park and the two palaces offer a degree of tranquillity and majesty you won't find in the capital itself.

Friedrich the Great's **summer palace** sits atop six vineyard terraces. The verdigris of the copper dome peeks out above a wide staircase of 132 steps, sandwiched between the blue of the sky and the green of the plants below. Stone figures draped in vines support the colourful rococo structure with ease. Measuring in at 97m (318ft) long and just 12m (40ft) high, the palace was designed by Friedrich himself and built from 1745 to 1747 by Georg Wenzeslaus von Knobelsdorff, the most prominent north German architect of his age. The 12 rooms are artistically decorated with gilt wood carving, reliefs, paintings, mirrors and inlaid floors.

Potsdam: Sanssouci

A star in Sanssouci Park

A Prussian Arcadia

Art historians have long puzzled over why Friedrich built a summer palace that was so small, impractical, old fashioned and unpretentious for its time. After all, he wasn't as thrifty as his father, the Soldier King (whose gout was popularly blamed on the palace's lack of a cellar – after all, wine that can't be stored must be drunk...). Perhaps the picture above the door in the concert room gives us a clue. It depicts a palace in a vineyard by a river, with boats, sheep… and a tomb with the inscription "Et in Arcadia ego".

The King didn't get the simple grave at Sanssouci he'd dreamt about and stipulated in his Will until 1991, however. Even then, the burial – his fifth in total – wasn't the modest affair he wanted: His remains were brought to Sanssouci from Hohenzollern Castle and given an elaborate state funeral. The 300ha (741 acre) park doesn't have any sheep, either – only statues arranged in artistically tamed natural surroundings.

Nature, Tamed

Sanssouci boasts one of Peter Joseph Lenné's most beautiful landscaped gardens. By walking just a few steps, you can enjoy a host of different views leading to two palaces, a church, a mill, a fountain and a ruin. Lenné called these linear views "lines of sight."

You should approach Sanssouci through the wrought iron Green Gate in the **Marlygarten**, the vegetable plot planted by Friedrich Wilhelm I and ironically named after Louis XIV's enormous gardens at Marly. Wilhelm's son Friedrich II was 32 and had ruled for 4 years when he created the Wüsten Berg vineyard terraces on the edge of these vegetable fields in 1744. This set off a veritable whirlwind of building. The **Friedenskirche** (Church of Peace, 1845–54), a columnar basilica with a bell tower and cloister, was designed by

A tea ceremony under golden palms

Excursions

Ludwig Persius. In true baroque style, the walls of one of the oldest art galleries in Europe, the **Bildergalerie** (Picture Gallery, 1755–63) next to the palace, are covered in baroque and Renaissance historical paintings. The **Neue Orangerie** (New Orangery, 1851–61) is reminiscent of an Italian Renaissance villa. It was built as a guesthouse for Tsar Nicholas and his wife, Friedrich Wilhelm IV's sister. Tropical and subtropical plants flourish in the Botanic Garden's greenhouses below the Orangery.

Pure Bravado – the Neues Palais

A path from the Orangery's upper terrace leads to the **Drachenhaus** (Dragon House, 1770–72), designed by Carl von Gontard in the then-popular Chinese style. It was home to the wine grower who tended the vines. The purely decorative **Chinesisches Teehaus** (Chinese Teahouse, 1754–56) across Maulbeerallee Avenue has a cloverleaf floor plan, a portico held up by golden palms, and a group of gleaming, life-sized gilt statues enjoying some tea and music. 18th-century porcelain is on show inside.

In the eyes of the public, the 240m-long, three winged, bombastically adorned **Neues Palais** (New Palace) plays second fiddle to Schloss Sanssouci. Friedrich wanted it to show the might of Prussia after the Seven Years' War (1763–69). It's hard to tell if the palace, cluttered with 400 sculptures and crammed with marble and shells, has more of a baroque or rococo style. Friedrich himself called it a "fanfare" – pure bravado made manifest in stone.

Before you leave, take some time to enjoy the greenery, the bubbling of the fountains and the twittering of the birds.

✉ Schloss Sanssouci
☎ 0331 9 69 42 00 🕐 Apr–Oct, Tue–Sun 10–6pm; Nov–Mar 10–5pm (Damenflügel/Ladies' Wing, May–Oct, Sat–Sun 10–6pm) 💶 €12 (Damenflügel €2), €19 ticket for one-time entry to all of Potsdam's palaces
Bildergalerie 🕐 May–Oct, Tue–Sun 10–6pm 💶 €6
New Chambers 🕐 Apr–Oct, Tue–Sun 10am–6pm 💶 €4
Historic Mill 🕐 Apr–Oct, 10am–6pm; Nov, Jan–Mar, Sat–Sun 10am–4pm 💶 €3
Orangery Palace 🕐 Apr Sat–Sun, 10–6pm; May–Oct, Tue–Sun, 10–6pm 💶 €4
Chinese House 🕐 May–Oct, Tue–Sun 10–6pm 💶 €2. Friedenskirche
🕐 May–Sep, Mon–Sat 10–6pm, Sun noon–6pm; Oct–Apr, Mon–Sat 11–4pm, Sun 11.30–4pm 💶 Free. New Palace 🕐 Apr–Oct, Wed–Mon 10am–6pm, Nov–Mar, Wed–Mon 10am–5pm 💶 €8. Schloss Charlottenhof 🕐 May–Oct, Tue–Sun 10am–6pm (only on a guided tour) 💶 €4. Roman Baths 🕐 Mid Apr–Oct, Tue–Sun 10am–6pm 💶 €5 🚉 Potsdam Hauptbahnhof 🚌 650 or 695

Rheinsberg

Complete with a palace, a park and a charming small town set in a landscape filled with lakes, Rheinsberg was the happiest place on earth for both the young Prince Friedrich – later known as Old Fritz – and for the famous German poet Kurt Tucholsky.

A statue of the young *Kronprinz* (Crown Prince) Fritz greets you when you arrive at the palace. His father, the strict Soldier King, gave him the building as a present, and Friedrich had it extended and furnished in a rococo style. He only lived here for four years (1736–40), but it's said that it was a very happy time. He had to move to Berlin when he became King.

Next to the beautiful **Grienericksee** (Lake Grienerick) you'll find sculptor Giovanni Antonio Cybei's marble statues (1766) of the god Apollo and the four elements – water, fire, earth and air – keeping watch over Rheinsberg Palace. Prince Heinrich, Friedrich's brother, was lord of the manor here until he passed away in 1802. He's interred in the pyramid tomb he had erected shortly before his death.

"The lake lapped in lazy wavelets against the reedy shore" – so wrote Kurt Tucholsky in his 1912 work, *Rheinsberg, a Storybook for Lovers*, bringing the lake and palace literary fame. Tucholsky's love story between his characters Wolfgang and Claire became a bestseller, and attracted a stream of visitors that shows no sign of stopping to this day. There's a memorial to the poet in the palace.

Schloss Rheinsberg
☎ 033931 72 60
🕐 Apr–Oct, Tue–Sun 10am–6pm; Nov–Mar, Tue–Sun 10–5pm 🎫 €8

The former palace of Friedrich and his brother Heinrich

Kurt Tucholsky Museum of Literature, Schloss Rheinsberg
☎ 033931 3 90 07 🕐 Tue–Sun 10am–5.30pm 🎫 €4

Directions: 85km (53mi) NW of Berlin. Take the A 24 (exit Neuruppin) or the B 96 to Gransee then take secondary roads. Regional trains travel from Berlin.

Buckow

The Märkische Schweiz Nature Park is a landscape of lakes and hills to the east of Berlin. It was once a favourite haunt of poets, and is still one of the most popular spots for city day trippers today.

Situated on the bank of Lake Schermützel, Buckow is both the centre and the pearl of the Märkische Schweiz. Berliners built villas here at the end of the 19th century, and people from East Berlin visited their holiday cottages in Buckow during the GDR era. Many poets, including Adelbert von Chamisso and Theodor Fontane, made thoughtful literary contributions to building up the area's reputation. Bertolt Brecht's summer residence from 1952 to 1956 – described in his journal as "a not inelegantly built cottage" – still stands here today. It's been a memorial since 1977.

You enter Brecht's house via a high, well-lit salon with a heavy wooden table and chests and benches from the 18th and 19th centuries. The black-stained floorboards in front of the hearth creak underfoot. Readings and musical performances are sometimes held here in summer. Brecht is said to have preferred working out in the boat house, which is now home to the covered wagon that pulled his wife, Helene Weigel, across the stage of the Berlin Ensemble in her role as *Mother Courage* for the very first time in 1949. Copper plaques display poems from Brecht's famous *Buckow Elegies*, which were written here in 1953.

Brecht-Weigel-Haus
✉ Bertolt-Brecht-Str. 30 ☎ 033433 4 67 🕐 Apr–Oct, Wed–Fri 1pm–5pm, Sat–Sun 1pm–6pm; Nov–Mar, Wed–Fri 10am–noon & 1pm–4pm, Sat–Sun 11am–4pm 💶 €3

Directions: 60km (37mi) E of Berlin, take the B 1. Train: Müncheberg; Bus 928

A memorial to "Mother Courage", Helene Weigel

Walks & Tours

1 FROM SPANDAU TO POTSDAM

Boat Tour

DISTANCE: c. 17km (10.5mi) **TIME:** 2.5 hours
START: Spandau Lindenufer (Stern und Kreis Schifffahrt,
tel: 030 5 36 36 00, noon–midnight. Apr, Thu, Sat; 5 May–4 Oct,
Mon, Wed, Fri, Sat (except holidays), €15.50
🚇 Rathaus Spandau **END:** Potsdam

If you miss out on taking a ride on a Dampfer (steam boat) in Berlin, you won't truly get to know the city. Seen from the water, the metropolis looks less severe and seems more relaxed, idyllic and sometimes even rural.

❶–❷

The trip begins on the **Lindenufer** at the edge of the attractive Altstadt Spandau (Spandau's old town). Spandau has been part of Berlin since 1920, but its low-rise houses and vast pedestrian zone lend it a more provincial atmosphere. The 15th-century **Gotisches Haus** (Gothic House), once home to a merchant, is the oldest preserved residential building in the city. The **St Nikolaikirche** (Church of St Nicholas) was where Elector Joachim II put an end to Catholicism and introduced Lutheran teachings to the territory in 1539. The town's fortifications once stood where the passenger ships to Wannsee and Potsdam depart from today. A little further north, the Spree flows quietly between industrial complexes

Tiefwerder: An idyllic place behind shipyards and a residential area

into the Havel before hitching a ride to the south.

2-3

The boat first travels round to the more industrial back of Spandau. You'll see the Südhafen (southern harbour) to your left. The idyllic former fishing port of **Tiefwerder** lies by the Unterhafen (lower harbour), a mix of shipyards and boat-houses, club buildings and apartment blocks. Tiny gardens with caravans or small summerhouses stand side by side all along the 4–5m (13–16ft)-wide branches of the river.

On the right-hand side after the bridge (over which Heerstraße runs),

you'll see a historic village inn amidst some awful 1960s residential blocks. Boats to suit every conceivable budget bob up and down in the enormous marinas. It's hard to believe that the first steamship built in Europe, the *Princess Charlotte of Prussia*, was launched here in September 1816.

3-4

Pichelswerder to your left was a wood-trading yard in the 18th cen-

tury and has been a popular day trip destination for 200 years. The inns here were once famous. Water sport clubs took over the area long ago, and on fine weekends it's as busy here as on the Ku'damm in central Berlin. The Havel grows wider at this point, and its various branches flow together. Looking back to the right, you'll see the particularly

TAKING A BREAK
If you're feeling a little bit peckish, you'll be pleased to know that some snacks and drinks are available for sale on the **boats**.

Walks & Tours

chic boats in **Scharfe Lanke**, the most famous of Spandau's bays. Its expensive moorings can be reached quickly and easily from Heerstraße. The German Life Saving Association's prominent diving tower is used by lifesavers practising in deep water.

4–5

To the right you'll see the **Weinmeisterhorn** where nuns grew vines in the Middle Ages. Around 35 years ago, the site – which served for decades as a shipyard for building and repairing barges – was converted into Berlin's first marina. Today, the Marina Lanke provides services for waterway users and a boat fuelling station.

According to legend, the **Schildhorn**, a promontory on the left, is where Albrecht the Bear defeated the Slavic Prince Jaczo in 1157. Rising up from the trees on Karlsberg hill (also left) is the **Grunewaldturm** (Grunewald Tower). It was a gift from Teltow (a district south of Berlin) to mark the

100th birthday of Kaiser Wilhelm I, after whom it was originally named. The white **Villa Lemm** to the right, which lies on the Gatow rowing route, was the seat of the British military governors until the early 1990s. In June every year, West Berliners enjoyed looking on as officers dressed in red and ladies in hats gathered on the manicured lawn to celebrate the birthday of their Queen. It belongs to a businessman today.

5–6

The beautiful **Schwanenwerder** peninsula beyond the sailing school and windsurfing club was praised as being "full of charm" in the 19th century by French novelist and Napoleonic officer, Henri Stendhal. It was known as "fat cat island" in Berlin after 1933: Joseph Goebbels and Hitler's architect Albert Speer both resided here. "Father of the Airlift" Lucius D. Clay lived on the peninsula after the Americans took control.

Strandbad Wannsee: Berlin's Lido

Ruins were in fashion when this little castle was built on Peacock Island

founded in 1822, later formed the basis of Berlin's Zoological Garden (► 131). Around 60 peacocks live on the quiet island today.

8–9

The Havel widens out to become the **Sacrower See** (Lake Sacrow) beyond the former East-West border. Where the houses stop here was where the "Death Strip" began. The **Heilandskirche** (Church of the Saviour) by the lake was inaccessible until the Wall came down. The basilica (1841–44), considered a prototype for the Friedenskirche (Church of Peace) at Sanssouci, was designed by Ludwig Persius.

9–10

The **Volkspark Klein-Glienicke** (People's Park) glides by on your left. Look for the columns of architect Karl Friedrich Schinkel's Casino. You'll also see his *Große Neugierde* (Great Curiosity), a teahouse with a view, before going under Glienecke Bridge connecting Berlin with Potsdam. New buildings stand out like a sore thumb in the idyllic old Prussian cultural landscape, robbing the scene of some of its beauty. Traffic roars past the **jetty in Potsdam** and seems incredibly loud at first.

6–7

The boat passes **Strandbad Wannsee** (Wannsee Lido) and anchors in **Wannsee**. The cool breeze up on deck suddenly dies away, and passengers have to board and disembark in the sweltering heat of the harbour. No sooner has the boat set off than it becomes pleasantly cool once again.

7–8

The next stop is **Pfaueninsel** (Peacock Island). If you want to visit it, you'll have to transfer to a ferry. At 98ha (237 acres) in size, this "Pearl of the Havel" became famous as the secret love nest of Friedrich Wilhelm (Prussian Crown Prince and nephew of Friedrich II) and Wilhelmine Enke, whom he later made Countess of Lichtenau and who bore him 5 children. He died in her arms in 1797. The Countess is said to have inspired and furnished the island's small, fashionably ruined castle. Peter Joseph Lenné designed the landscaped park here at the start of the nineteenth century. The animals of the exotic menagerie,

A lion fountain in the park at Schloss Klein-Glienicke

2 THROUGH KÖPENICK
Walk

DISTANCE: 2km (1.4mi) **TIME:** 1.5 hours
Start: Köpenick Town Hall 🚋 Köpenick, Tram 61, 62
END: Gartenstraße river beach

A robbery and a "daring escapade" made Köpenick famous 100 years ago. Berlin's southeasternmost district is a beautiful place, boasting waterways, chains of hills, woods and a heath landscape. Take a walk through the Old Town and you'll feel like you're visiting the countryside.

❶–❷

Köpenick gained international notoriety in 1906 thanks to the "Captain of Köpenick", a shoemaker dressed in uniform who arrested the mayor with a few soldiers and "dispatched" him to Berlin with his wife. He then seized the town's treasury and headed off to the capital himself. The escapade is recorded in the files at the police headquarters and is also told in Carl Zuckmayer's well-known play, the *Captain of Köpenick*, performed for the first

> **TAKING A BREAK**
> Go to the "Krokodil" **Flussbadeanstalt** (river beach), grab a drink and admire the view of Palace Island.

time in 1931. Berliners still jostle for a seat when it appears at a theatre nowadays. The **Backsteinrathaus** (Brick Town Hall) was just a year old at that time – it still stands today. A permanent exhibition documents the episode, and a bronze statue of the counterfeit captain stands out front.

❷–❸

The island on which Köpenick's idyllic old town stands is buffeted by traffic. Henriette Lustig – the washerwoman whose likeness you'll see on a washboard-wielding monument in front of the palace on the Frauentog – lived at **Alter Markt 4**. You'll spot renovated colonial houses if you head to **Katzengraben**: No. 6 dates back to 1683, and No. 11 was remodelled as early as 1869.

The Electoral Prince had the ground raised and built houses for 70 Huguenots in Freiheit street at the end of the 17th century. The street was named **Freiheit** ("Freedom") because its residents were not subject to tax. When the bus drove here from the New District to the Old Town in the GDR era, this stop was called out as usual. Sometimes the

In front of Köpenick Town Hall

driver would shout "Freedom for everyone!" – pause – "who wants to get off here!" It was pretty daring, and not everyone smiled…

3–4

The entrance to the **Schlossinsel** (Palace Island) is found opposite Alt-Köpenick street. The site was previously home to Slavic ramparts and a 12th-century fort. The island's current baroque palace was commissioned by Elector Friedrich Wilhelm for his son Friedrich III. He moved to Berlin after his father's death, however, and the palace remained unfinished. What you see today is just the right wing of the planned building. Following renovation work, an arts and crafts museum (▶ 110) has taken residence here with its valuable collection of rococo, baroque and Renaissance work.

The last river beach in Berlin

4–5

The route leads past the Frauentog (a bay in the Dahme river) to **Kietz**, a fishing settlement that's mentioned as far back as 1209. It boasts rough cobbles and small, attractively renovated houses with decorated doors and eaves, some of which bear the emblems of guilds. There's been a **Flussbadeanstalt** (river beach) at Gartenstraße 5 since 1877. You can rent a canoe here or cool off by jumping into the Dahme.

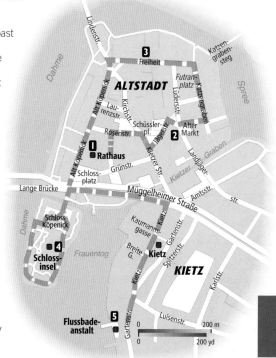

3 ALONG THE WALL TRAIL
Cycle Tour

DISTANCE: 7km (4mi) (Bike Hire ➤ 40)   **TIME:** 1.5 hours
START: Potsdamer Platz ✚ 200 A1 🚇 Potsdamer Platz
END: Oberbaumbrücke bridge ✚ 206 C3 🚇 Warschauer Straße

The Wall ran for 160km (99mi) around West Berlin, but even Berliners often don't recall where it stood. Although more than 25 years have passed since the bulwark dividing East from West was torn down, you'll still recognise the border in places. The position of 43.1km (27mi) of Wall are marked out with cobblestones in the city centre. You'll also see it breaking up the greenery on the outskirts of town. This tour runs along the most interesting section of the Mauerweg (Wall Trail).

TAKING A BREAK
There are numerous cafés around Checkpoint Charlie where you can stop to take a break.

and Köthener Straße. The cycle route follows the west side of **Stresemannstraße**, which lay in the border zone. The Hinterland

❶–❷
The route begins at **Potsdamer Platz** (➤ 101–118). Several segments of the Wall have been kept in front of the Ritz-Carlton Hotel. A double row of cobblestones marks the Wall's path on the corner of Stresemann Straße

Wall stood on the east side of the street. Three of its original segments, presented to former

POTSDAMER PLATZ
Potsdamer Platz was the most traffic-intensive intersection in the city up until World War II. It was destroyed by bombs in 1943 – the Weinhaus Huth, a modern steel frame construction built in 1912, was the only building to withstand the barrage of attacks. It was later due for demolition to make way for a city highway, but this was never built. A flea market was held here for some time after the Wall came down. Today, Potsdamer Platz is a new centre for a reunified Berlin. You'll find shopping malls and offices (➤ 102) on the former site of Potsdamer Bahnhof station, from where Prussia's first rail route (to Potsdam) ran from 1838.

The start of the Wall Trail

UN Secretary General Kofi Annan by the Berlin Senate, have been erected in front of the UN building

1899 to 1934. It was also used for meetings of Otto Grotewohl's first GDR government. The Stasi (secret police) also installed listening devices on the roof to intercept radio communication from West Berlin.

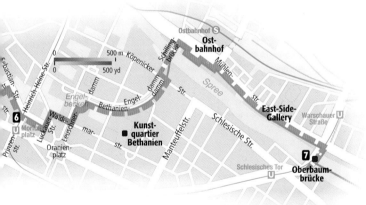

in New York. It's worth making a short detour into **Erna-Berger-Straße**, where you'll find one of the few remaining watchtowers.

The first session of Berlin's House of Representatives took place here on 29 April, 1993.

2–3

The Wall continued into Niederkirchnerstraße and past the **Martin-Gropius-Bau** (➤ 189). Opposite (over the other side of the Wall) is the **Preußischer Landtag**, the seat of the Prussian parliament from

3–4

A 200m (656ft)-long stretch of the **Berlin Wall** runs directly by the Martin-Gropius-Bau. Right behind it – in the former grounds of the Prinz Albrecht Palace – was where the SS, the Gestapo and the

Once a warning, now a memorial to the border in Berlin

Ministry of Reich Security were located in the Nazi era. The "Topography of Terror" exhibition (➤ 115) documents this period today. A sign at the intersection of Wilhelmstraße and Zimmerstraße points out the Nazi's Ministry of Aviation (1935–6) where the GDR was founded in 1949. It's now home to the **Ministry of Finance**. The frieze of marching workers (1952) is made of Meissen porcelain. In 2001, Wolfgang Rüppel contrasted this image with a 24m (79ft)-long artwork sunk into the ground in memory of the People's Revolt of 17 June, 1953.

4–5

The border's former route is marked with cobbles in Zimmerstraße. The "border crossing for foreigners" – **Checkpoint Charlie** (➤ 165) – was located at the corner of Friedrichstraße nearby. The memorial in front of Zimmerstraße 26 is dedicated to Peter Fechter who was shot in August 1962 as he tried to escape to the West. A colourful

new housing block (1994–6) was designed for **Charlottenstraße** and **Markgrafenstraße** by architect Aldo Rossi. Border policeman Reinhold Huhn was shot by a collaborator in June 1962 as he tried to stop people escaping to the West through a tunnel. The GDR renamed a nearby street "Schützenstraße" (Marksman Street) in honour of this "Socialist Hero".

5–6

In 1966, publisher Axel Springer had his **publishing house** built right next to the Wall in Kreuzberg to show how much he believed in reunification. The part of Lindenstraße on which it stands was renamed Axel-Springer-Straße in 1995, 10 years after his death. The Wall trail cobbles turn into Kommandantenstraße and behind the school (which lay in the East) at the end of Alexandrinenstraße. The residents of Sebastianstraße could see nothing but Wall for 28 years. The **Heinrich-Heine-Straße Border Crossing** for German citizens lay at the intersection with Prinzenstraße. There's an installation about it in the U-Bahn tunnel.

6–7

Follow the cobblestones to the junction of Waldemar Straße and Luckauer Straße, go over the Luisenstädtischer Canal, turn left into Leuschnerdamm and head past the Kreuzberg 👬 Kid's Farm en route to Engelbecken pond. The Wall ran along Bethaniendamm behind the **Kunstquartier Bethanien** (Bethanian Art Quarter; ➤ 151). Cross Köpenicker Straße and the **Schillingbrücke** bridge to Friedrichshain, where the Wall and the border ran along opposite sides of the Spree. Pass Ostbahnhof station on Mühlenstraße to get to the **East Side Gallery** (➤ 169) and the former **Oberbaumbrücke Crossing for West Berliners**.

Practicalities

Practicalities

WHAT YOU NEED

	● Required ○ Suggested ▲ Not required	Some countries require a passport to remain valid for a minimum period (usually at least six months) beyond the date of entry – check beforehand.	UK	USA	Canada	Australia	Ireland	Netherlands
Passport/National Identity Card			●	●	●	●	●	●
Visa (regulations can change – check before booking)			▲	▲	▲	▲	▲	▲
Onward or Return Ticket			▲	●	●	●	▲	▲
Health Inoculations (tetanus and polio)			▲	▲	▲	▲	▲	▲
Health Documentation (► 196, Health)			●	▲	▲	▲	●	●
Travel Insurance			○	○	○	○	○	○
Driving Licence (national)			●	●	●	●	●	●
Car Insurance Certificate			●	●	●	●	●	●
Car Registration Document			●	●	●	●	●	●

WHEN TO GO

High season   Low season

JAN	FEB	MAR	APRIL	MAY	JUNE	JULY	AUG	SEP	OCT	NOV	DEC
2°C	3°C	8°C	13°C	19°C	22°C	24°C	23°C	19°C	13°C	7°C	3°C
36°F	37°F	46°F	55°F	66°F	72°F	75°F	73°F	66°F	55°F	45°F	37°F

☀ Sun   ☁ Cloud   🌤 Sun/Showers

The temperatures indicated are the average **daytime temperatures** in the respective months. The **most pleasant time to visit** Berlin is from May to September. Berlin is a summer city: It offers a wealth of events and exhibits the flair usually associated with places in more southerly latitudes during the warmer months. Nevertheless, the city also has an abundance of cultural attractions that entice people to visit during the autumn and winter. The dry cold, which is sometimes cutting and gets right through to your bones, can be avoided by taking shelter in the city's museums and restaurants – Berlin is attracting an increasing number of visitors around Christmas and New Year as a result. The Easter holidays are also a popular time to visit.

GETTING ADVANCE INFORMATION

Websites
■ www.berlin.de
■ www.visitberlin.de

GETTING THERE

By Air: Berlin has air links with 165 cities in 48 countries. Passengers from the USA, Germany and Western Europe land at **Tegel** (TXL). Flights from Eastern Europe, Asia and most charter flights go to **Schönefeld** (SXF).

Prices: Domestic German flights are relatively cheap if they are booked in advance. The same is true of flights from some European countries. Ask the airline directly, visit a travel agent or check out what's on offer on the Internet.

By Train: Berlin can be reached from all directions on IC, ICE and EuroCity trains. The Hauptbahnhof (Central Station) is the largest in Europe. The eastern inner city can be accessed via the **Ostbahnhof** at Straße der Pariser Kommune 5 in Friedrichshain. Some trains from the east terminate at **Bahnhof Lichtenberg** at Weitlingstraße 22. Train services to and from Hamburg often make use of **Bahnhof Spandau** found on Seegefelder Straße.

By Car: Autobahns (motorways) run to Berlin from Hamburg and Rostock (A 24), Hannover (A 2), Munich via Leipzig (A 9), from Dresden (A 13), Frankfurt/Oder (A 12) and Stettin (A 11). Exits on the Berliner Ring road lead to the city's individual districts.

CUSTOMS / IMMIGRATION

EU citizens may import and export goods for their personal use tax-free (800 cigarettes, 90L of wine). The duty-free limits for non-EU citizens are: 50g perfume, 2L of wine, 1L of spirits and 200 cigarettes. Non-EU citizens require a visa (valid up to 90 days) or a residence or settlement permit.

TIME

Berlin lies within the Central European time zone (CET), i.e. one hour ahead of Greenwich Mean Time (GMT). Clocks are adjusted forwards one hour for summer time in March (GMT+1). They're put back again in October.

CURRENCY & FOREIGN EXCHANGE

Currency: The official abbreviation for the euro is EUR. Euro notes are available in denominations of €5, €10, €20, €50, €100, €200 and €500. Coins come in 1 and 2 euros and 50, 20, 10, 5, 2 and 1 cents.

An **exchange rate calculator** is available for various currencies on the Internet: www.oanda.com.

ATMs: Cash machines (ATMs) are found all over the city.

Credit cards are accepted in larger hotels, restaurants and shops.

Blocked Credit/Debit cards: Have the emergency number of your bank handy just in case your credit or debit card is blocked while you're abroad – banks sometimes view spending away from home as suspicious activity. To help prevent this from happening, you can contact most banks ahead of time to let them know the dates of your trip.

GERMAN NATIONAL TOURIST OFFICE: www.germany.travel

In the UK
60 Buckingham Palace Road
London SW1W 0AH
☎ 020/7317-0908

In the US
122 East 42nd Street, 52nd Floor
New York, NY 10168
☎ 800-651-7010

In Canada
480 University Avenue
Toronto, Ontario M5G 1V2
☎ 416/968-1685

Practicalities

WHEN YOU ARE THERE

NATIONAL HOLIDAYS

1 January	New Year's Day
March/April	Good Friday,
	Easter Sunday/Monday
1 May	Labour Day
May/June	Ascension Day, Pentecost
3 October	The Day of German Unity
24 December	Christmas Eve
25/26 December	Christmas
31 December	New Year's Eve

ELECTRICITY

 The power supply in Germany is 220 volts. Travellers from outside continental Europe should use an adaptor.

OPENING HOURS

○ Shops   ● Museums/Monuments   ● Pharmacies
● Offices   ● Post offices   ● Banks

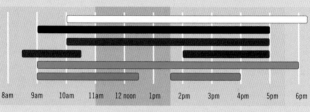

8am 9am 10am 11am 12 noon 1pm 2pm 3pm 4pm 5pm 6pm

☐ Daytime   ■ Midday   ☐ Evening

Shops: Most shops are open Monday to Saturday, 10am–8pm. Unusually for Germany, however, Berlin's shops are actually allowed to open round the clock from Monday to Saturday. Shops catering to various tourist needs can also open on Sundays.
Banks: Banks and *Sparkassen* (Savings Banks) are usually open Mon–Fri from 9am till 2pm or 3pm and until 6pm one day a week. Some also open Saturday morning.
Museums: Almost all museums open Tue–Sun, 10am–6pm. Some state museums open until 8pm on Thursdays. Museums that open on Mondays close on Tuesdays instead.

TIPS/GRATUITIES

People generally round up bills for restaurants, drinks and taxis.
If in doubt, you won't go wrong if you tip 10%.

Hotel Porters	€1–€2 per bag	Tour Guides	at own discretion
Housekeeping (hotels, etc.)	€1–€2 per day	Toilets	50 cents

TIME DIFFERENCES

Berlin (CET)
12 noon

 ←
London (GMT)
11am

 ←
New York (ET)
6am

 ←
Los Angeles (PT)
3am

 →
Sydney (AEST)
8pm

STAYING IN TOUCH

Post You'll find post offices in all city districts. Branches have been set up in many stationery shops and supermarkets, etc., where you can buy stamps, send letters,  small packages and parcels, and withdraw money. The branch right next to the Friedrichstraße U-Bahn is open until 10pm. It's also open on Sundays and public holidays.

Public telephones There are still two different sorts of public phone box in Berlin – traditional yellow enclosed boxes and open pink-and-grey booths. Almost all require a *Telefonkarte* (telephone card), available at post offices, stationery shops and newsagents. For overseas calls, dial the country code followed by the number (omit the first "0" from the area code.)

International Dialling Codes:

United Kingdom:	0044
Republic of Ireland:	00353
USA/Canada:	001
Australia:	0061

Mobile phones Making local calls and phoning other European countries is no longer very expensive for EU visitors thanks to European roaming tariffs. Check the prices and T&Cs with your operator in advance. Costs may be higher for non-European travellers. Network providers in Germany include E-Plus, O2, Vodafone and T-Mobile. There's great reception all over the city.

WiFi and Internet Berlin doesn't have a free, city-wide WiFi network. You can nevertheless get online free of charge in many cafés. Hotels, hostels and guesthouses generally also offer free Internet access – many even make computers available for guests to use.

PERSONAL SAFETY

Berlin is a relatively safe city for tourists. Small-scale criminal activity is limited to very busy areas such as Breitscheidplatz and Bus Route 100, which are often frequented by pickpockets.

- Drivers needn't be alarmed by the young people waiting at traffic lights. They wash windscreens for 1 euro. You're most likely to see them at the Großer Stern or at Kreuzberg intersections.
- Empty S-Bahn trains heading towards the east at night have occasionally witnessed scenes of racist behaviour.
- Avoid going into such parks as Hasenheide Park at night – drug dealers operate there.

Police assistance:
☎ 110 from any phone

☎	EMERGENCY	110
	POLICE	110
	FIRE, AMBULANCE	112
	POISON EMERGENCIES	1 9240

Practicalities

HEALTH

 Insurance: In case you have to see a doctor, it's recommended that Non-EU visitors obtain special travel health insurance. You'll find doctors' addresses in telephone directories' yellow pages. For emergency on-call doctors (Ärtzlicher Bereitschaftsdienst) call 030 31 00 31.

 Dental services: Dental treatments for non-German visitors can be expensive. Patients are given a bill which can be claimed against health insurance on arrival back home. For the emergency dental service *(Zahnärztlicher Bereitschaftsdienst)* call 030 89 00 43 33.

 Weather: Berlin can be hot in the middle of summer. Protect yourself against the sun and drink plenty of fluids.

 Drugs: There are numerous pharmacies *(Apotheke)* in Berlin selling prescription and non-prescription drugs, homeopathic remedies, medicinal herbs and drugstore products.

 Safe water: All tap/faucet water is readily drinkable. The water from historic green pumps should not be consumed.

TRAVELLING WITH A DISABILITY

Lifts and ramps for easy access to platforms are installed at 67 U-Bahn and 120 S-Bahn stations (marked out on the BVG transport network maps). More than 100 routes have buses with lowerable access ramps. Low-floored trams with ramps that can be lowered to the ground run on 14 routes. Vehicles for visitors with disabilities are identified on timetables.

CHILDREN

Children's theatres, cinemas, farms and events for kids in museums are all commonplace in Berlin. Special kids' attractions are marked out in this book with the logo shown above.

CONCESSIONS

Concessions for **entry tickets** are usually only granted to German residents who are unemployed, students, welfare recipients, soldiers, trainees or who have severe disabilities. ID is required.
The **Berliner Museumspass** (Berlin Museum Pass) lets you see all the permanent exhibitions at state museums that are part of the Preußischer Kulturbesitz (► 84). **Kids and young people** up to the age of 18 get into state museums free.
The **WelcomeCard** and the **CityTourCard** both allow you to make unlimited journeys on public transport and enjoy discounts for numerous sights in the city for a pre-determined period of time.

PUBLIC LAVATORIES

There are often toilets at the major sights. Some green street pavilions (urinals) still exist.

LOST & FOUND

Central Office: Platz der Luftbrücke 6, tel: 030 9 02 77 31 01. **BVG** (Transport): Potsdamer Str. 182, tel: 030 1 94 49.

EMBASSIES AND CONSULATES

UK
☎ 030 20 45 70
www.ukingermany.
fco.gov.uk

USA
☎ 030 8 30 50
germany.usembassy.gov

Ireland
☎ 030 22 07 20
www.dfa.ie/irish-embassy/Germany

Canada
☎ 030 20 31 20
www.canadainternational.
gc.ca

Useful Words and Phrases

You'll often see the German "sharp S" (ß) in words like Straße (street) etc. on signs throughout the city. It's pronounced (and also frequently written) as a double 'ss'. Str. is an abbreviation of Straße. In German addresses, the house number comes after the name of the street (e.g. Musterstraße 12/Musterstr. 12). The following German terms have been used throughout this book:

U-Bahn underground railway (subway)
S-Bahn overground (often overhead) local and regional railway
Bahnhof railway station
Reichstag the Federal German Parliament

SURVIVAL PHRASES

Yes/no **Ja/nein**
Good morning **Guten Morgen**
Good afternoon **Guten Tag**
Good evening **Guten Abend**
Goodbye **Auf Wiedersehen**
How are you? **Wie geht es Ihnen?**
You're welcome **Bitte schön**
Please **Bitte**
Thank you **Danke**
Excuse me **Entschuldigung**
I'm sorry **Es tut mir Leid**
Do you have…? **Haben Sie…?**
I'd like… **Ich möchte…**
How much is that? **Was kostet das?**
I don't understand **Ich verstehe nicht**
Do you speak English?
   Sprechen Sie Englisch?
Open **Geöffnet**
Closed **Geschlossen**
Push/pull **Drücken/Ziehen**
Women's lavatory **Damen**
Men's lavatory **Herren**

OTHER USEFUL WORDS & PHRASES

Yesterday **Gestern**
Today **Heute**
Tomorrow **Morgen**
Could you call a doctor please?
   Könnten Sie bitte einen Arzt rufen?

Do you have a vacant room?
   Haben Sie ein Zimmer frei?
   with a bath/shower **mit Bad/Dusche**
Single room **Das Einzelzimmer**
Double room **Das Doppelzimmer**
One/two nights **Eine Nacht/Zwei Nächte**
How much per night? **Was kostet es pro Nacht?**

DIRECTIONS & GETTING AROUND

Where is…? **Wo ist…?**
   the train/bus station **die Bahnhof/Busbahnhof**
   the bank **die Bank**
Where are the nearest toilets? **Wo sind die nächsten Toiletten?**
Turn left/right **Biegen Sie links ab/rechts ab**
Go straight on **Gehen Sie geradeaus**
Here/there **Hier/da**
North **Nord**
East **Ost**
South **Süd**
West **West**

DAYS OF THE WEEK

Monday **Montag**
Tuesday **Dienstag**
Wednesday **Mittwoch**
Thursday **Donnerstag**
Friday **Freitag**
Saturday **Samstag**
Sunday **Sonntag**

NUMBERS

1	eins	12	zwölf	30	dreißig	102 ein hundert zwei
2	zwei	13	dreizehn	31	einunddreißig	200 zwei hundert
3	drei	14	vierzehn	32	zweiunddreißig	300 drei hundert
4	vier	15	fünfzehn	40	vierzig	400 vier hundert
5	fünf	16	sechszehn	50	fünfzig	500 fünf hundert
6	sechs	17	siebzehn	60	sechszig	600 sechs hundert
7	sieben	18	achtzehn	70	siebzig	700 sieben hundert
8	acht	19	neunzehn	80	achtzig	800 acht hundert
9	neun	20	zwanzig	90	neunzig	900 neun hundert
10	zehn	21	einundzwanzig	100	ein hundert	1,000 tausend
11	elf	22	zweiundzwanzig	101	ein hundert eins	

Useful Words and Phrases

EATING OUT

A table for... please **Einen Tisch für... bitte**
We have/haven't booked **Wir haben/haben nicht reserviert**
I'd like to reserve a table for... people at...
Ich möchte einen Tisch für... Personen um... reservieren
I am a vegetarian **Ich bin Vegetarier**
May I see the menu, please?
Die Speisekarte bitte?
Is there a dish of the day, please?
Gibt es ein Tagesgericht?
We'd like something to drink
Wir möchten etwas zu trinken
Do you have a wine list in English?
Haben Sie eine Weinkarte auf Englisch?
This is not what I ordered
Das habe ich nicht bestellt
Could we sit there? **Können wir dort sitzen?**
When do you open/close?
Wann machen Sie auf/zu?
The food is cold **Das Essen ist kalt**
The food was excellent
Das Essen war ausgezeichnet

Can I have the bill, please?
Wir möchten zahlen, bitte
Is service included? **Ist das mit Bedienung?**

Breakfast **Das Frühstück**
Lunch **Das Mittagessen**
Dinner **Das Abendessen**
Starters **Die Vorspeise**
Main course **Das Hauptgericht**
Desserts **Die Nachspeisen**
Fish dishes **Fischgerichte**
Meat dishes **Fleischgerichte**
Fruit **Obst**
Vegetables **Gemüse**
Dish of the day **Das Tagesgericht**
Wine list **Die Weinkarte**
Salt **Das Salz**
Pepper **Der Pfeffer**
Knife **Das Messer**
Fork **Die Gabel**
Spoon **Der Löffel**
Waiter **Kellner**
Waitress **Kellnerin**

MENU A–Z

Äpfel Apples
Apfelsaft Apple juice
Apfelsinen Oranges
Aufschnitt Sliced cold meat
Austern Oysters
Belegte Brote Sandwiches
Birnen Pears
Blumenkohl Cauliflower
Brathähnchen Roast chicken
Bratwurst Fried sausage
Brokkoli Broccoli
Brötchen Bread roll
Creme Cream
Eintopf Stew
Eisbein Pork knuckle
Ente Duck
Erbsen Peas
Erdbeeren Strawberries
Fasan Pheasant
Fenchel Fennel

Flunder Flounder
Forelle Trout
Frühstücksspeck Grilled bacon
Gans Goose
Gekochtes Ei Boiled egg
Gulasch Goulash
Grüne Bohnen Green beans
Heilbutt Halibut
Hering Herring
Himbeeren Raspberries
Honig Honey
Hummer Lobster
Kabeljau Cod
Kaffee Coffee
Kalbsleber Calf's liver
Karotten Carrots
Karoffeln Potatoes
Käse Cheese
Käsekuchen Cheesecake
Kasseler Smoked pork loin

Kirschen Cherries
Krabben Shrimps
Kohl Cabbage
Konfitüre Preserves
Kopfsalat Lettuce
Lachs Salmon
Lammbraten Roast lamb
Lauch Leeks
Mais Sweet corn
Milch Milk
Obsttorte Fruit tart
Obstsalat Fruit salad
Orangensaft Orange juice
Paprika (Bell) Pepper
Pfirsiche Peaches
Pflaumen Plums
Pilze Mushrooms
Rinderbraten Roast beef
Rotkohl Red cabbage
Rührei Scrambled egg

Schinken Ham
Scholle Plaice
Schokoladentorte Chocolate cake
Schweinebraten Roast pork
Schweinekotelett Pork chop
Seezunge Sole
Spargel Asparagus
Spiegelei Fried egg
Spinat Spinach
Suppen Soups
Tee Tea
Tomaten Tomatoes
Vanillepudding Custard
Wiener Schnitzel Veal escalope
Weintrauben Grapes
Wild Game
Zucchini Courgettes/ Zucchini
Zwiebeln Onions

Street Atlas

For chapters: See inside front cover

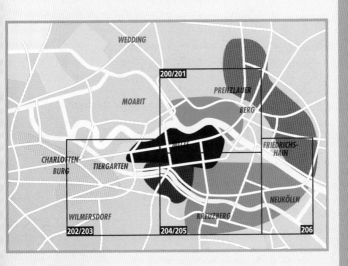

WEDDING

200/201

PRENZLAUER

BERG

MOABIT

CHARLOTTEN-
BURG

TIERGARTEN

FRIEDRICHS-
HAIN

WILMERSDORF

202/203

KREUZBERG

204/205

NEUKÖLLN

206

Key to Street Atlas

ℹ Information

M̂ Museum

🎭 Theatre / Opera house

👤 Monument

⊕ Hospital

✡ Police station

✉ Post office

✝ Church / Chapel

✡ Synagogue

★ Sight / Attraction

🗼 Tower

⚓ Jetty

🏠 🏖 Indoor / Open air pool

P Parking area

– – – Former border (Berlin Wall)

🐘 Zoo

—U— U-Bahn line/station

—S— S-Bahn line/station

⬜ Pedestrian precinct

⬛ Public building /
Building of interest

★ TOP 10

26 Don't Miss

22 At Your Leisure

1 : 17.600

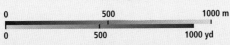

| 0 | 500 | 1000 m |

| 0 | 500 | 1000 yd |

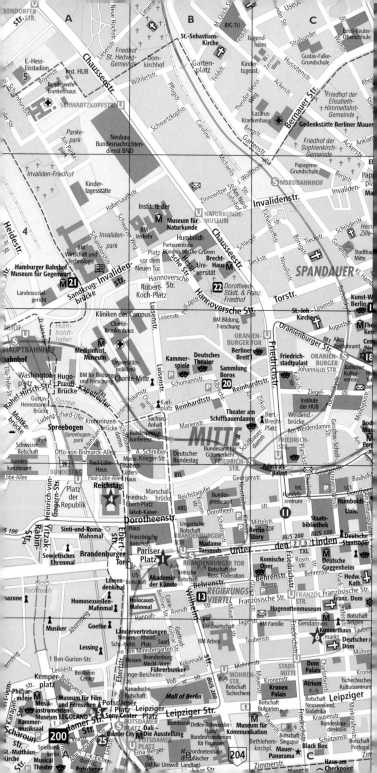

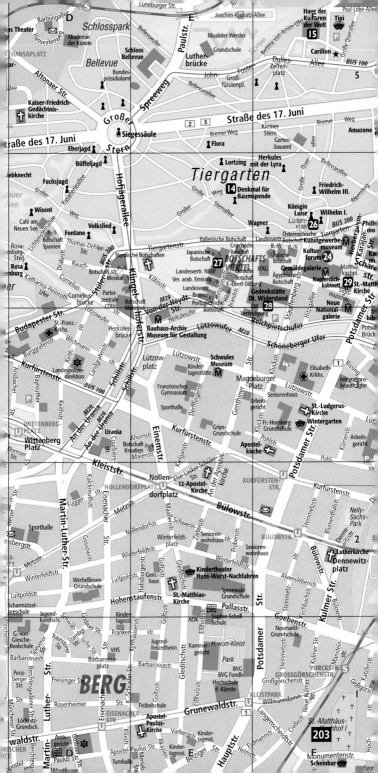

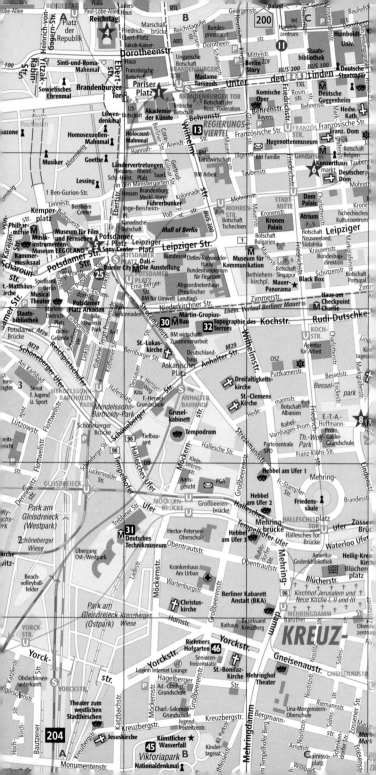

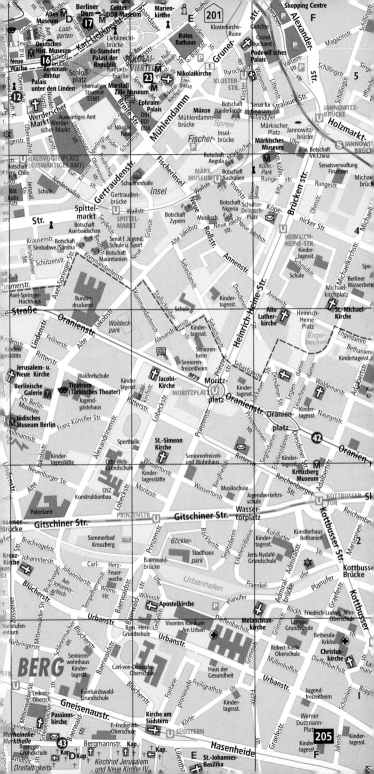

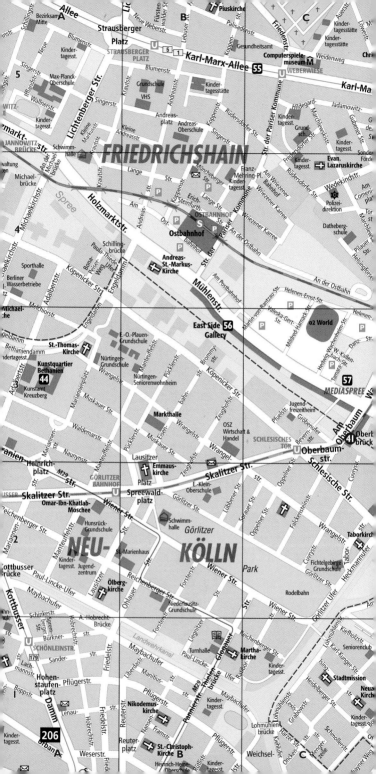

Street Index

Index

Index

Index

Events Throughout the Year

JANUARY

The Berlin New Year's Run: This 4km run from the Brandenburg Gate ushers in the new sporting year.

International Green Week: Berliners flock to the Exhibition for Food, Agriculture and Horticulture and sample tasty treats from around the world.

The Six-Day Race: Berlin's traditional track cycling race, also known as "Sixdays".

FEBRUARY

International Film Festival: Thousands of visitors flock to see films from all over the world in an event that's been giving Berlin's grey Februaries a touch of glamour since 1951.

MARCH

International Travel Trade Fair: Countries you've never even heard of present themselves as this, the world's largest travel fair. Visitors are drawn from hall to hall by exotic scents and sounds before heading home, tired from their "travels" and laden with brochures. After they've gone, the experts discuss how best to entice them out for a real trip.

APRIL

Opera Festival: Enjoy some great performances from the Berlin State Opera (held in the Schiller Theater until the end of 2015 at the earliest).

MAY

Theatre Festival: Selected guests give theatrical performances on a wide variety of stages.

Carnival of Cultures: This four-day festival around Pentecost reflects the cultural diversity of Berlin. There's dancing, music, art and culture from all over the world.

Gallery Weekend: Around 50 galleries – including many high-calibre establishments – invite you in to tour Berlin's art scene for a whole weekend.

Long Night of the Museums: More than 100 museums draw in visitors until late at night with concerts, readings, theatre and special exhibitions.

JUNE

Christopher Street Day: Rainbow flags summon people to this gay and lesbian parade (mainly held in Schöneberg and around Nollendorfplatz).

Fête de la Musique is a city-wide spectacle on June 21st. Free musical performances are held on hundreds of outdoor stages.

German-French Folk Festival: This giant festival of friendship has been held since 1963. There's a French village, carousels and a varied programme of entertainment.

JULY

Classic Open Air sees the Gendarmenmarkt turn into a concert hall.

German-American Folk Festival: Although the Allies took their leave in 1994, Berliners still come out to celebrate this formerly joint event.

AUGUST

ISTAF: The world's best athletes compete at the Olympiastadion.

International Berlin Beer Festival: You can try around 2,000 beers from all four corners of the world at stalls spread out along Karl-Marx-Allee.

Dance in August: Aficionados go to the Hebbel theatre to see dance from all over the world.

SEPTEMBER

Berlin Music Week: Festivals, concerts, club nights, workshops and business events dedicated to music take place at a wide variety of venues spread out all over the city.

International Radio Exhibition: The tech of the future is scrutinised by amateurs and experts alike.

Berlin Marathon: Fancy taking part? Make sure you book as early as you can – the number of runners is growing every year.

OCTOBER

The Day of German Unity: Germans celebrate reunification every year on 3rd October.

NOVEMBER

Jazzfest: Jazz legends and their fans have come together for one of Europe's most tradition-soaked music festivals since 1964. Berlin's many jazz clubs also offer a variety of treats throughout the year.

Boat & Fun Berlin: A trade fair that makes it perfectly clear that Berlin is a city with a wealth of waterways!

DECEMBER

Christmas Markets: The most beautiful Christmas markets in Berlin can be found in Sophienstraße, on the Gendarmenmarkt and around Neukölln's Richardplatz.

New Year's Eve Party: A big celebration takes place around the Brandenburg Gate.

Picture Credits

1st Edition 2016

Worldwide Distribution: Marco Polo Travel Publishing Ltd
Pinewood, Chineham Business Park
Crockford Lane, Chineham
Basingstoke, Hampshire RG24 8AL, United Kingdom.
© MAIRDUMONT GmbH & Co. KG, Ostfildern

Authors: Gisela Buddée, Christine Berger, Andrea Schulte-Peevers
Editor: Bintang Buchservice GmbH (Jessika Zollickhofer),
www.bintang-berlin.de
Revised editing and translation: Jon Andrews, jonandrews.co.uk
Program supervisor: Birgit Borowski
Chief editor: Rainer Eisenschmid

Cartography: © MAIRDUMONT GmbH & Co. KG, Ostfildern
3D-illustrations: jangled nerves, Stuttgart

Printed in China

Despite all of our authors' thorough research, errors can creep in.
The publishers do not accept any liability for this. Whether you
want to praise us, alert us to errors or give us a personal tip –
please don't hesitate to email or post to:

MARCO POLO Travel Publishing Ltd
Pinewood, Chineham Business Park
Crockford Lane, Chineham
Basingstoke, Hampshire RG24 8AL
United Kingdom
Email: sales@marcopolouk.com

FSC
www.fsc.org
MIX
Paper from
responsible sources
FSC® C020056

Mar 2016

10 REASONS
TO COME BACK AGAIN

1. **Berlin is so cheap** that you can experience a great deal on a budget.

2. The city's **theatres**, **museums** and **events** are enough to keep you coming back year after year.

3. Want to hear German swearing at its creative best? Listen to the **bus drivers!**

4. An **idyllic boat tour** on the Spree is too beautiful not to be experienced a a second time.

5. Berlin quite simply has the best **Currywurst** (sausage with curry sauce) in the world.

6. The city's lively **nightlife** stops for nothing – not even sunrise!

7. There are so many **beautiful parks** waiting to be discovered in Germany's greenest city.

8. **Enjoy the sunset from the Reichstag dome** – it'll melt your heart time and time again.

9. With more **100 markets and flea markets**, there are always more bargains to be found.

10. Stay in one of **Berlin's neighbourhoods** and you'll quickly feel right at home.